WHAT IS ANCIENT PHILOSOPHY?

WHAT IS ANCIENT PHILOSOPHY?

PIERRE HADOT

Translated by Michael Chase

THE BELKNAP PRESS OF
HARVARD UNIVERSITY PRESS

Cambridge, Massachusetts
London, England
2002

This book was originally published as *Qu'est-ce que la
philosophie antique?* by Éditions Gallimard, copyright © 1995
by Éditions Gallimard.

Library of Congress Cataloging-in-Publication Data

Hadot, Pierre.
[Qu'est-ce que la philosophie antique? English]
What is ancient philosophy? / Pierre Hadot; translated by Michael Chase.
p. cm.
Includes bibliographical references and index.
ISBN 0-674-00733-6 (alk. paper)
1. Philosophy, Ancient.   1. Title.
B172.H33513 2002
180—dc21   2002017193

Designed by Gwen Nefsky Frankfeldt

TO THE MEMORY OF A.-J. VOELKE

CONTENTS

P A R T   T H R E E

Interruption and Continuity: The Middle Ages and Modern Times

Acknowledgments

The considerations I offer to the reader are the fruit of lengthy labors devoted to ancient philosophers and philosophy. In the course of this research, two books particularly influenced me. The first was P. Rabbow's *Seelenführung: Methodik der Exerzitien in der Antike* (Spiritual Guidance: Methods of Spiritual Exercise in Antiquity), published in Munich in 1954, which set forth the various forms which these practices could assume among the Epicureans and the Stoics. This work had the merit of pointing out the continuity which exists between ancient and Christian spirituality, but it may have limited itself too exclusively to the rhetorical aspects of these spiritual exercises. The other work was written by my wife, Ilsetraut Hadot, before we met. Entitled *Seneca und die griechisch-römische Tradition der Seelenleitung* (Seneca and the Greco-Roman Tradition of Spiritual Guidance; Berlin, 1969), it resituated the Stoic philosopher's work within the global perspective of ancient philosophy.

I also had the pleasure of meeting two philosophers who, independently from me, were likewise interested in these problems. One was the late André-Jean Voelke, whose studies on philosophy as therapy of the soul have recently been published (*La philosophie comme thérapie de l'âme;* Paris, 1993). The other was my Polish colleague J. Domański, whose work on the concept of philosophy in the Middle Ages and the Renaissance has recently been published (*La philosophie: Théorie ou manière de vivre? Les controverses de l'Antiquité à la Renaissance* [Fribourg and Paris, 1996]). In it, the author shows how the ancient notion of philosophy was concealed—but only partially—in the Middle Ages, and how it was reborn in the Renaissance, for instance in the work of Petrarch and Erasmus. Moreover, I believe that my 1977 article "Exercices spirituels et philosophie antique" (Spiritual Exercises and Ancient Philosophy; in English in Hadot, *Philosophy as a Way of Life* [Oxford, 1995]) had some influence on Michel Foucault's idea of the "culture of the self," presented in his book *Le souci de soi* (1984). I have spoken elsewhere of the convergences as well as the divergences between us; see my essay "Réflexions sur la notion de culture de soi" (Reflections on the Notion of the Culture of the Self; also in *Philosophy as a Way of Life*).

I must express my heartfelt gratitude to Eric Vigne, who suggested I write this book, advised me on its structure, and showed exemplary patience with me. My dear colleague Roberte Hamayon, through her advice and her writing, has enlightened me concerning the very complex problems posed by shamanism; I would like to express my deep gratitude to her. My warmest thanks also go to Sylvie Simon, Gwenaëlle Aubry, Jeannie Carlier, and Ilsetraut Hadot, who read the manuscript in order to eliminate as many awkwardnesses and errors as possible.

Translator's Note

This translation is based on the 1995 edition of *Qu'est-ce que la philosophie antique,* published by Gallimard, but it incorporates several corrections which Pierre Hadot transmitted to me.

A word about citations from ancient authors. It is customary in works like the present one to substitute "standard" English translations in those places where the author has given French versions. But this won't do in the case of Pierre Hadot, whose method is profoundly philological; that is, he believes the process of understanding ancient philosophical texts begins when one translates them from the original Greek and Latin. Hadot's understanding of ancient philosophy has thus been shaped by his own interpretation and translation of ancient texts, so that to replace his translations by those from some "standard" English version would, I feel, render his thought incomprehensible.

Therefore, as in my other translations of works by Pierre Hadot, I have proceeded as follows when he cites ancient works in Greek or Latin. I first give as literal a translation as possible of his French version; then I check this version against the original Greek or Latin. In cases of wide divergence from Hadot's rendering, I have consulted with Hadot himself on the final translation.

This procedure sometimes results in English translations which are quite different from the "standard" English versions of the ancient texts cited. If the reader should wish to consult the latter, we have provided a basic English bibliography of the classical texts cited.

The translator would like to express his thanks to Maria Ascher, sharp-sighted representative of that invaluable yet endangered profession, the copy editor.

The time will come when, in order to perfect ourselves morally and rationally, we will prefer to have recourse to Xenophon's *Memorabilia* rather than the Bible, and we will use Montaigne and Horace as guides along the path which leads to the understanding of the sage, and of Socrates, the most imperishable of them all.

—Nietzsche, *Human, All Too Human*

The ancient Greek philosophers, such as Epicurus, Zeno, and Socrates, remained more faithful to the Idea of the philosopher than their modern counterparts have done. "When will you finally begin to *live* virtuously?" said Plato to an old man who told him he was attending classes on virtue. The point is not always to speculate, but also ultimately to think about applying our knowledge. Today, however, he who lives in conformity with what he teaches is taken for a dreamer.

—Kant, *Lectures on the Philosophical Encyclopedia*

It is desire that engenders thought.

—Plotinus, *Enneads,* V, 6 (24), 5, 9

What place shall the philosopher occupy within the city? That of a sculptor of men.

—Simplicius, *Commentary on the Manual of Epictetus*

The results of all the schools and of all their experiments belong legitimately to us. We will not hesitate to adopt a Stoic formula on the pretext that we have previously profited from Epicurean formulas.

—Nietzsche, *Posthumous Fragments,* Autumn 1881

It is more important to want to do good than to know the truth.

—Petrarch, "On His Own Ignorance and That of Many Others"

I think there is no one who has rendered worse service to the human race than those who have learned philosophy as a mercenary trade.

—Seneca, *Letters to Lucilius,* 108, 36

Plato and Aristotle can only be imagined dressed in the long robes of pedants. They were honest men, and, like the others, they laughed with their friends; and when they amused themselves by writing their *Laws* and their *Politics,* they did it as an amusement. This was the least philosophical and serious part of their lives; the most philosophical part was living simply and quietly.

—Pascal, *Pensées,* no. 331

If philosophical theories seduce you, sit down and go over them again and again in your mind. But never call yourself a philosopher, and never allow yourself to be called a philosopher.

—Epictetus, *Discourses,* III, 21, 23

Nowadays, there are philosophy professors, but no philosophers.

—Thoreau, *Walden*

Without virtue, God is a mere name.

—Plotinus, *Enneads,* II, 9 (33), 15, 39

"I did nothing today."—"What? Did you not live? That is not only the most fundamental but the most illustrious of your occupations."

—Montaigne, *Essays,* III, 13, "On Experience"

Introduction

Seldom do we reflect upon what philosophy is in itself.[1] Indeed, it is extremely difficult to define it. What philosophy students are introduced to is above all *philosophies*. After the "darkness" of the Middle Ages, which are too often ignored in official courses of study, we find Descartes, Malebranche, Spinoza, Leibniz, Kant, Hegel, Fichte, Schelling, Bergson, and a few contemporaries. For their exams, students often have to write an essay showing that they are quite familiar with the theories of such-and-such an author. Another essay is designed to test students' ability to reflect on a problem which is called "philosophical," because it has usually been discussed by ancient or contemporary philosophers.

In itself, there is nothing wrong with all this. It certainly seems that the way one can come to have an idea of *philosophy* is by studying *philosophies*. Yet the history of "philosophy" is not the same as the history of philosophies, if what we understand by "philosophies" are theoretical discourses and philosophers' systems. In addition to this history, however, there is room for the study of philosophical modes of life.

The present work attempts to describe, in its general and common features, the historical and spiritual phenomenon represented by ancient philosophy. The reader may ask: Why should we limit ourselves to ancient philosophy, which is so far from us? I would like to offer several responses. In the first place, this is a field in which I hope to have acquired a certain competence. Second, in the words of Aristotle, if one wishes to understand things, one must watch them develop[2] and must catch them at the moment of their birth. If we now speak about "philosophy," it is because the Greeks coined the word *philosophia,* which means "love of wisdom," and because Greek philosophy was transmitted to the Middle Ages and thence to modern times. Our goal, then, is to seize this phenomenon at its origin, remaining quite aware that philosophy is a historical phenomenon which arose at a particular point in time and has evolved up to the present.

In this book, I intend to show that a profound difference exists between the representations which the ancients made of *philosophia* and the representation which is usually made of philosophy today—at least in the case of the image of it which is presented to students, because of the exigencies of university teaching. They get the impression that all the philosophers they study strove in turn to invent, each in an original way, a new construction, systematic and abstract, intended somehow or other to explain the universe, or at the least, if we are talking about contemporary philosophers, that they tried to elaborate a new discourse about language. These theories—which one could call "general philosophy"—give rise, in almost all systems, to doctrines or criticisms of morality which, as it were, draw the consequences, both for individuals and for society, of the general principles of the system, and thus invite people to carry out a specific choice of life and adopt a certain mode of behavior. The problem of knowing whether this choice of life will be efficacious is utterly secondary and accessory; it doesn't enter into the perspective of philosophical discourse.

I think that such a representation is mistaken if it is applied to the philosophy of antiquity. Obviously, there can be no question of denying the extraordinary ability of the ancient philosophers to develop theoretical reflection on the most subtle problems of the theory of knowledge, logic, or physics. This theoretical activity, however, must be situated within a perspective which is different from that which corresponds to the idea people usually have of philosophy. In the first place, at least since the time of Socrates, the choice of a way of life has not been located at the end of the process of philosophical activity, like a kind of accessory or appendix. On the contrary, it stands at the beginning, in a complex interrelation with critical reaction to other existential attitudes, with global vision of a certain way of living and of seeing the world, and with voluntary decision itself. Thus, to some extent, this option determines the specific doctrine and the way this doctrine is taught. Philosophical discourse, then, originates in a choice of life and an existential option—not vice versa. Second, this choice and decision are never made in solitude. There can never be a philosophy or philosophers outside a group, a community—in a word, a philosophical "school." The philosophical school thus corresponds, above all, to the choice of a certain way of life and existential option which demands from the individual a total change of lifestyle, a conversion of one's entire being, and ultimately a certain desire to be and to live in a certain way. This existential option, in turn, implies a certain vision of the world, and the task of philosophical discourse will therefore be to reveal and rationally justify this existential option, as well as this representation of the world. Theoretical philosophical discourse is thus born from this initial existential option, and it leads back to it, insofar as—by means of its logical and persuasive force, and the action it tries to exert upon the interlocutor—it incites both masters and disciples to live in genuine conformity with their initial choice. In other words, it is, in a way, the application of a certain ideal of life.

I mean, then, that philosophical discourse must be understood from the perspective of the way of life of which it is both the expression and the means. Consequently, philosophy *is* above all a way of life, but one which is intimately linked to philosophical discourse. One of the fundamental themes of this book will be the distance which separates philosophy from wisdom. Philosophy is merely a preparatory exercise for wisdom. We will not be concerned with opposing, on the one hand, philosophy as a theoretical philosophical discourse, and, on the other, wisdom as the silent way of life which is practiced from the moment in which discourse achieves its completion and perfection. This is the scheme E. Weil had in mind when he wrote: "The philosopher is not 'wise'; he neither has wisdom nor is wisdom. He speaks, and even if his discourse aims solely at its own suppression, he will still go on speaking until he reaches the end, and beyond the perfect instants in which he ends."[3]

This would be a situation analogous to that of Wittgenstein's *Tractatus Logico-Philosophicus,* where the philosophical discourse of the *Tractatus* is finally transcended in silent wisdom.[4] Beginning with Plato's *Symposium,* ancient philosophy admits, in one way or another, that the philosopher is no sage. Yet it does not consider itself a pure discourse which stops when wisdom appears. Rather, it is, at the same time and indissolubly, a discourse *and* a way of life which tend toward wisdom without ever achieving it. It is also true, however, that the discourse of Plato, Aristotle, and Plotinus stops at the threshold of certain experiences which, if they are not wisdom, are at least a kind of foretaste of it.

Nor should we oppose discourse and way of life, as though they corresponded to theory and practice, respectively. Discourse can have a practical aspect, to the extent that it tends to produce an effect on the listener or reader. Insofar as way of life is concerned, it cannot, of course, be theoretic, but it can be theoretical—that is to say, contemplative.[5]

In order to be clear, I must specify that I understand "discourse" in the philosophical sense of "discursive thought" expressed in written or oral language, and not in the currently widespread sense of "a way of speaking which reveals an attitude" (as in "racist discourse," for example). For instance, I refuse to conflate language and cognitive functions. In this context, let me quote the following illuminating lines by J. Ruffié:[6]

> In fact, it is perfectly possible to think and to know without language; in some ways, perhaps it is possible to know in a superior way. Thought can be recognized by its capacity to define reasonable conduct, the faculty of mental representation, and abstraction. Animals, which are capable of distinguishing triangular shapes, or certain combinations of objects, can think, as can young children who do not yet speak and deaf-mutes who have not been educated. . . . Clinical studies have demonstrated that there is no correlation between the development of language and that of intelligence: people who are mentally defective can talk, and people suffering from aphasia can be highly intelligent. . . . Even in normal people, the faculties of elaboration can appear to be more or less stifled by the faculties of expression. Great discoveries, it seems, can be made independently of language, from patterns which are elaborated within the brain.

I have insisted on this point because in the course of this book we shall encounter situations in which philosophical activity continues to be carried out, even though discourse cannot express this activity.

We will not be concerned with opposing and separating philosophy as a way of life, on the one hand, and, on the other, a philosophical discourse that is somehow external to philosophy. On the contrary: we wish to show that philosophical discourse is a *part* of this way of life. It must be admitted, however, that the philosopher's choice of life determines his discourse. This is to say that philosophical discourses cannot be considered realities which exist in and for themselves, so that their structure could be studied independently of the philosopher who developed them. Can Socrates' discourse be separated from the life and death of Socrates?

The notion of *spiritual exercises* will appear frequently in the following pages.[7] By this term, I mean practices which could be physical, as in dietary regimes, or discursive, as in dialogue and meditation, or intuitive, as in contemplation, but which were all intended to effect a modification and a transformation in the subject who practiced them. The philosophy teacher's discourse could also assume the form of a spiritual exercise, if the discourse were presented in such a way that the disciple, as auditor, reader, or interlocutor, could make spiritual progress and transform himself within.

The argument will be developed in three stages. The first will consist in retracing the history of the first uses of the word *philosophia*. We will try to understand the meaning of Plato's philosophical definition of this word in the *Symposium,* where he defines *philosophia* as the love of wisdom. Then we will try to rediscover the characteristics of the various philosophies of antiquity, considered as ways of life; this will lead us to consider the common features which unite them. In a third section, we will examine for what reason and to what extent philosophy was conceived, from the Middle Ages onward, as a purely theoretical attitude. Finally, we will ask whether it is possible to return to the ancient ideal of philosophy. In order to justify our answer, we will rely a great deal on the texts of ancient philosophers. This, I think, will be of benefit to students who do not always have easy access to the sources.

PART ONE

THE PLATONIC DEFINITION OF "PHILOSOPHER" AND ITS ANTECEDENTS

Philosophy before Philosophy

THE *HISTORIA* OF THE FIRST THINKERS OF GREECE

"Philosophy before philosophy." The words belonging to the *philosophia* family did not in fact appear until the fifth century B.C., and the term *philosophia* itself was not defined until the fourth century B.C., by Plato. Aristotle, however, and with him the entire tradition of the history of philosophy, applied the word "philosophers" to the first Greek thinkers[1] who appeared at the beginning of the sixth century, in the colonies of Asia Minor, at the periphery of the Greek zone of influence. More precisely, they appeared in the town of Miletus: first the mathematician and engineer Thales, one of the Seven Sages, famous for having predicted the solar eclipse of May 28, 585 B.C.; followed by Anaximander and Anaximenes. This intellectual movement then spread to other Greek colonies, in Sicily and southern Italy. In the sixth century B.C. Xenophanes of Colophon emigrated to Elea; and late in the century Pythagoras, who originally came from Samos (not far from Miletus), settled in Crotona, and then in Metapontum. Gradually, southern Italy and Sicily became the center of an extraordinarily vital intellectual culture, exemplified by, among others, Parmenides and Empedocles.

All these thinkers proposed a *rational* explanation of the world—and this was a milestone in the history of thought. To be sure, there had been cosmogonies before them, in the Near East and elsewhere in Archaic Greece as well. Yet those had been mythical—that is to say, they described the history of the world as a battle among personified entities. They were "geneses" in the biblical sense of the Book of Genesis (or Book of Generations), which was intended to bring a people back to the memory of its ancestors, and to reconnect it with the cosmic forces and the generations of the gods. Creation of the world, creation of man, creation of a people: such had been the object of those cosmogonies. As G. Naddaf has shown,[2] although the first Greek thinkers substituted a rational theory of the world for such mythical narratives, they still preserved the three-part schema which had structured the older cosmogonies. They proposed a theory to explain the origins of the world, of mankind, and of the city. This theory was rational, in that it sought to account for the world by positing not a battle among personified elements but a battle among "physical" realities, and the predominance of one of these over the others. This radical transformation is summed up in the Greek word *phusis,* which originally meant the beginning, the development, and the result of the process by which a thing constitutes itself. The object of this intellectual undertaking, which they called *historia,*[3] was universal *phusis.*

Throughout the Greek philosophical tradition, thinkers proposed rational theories influenced by this original cosmogonic schema. Here we will give only the example of Plato who, in a series of dialogues entitled *Timaeus, Critias,* and *Hermocrates* (this last one planned, but superseded by the *Laws*), wished to write a great treatise on the entire range of *phusis,* from the origin of the world and of man to the origin of Athens. Here again we find a book of "generations," which brought the Athenians back to the memory of their origins and their ancestors, in order to root them in the universal order and the foundational act of the creator-deity. Plato makes no secret of it: in the *Timaeus,* he proposes what he calls a likely "fable" in which the mythical figure of the Demiurge creates the World as he looks at the eternal Model constituted by the Ideas.[4] In Book X of the *Laws,* however, Plato is no longer content to propose a mythical story; he wants to found his cosmogony on a rigorous demonstration, based on arguments acceptable to everyone. In the course of this rational effort, Plato relies explicitly on the concept of *phusis,* conceived as "nature-process" by the first Greek thinkers, and he insists on the primordial, originary character of this process. Yet, for Plato,[5] what is primordial and originary is movement, the process which engenders itself and is self-moving—that is to say, the soul. Thus, a creationist schema is substituted for the evolutionist schema. The universe is no longer born of the automatism of *phusis,* but is a product of the rationality of the soul; and the soul, as the first principle, prior to everything else, is thus identified with *phusis.*

PAIDEIA

We can also speak of "philosophy before philosophy" with regard to another current of Presocratic Greek thought—namely, the practices and theories which relate to a fundamental demand of the Greek mentality: the desire to form and to educate,[6] or the concern for what the Greeks called *paideia.*[7] Since the distant time of Homeric Greece, the education of the young had been the great preoccupation of the class of nobles, or those who possessed *arete.* This was the excellence required by the nobility of blood,[8] which, later on, among the philosophers, would become virtue, or the nobility of the soul. We can obtain an idea of this aristocratic education thanks to the poems of Theognis, which constitute a collection of moral precepts.[9] This education was imparted by adults, within the social group itself. According to its precepts, young men strove to acquire the qualities—physical strength, courage, sense of duty and honor—which were suitable for warriors and which were incarnate in great, divine ancestors taken as models. Beginning in the fifth century, as democracy began to flourish, the city-states showed the same concern for forming their future citizens by physical exercises, gymnastics, music, and mental exercises. Yet democratic life engendered struggles for power; it was necessary to know how to persuade the people, and how to induce them to make specific decisions in the Assembly. If one wanted to become a leader of the people, one thus had to acquire a mastery of language—and it was to this need that the Sophistic movement would respond.

THE FIFTH-CENTURY SOPHISTS

With the flourishing of Athenian democracy in the fifth century B.C., all the intellectual activity which had spread throughout the Greek colonies of Ionia, Asia Minor, and Southern Italy came to set up shop in Athens. Thinkers, professors, and intellectuals converged on the city, importing with them modes of thought which had until then been almost unknown, and which were received with varying degrees of favor. For instance, the fact that Anaxagoras,[10] who came from Ionia, was accused of atheism and had to flee into exile shows that the spirit of investigation which had developed in the Greek colonies of Asia Minor was deeply unsettling for the Athenians. The famous Sophists of the fifth century were also often strangers: Protagoras and Prodicus came from Ionia; Gorgias, from South Italy. The intellectual moment which they represented appears both as a continuation of and as a break with what preceded it. There was continuity, insofar as the argumentative method of Parmenides, Zeno of Elea, and Melissus could be found in the Sophists' paradoxes; and also insofar as the Sophists sought to gather together all the scientific and historical knowledge which had been accumulated by the thinkers who went before them. There was also a break, however, in that they submitted this accumulated knowledge to a radical critique, each of them insisting, in his own way, on the conflict between nature *(phusis)* and human conventions *(nomoi)*. Furthermore, their activity was directed particularly toward the training of youth, with a view to success in political life. The Sophists' teachings thus responded to a need. The flourishing of democratic life demanded that its citizens, especially those who wanted to achieve positions of power, have a perfect mastery of language. Up until this point, young people had been trained for the acquisition of excellence *(aretē)* by means of *sunousia,* or nonspecialized contact with the adult world.[11] The Sophists, by contrast, invented education in an artificial environment—a system that was to remain one of the characteristics of our civilization.[12] They were professional teachers, pedagogues first and foremost, although we must recognize the remarkable originality of Protagoras, Gorgias, and Antiphon. For a salary, they taught their students the formulas which would enable them to persuade their audience, and to defend both the *pro* and the *contra* sides of an argument *(antilogia)* with equal skill. Plato and Aristotle would reproach them with being salesmen of knowledge, mere retail-wholesale businessmen.[13] They taught not only the technique of persuasive discourse, but also everything which could help an individual attain that loftiness of vision which always seduces an audience—in other words, overall culture. This entailed just as much science, geometry, and astronomy as it did history, sociology, and legal theory. They did not found permanent schools; rather, in exchange for payment, they offered series of courses. In order to attract audiences, they advertised their services by giving public lectures, at which they showed off their knowledge and skill. They were itinerant professors; and not only Athens, but other cities as well, benefited from their techniques.

Thus, *aretē* (excellence), conceived as competence intended to enable young people to play a role in the city, could now be the object of an apprenticeship, so long as the student had the right natural aptitudes and practiced hard enough.

The Inception of the Idea of "Doing Philosophy"

THE TESTIMONY OF HERODOTUS

It is almost certain that Presocratic philosophers of the seventh and sixth centuries B.C., such as Xenophanes and Parmenides, knew neither the adjective *philosophos* nor the verb *philosophein* ("to do philosophy"), much less the noun *philosophia*. Moreover, despite certain ancient but very controversial evidence to the contrary, this was probably also the case for Pythagoras[1] and Heraclitus.[2] In all likelihood, these words did not appear until the fifth century, the "Age of Pericles," when Athens shone by virtue of both its political dominance and its intellectual influence. This was the time of Sophocles, Euripides, and the Sophists, but it was also when the historian Herodotus, a native of Asia Minor, came to live in the famous city in the course of his numerous travels. It is perhaps in Herodotus' work that we find the first mention of "philosophical" activity. Herodotus tells of the legendary meeting between Solon (an Athenian legislator of the seventh–sixth centuries, and one of the so-called Seven Sages) with Croesus, king of Lydia. The latter, proud of his power and wealth, speaks to Solon as follows: "My Athenian guest, the rumor of your wisdom [*sophiēs*] and your travels has reached us. We hear that since you have a taste for wisdom [*philosopheon*], you have visited many lands because of your desire to see."[3]

Here we can glimpse what wisdom and philosophy meant at that time. The only goal of Solon's travels was to know, to acquire vast experience of reality and of men, and to discover different lands and customs. We should note at this point that the Presocratics apparently designated their intellectual undertaking as a *historia*—that is, an inquiry.[4] Such experience can make the person who possesses it a good judge in matters concerning human life. This is why Croesus goes on to ask Solon who, in his opinion, is the happiest of men. Solon replies that no one can be called happy before the end of his life is known.

Thus, Herodotus reveals the existence of a word which was perhaps already fashionable, but in any case became so in fifth-century Athens, the Athens of democracy and of the Sophists. In general, since the time of Homer, compound words beginning with *philo-* had served to designate the disposition of a person who found his interest, pleasure, or *raison de vivre* in devoting himself to a given activity. *Philoposia*, for instance, was the pleasure and interest one took in drinking; *philotimia* was a propensity to acquire honors. *Philosophia*, therefore, would be the interest one took in wisdom.[5]

PHILOSOPHICAL ACTIVITY, THE PRIDE OF ATHENS

Fifth-century Athenians were proud of this intellectual activity and the interest in science and culture which flourished in their city. The Athenian statesman Pericles—in the funeral oration which, according to Thucydides, he delivered in memory of the first soldiers who fell in the Peloponnesian War—praised the way of life practiced in Athens: "We cultivate beauty with simplicity, and we do philosophy without lacking in firmness."

The two verbs used here are both compounds of *philo-*: *philokalein* and *philosophein*. We may note in passing that this text implicitly proclaims the triumph of democracy. It is no longer only exceptional personalities or nobles who are able to achieve excellence *(aretē);* all citizens can reach this goal if they love beauty and give themselves over to the love of *sophia.* At the beginning of the fourth century, the orator Isocrates took up the same theme in his *Panegyric:*[6] it is Athens which has revealed philosophy to the world.

Philosophical activity included everything relating to intellectual and general culture: the speculations of the Presocratics, the birth of the sciences, theories of language, rhetorical techniques, and the arts of persuasion. If we may judge from an allusion made by the Sophist Gorgias in his *Praise of Helen,* it was sometimes related more particularly to the art of argumentation. Helen, said Gorgias, was not responsible for her actions: she was led to act the way she did either by the will of the gods, or under threat of violence, or by the force of persuasion, or finally by passion. Gorgias goes on to distinguish three forms of persuasion by language, one of which consists, he says, "in jousts of philosophical discourse." No doubt this refers to the public discussions in which the Sophists confronted one another in order to show off their talents, offering competing discourses on subjects which were not linked to any particular juridical or political problem but which pertained to overall culture.

THE NOTION OF *SOPHIA*

The words *philosophos* and *philosophein* thus presuppose the notion of *sophia;* but we must admit that at this time there was no philosophical definition of the idea of *sophia.*

When trying to define *sophia,* modern commentators always

hesitate between the notion of knowledge and that of wisdom. Was the person who was *sophos* one who knew and had seen many things, had traveled a great deal, and was broadly cultured, or was he rather the person who knew how to conduct himself in life and who lived in happiness? As we shall see often in the course of this work, these two notions are not at all mutually exclusive. In the last analysis, real knowledge is know-how, and true know-how is knowing how to do good.

Since the time of Homer, the words *sophia* and *sophos* had been used in the most diverse contexts, with regard to modes of conduct and dispositions which apparently had nothing to do with those of "philosophers."[7] In the *Iliad*,[8] Homer speaks of a carpenter who, thanks to the advice of Athena, knows his way around all *sophia*—in other words, all know-how. Similarly, the *Homeric Hymn to Hermes*, after recounting the invention of the lyre, adds that Hermes himself modeled the instrument of another *sophia*, different from the art of the lyre—namely, the syrinx.[9] Here, then, we are dealing with *musical* art or know-how.

To judge by these examples, we may reasonably wonder whether, in the case of the shipbuilder and the musician, the word *sophia* might not designate, above all, activities or practices which are subject to measures and rules.[10] They presuppose instruction and apprenticeship, but they also demand the help of a god or divine grace which reveals the secrets of fabrication to the artisan and artist and helps them in the exercise of their art.

Sophiē is used in the same way by Solon[11] in the seventh century B.C. to designate poetic activity, which is the fruit both of lengthy practice by the poet and of inspiration by the Muses. This power of the poetic word, which is inspired by the Muses and gives the events of human life their meaning, appears at its clearest in Hesiod, at the beginning of the seventh century. Although he does not literally use the word *sophia*, Hesiod does give forceful expression to the content of poetic wisdom; and his testimony is all the more interesting in that it places the poet's *sophia* side by side with that of the king.[12] It is the Muses who inspire the sensible king. Likewise, they pour soft dew and sweet honey on the tongue and lips of the poet they have chosen. "All people have their eyes on [the king] when he dispenses justice in upright verdicts. His infallible language knows, as it ought, how to appease the greatest quarrels." The poet's words similarly transform men's hearts: "If someone has mourning in his heart new to care, and his soul is dried up in grief, let a singer, servant of the Muses, celebrate the deeds of the men of old or the blessed gods who hold Olympus. He quickly forgets his troubles and does not remember his cares, for the gift of the goddesses has quickly distracted him."

Here we can already glimpse the idea, fundamental in antiquity, of the psychagogic value of discourse and the capital importance of mastery of the word.[13] The word operates in two registers which seem very different: that of juridical and political discussion, in which kings dispense justice and appease quarrels; and that of poetic incantation, in which poets change people's minds by means of their songs. Mnemosyne, mother of the Muses, brings "forgetfulness of woes and a truce for worries."[14] In such incantations, we can discern a sketch of what would later become philosophical spiritual exercises, whether on the level of discourse or on that of contemplation. It is not only by the beauty of their songs and stories that the Muses make us forget our misfortunes; they also allow poets and their audience to attain cosmic vision. If they "give joy to the mighty mind of their father Zeus,"[15] this is because they sing to him and make him see "what is, what will be, and what was"; and this is precisely what Hesiod himself sang in the *Theogony.* An Epicurean saying, attributed to Epicurus' disciple Metrodorus, ran: "Remember that, born mortal and with a limited life, you have risen, thanks to the science of nature, as far as the infinity of time and space, and you have seen what is, what will be, and what was."[16] Before the Epicureans, Plato had already said

that the soul possessing elevation of thought and the contemplation of the whole of time and being will not view death as something to be feared.[17]

Sophia can also designate the skill with which a person behaves
with other people; it can go as far as ruses and dissimulation. For
instance, we find the following advice in a collection of sayings—
precepts codifying aristocratic education—which Theognis, who
wrote in the sixth century B.C. addressed to Cyrnos: "Cyrnos, turn
a different aspect of yourself to each of your friends; adapt yourself to the feelings of each. For a whole day attach yourself to one,
and then you'll know how to change characters; for skillfulness
[*sophiē*] is better than even a great excellence [*aretē*]."[18]

Here we see the richness and variety of the notion of *sophia*.
Components of this notion appear again in representations—first
popular and legendary, then historical—of the Seven Sages.[19] We
already find traces of these representations in some sixth-century
poets, and later in Herodotus and Plato. Thales of Miletus possessed what we could call encyclopedic knowledge: he predicted
the solar eclipse of May 28, 585, and affirmed that the earth rested
on water; yet he also possessed technical knowledge, since it was
claimed that he diverted the course of a river. He also displayed
political farsightedness: he tried to save the Ionian Greeks by proposing that they form a federation.

Only political activity is attested for Pittacus of Mytilene (seventh century), and Solon of Athens (seventh–sixth centuries), was,
as we have seen, a politician whose beneficent legislation was long
remembered. Yet he was also a poet who expressed his ethical and
political ideals in verse. Chilon of Sparta, Periander of Corinth,
and Bias of Priene (who all lived at the beginning of the sixth century) were also politicians, famous either for the laws they had de-
creed or for their oratorical and juridical activity. Our indications
concerning Cleobulus of Lindos are least certain of all: we know
only that some poems were attributed to him.

Maxims—or, as Plato said, "brief and memorable words"[20]—

were attributed to these Seven Sages. These dicta were uttered by each of them when they gathered at Delphi and wished to offer up to Apollo, in his temple, the first fruits of their wisdom. They devoted to him the admonitions which everyone repeats: "Know thyself," "Moderation in all things." In fact, a whole list of maxims, said to be the work of the Seven Sages, was inscribed near the temple of Delphi, and the custom of inscribing them, so that they could be read by all passers-by in the various Greek cities, was very widespread. When, in 1966, excavations were carried out at Ai Khanoum, on the border of modern Afghanistan (the ancient Greek kingdom of Bactriana), a mutilated stele was discovered. Louis Robert has showed that it originally bore a complete series of 140 Delphic maxims; Aristotle's disciple Clearchus had had them engraved in the third century B.C.[21] From this example, we get some idea of the importance which the Greeks attached to moral education.[22]

From the sixth century on, with the flourishing of the "exact" sciences (medicine, mathematics, geometry, and astronomy) another component was added to the notion of *sophia*. There were no longer "experts" *(sophoi)* only in the arts or in politics; they also existed in the domain of science. Moreover, since the time of Thales of Miletus, an increasingly precise mode of thought had developed around what the Greeks called *phusis*—that is, the phenomenon of the growth of living beings and of man, but also of the universe. This mode of thought, moreover, was often closely linked to ethical considerations, as it is in Heraclitus, and especially in Democritus.

The Sophists were so called because their goal was to teach young people *sophia*. The epitaph of Thrasymachus read: "My career is *sophia*."[23] For the Sophists, the word *sophia* meant first and foremost know-how in political life; but it also implied all the other components we have seen. In particular, it included scientific culture, at least insofar as this was a part of general culture.

The Figure of Socrates

The figure of Socrates had a decisive influence on the definition of the word "philosopher" which Plato sets forth in *The Banquet*—a dialogue that shows the first true awareness of the philosopher's paradoxical situation among his fellow human beings. For this reason, we shall have to spend considerable time not on the historical Socrates, who is difficult to know, but on the mythical figure of Socrates as presented by the first generation of his disciples.

THE FIGURE OF SOCRATES

Socrates has often been compared to Jesus Christ.[1] Among other analogies, it is quite true that both had immense historical influence, although they exercised their activity in times and places (a small city and a tiny country) which were minuscule compared to the world. They also had a very small number of disciples. Neither man wrote anything, but we do have "eyewitness" reports about them: Xenophon's *Memorabilia* and Plato's dialogues (concerning Socrates) and the Gospels (concerning Jesus). Nevertheless, it is extremely difficult for us to say anything definite about the historical Jesus or the historical Socrates. After they died, their disciples founded schools to spread their message,[2] but the schools founded by the "Socratics" vary much more widely than do the various forms of primitive Christianity; this indicates the complexity of the Socratic message. Socrates inspired Antisthenes, the founder of the Cynic school, who preached tension and austerity and was to have a profound influence on Stoicism; yet Socratic ideas also shaped the thought of Aristippus, founder of the Cyrenaic school, for whom the art of living consisted in taking the best advantage of each concrete situation as it presented itself. Aristippus did not disdain relaxation and pleasure, and was to have a considerable influence on Epicureanism; but he also inspired Euclides, the founder of the Megarian school, which was famous for its dialectics. Only one of Socrates' disciples—Plato—triumphed over history, and he did so because he was able to give his dialogues imperishable literary form, or rather because the school he founded survived for centuries, thereby saving his dialogues and developing, or perhaps deforming, his doctrine. In any case, all these schools seem to have one point in common: it is with them that the idea or concept of philosophy appears. As we shall see, it was conceived both as a specific discourse linked to a way of life, and as a way of life linked to a specific discourse.

We would perhaps have a wholly different idea of who Socrates was if the works produced in all the schools founded by his disciples had survived, and, in particular, if the entire literature of "Socratic" dialogues, which represented Socrates in dialogue with his interlocutors, had been preserved. We must recall, in any case, that the fundamental feature of Plato's dialogues—the presentation of dialogues in which Socrates almost always plays the role of questioner—was not invented by Plato. Instead, these famous dialogues belong to the genre of the Socratic dialogue, which was very much in fashion among Socrates' disciples.[3] The success of this literary form gives us some idea of the extraordinary impression which the figure of Socrates, and the way he carried out his discussions with his fellow citizens, produced on his contemporaries, especially on his disciples. In the case of the Socratic dialogues written by Plato, the originality of literary form consists not so much in the use of a discourse divided into questions and answers (dialectical discourse existed long before Socrates) as in the assigning of the central role to Socrates. The result is a unique relationship: between the author and his work, on the one hand, and, on the other, between the author and Socrates. The author pretends not to be involved in his work, apparently content merely to reproduce a debate which once opposed conflicting theses; at most, we can presume that he prefers the thesis which he makes Socrates defend. In a sense, then, he takes on the mask of Socrates.

Such is the situation we find in Plato's dialogues. Plato in his own individuality never appears in them. The author doesn't even intervene to say that it was he who composed the dialogues, and he does not include himself in the discussions which take place between the interlocutors. On the other hand, neither does he specify what, in the remarks which are recorded, belongs to Socrates and what belongs to him. In some dialogues, it is therefore often extremely difficult to distinguish what is Socratic from what is Platonic.

Thus, shortly after his death, Socrates appears as a mythical figure. And it is precisely this myth of Socrates which has indelibly marked the whole history of philosophy.

SOCRATIC IGNORANCE AND THE CRITIQUE OF SOPHISTIC KNOWLEDGE

In the *Apology,* Plato reconstructs, in his own way, the speech which Socrates gave before his judges in the trial in which he was condemned to death. Plato tells how Chaerephon, one of Socrates' friends, had asked the Delphic oracle if there was anyone wiser *(sophos)* than Socrates.[4] The oracle had replied that no one was wiser than Socrates. Socrates wondered what the oracle could possibly have meant, and began a long search among politicians, poets, and artisans—people who, according to the Greek tradition discussed in the previous chapter, possessed wisdom or know-how—in order to find someone wiser than he. He noticed that all these people thought they knew everything, whereas in fact they knew nothing. Socrates then concluded that if in fact he was the wisest person, it was because he did *not* think he knew that which he did not know. What the oracle meant, therefore, was that the wisest human being was "he who knows that he is worth nothing as far as knowledge is concerned."[5] This is precisely the Platonic definition of the philosopher in the dialogue entitled the *Symposium:* the philosopher knows nothing, but he is conscious of his ignorance.

Socrates' task—entrusted to him, says the *Apology,* by the Delphic oracle (in other words, the god Apollo)—was therefore to make other people recognize their lack of knowledge and of wisdom. In order to accomplish this mission, Socrates himself adopted the attitude of someone who knew nothing—an attitude of naiveté. This is the well-known Socratic irony: the feigned ignorance and candid air with which, for instance, he asked questions in order to find out whether someone was wiser than he. In the words of a character from the *Republic:*[6] "That's certainly Socrates' old familiar irony! I knew it. I predicted to everyone present, Socrates, that you'd refuse to reply, that you'd feign ignorance, and that you'd do anything but reply if someone asked you a question."

This is why Socrates is always the questioner in his discussions. As Aristotle remarked, "He admits that he knows nothing."[7] According to Cicero, "Socrates used to denigrate himself, and conceded more than was necessary to the interlocutors he wanted to refute. Thus, thinking one thing and saying another, he took pleasure in that dissimulation which the Greeks call 'irony.'"[8] In fact, however, such an attitude is not a form of artifice or intentional dissimulation. Rather, it is a kind of humor which refuses to take oneself or other people entirely seriously; for everything human, and even everything philosophical, is highly uncertain, and we have no right to be proud of it. Socrates' mission, then, was to make people aware of their lack of knowledge.

This was a revolution in the concept of knowledge. To be sure, Socrates could and willingly did address himself to the common people, who had only conventional knowledge and acted only under the influence of prejudices without any basis in reflection, in order to show them that their so-called knowledge had no foundation. Above all, however, Socrates addressed himself to those who had been persuaded by their education that they possessed Knowledge. Prior to Socrates, there had been two types of such people. On the one hand, there had been the aristocrats of knowledge, or masters of wisdom and truth, such as Parmenides, Empedocles, and Heraclitus, who opposed their theories to the ignorance of the mob. On the other hand, there had been the democrats of knowledge, who claimed to be able to sell their knowledge to all comers; these were, of course, the Sophists. For Socrates, knowledge was not an ensemble of propositions and formulas which could be written, communicated, or sold ready-made. This is apparent at the beginning of the *Symposium*. Socrates arrives late because he has been outside meditating, standing motionless and "applying his mind to itself." When he enters the room, Agathon, who is the host, asks him to come sit next to him, so that "by contact with you . . . I may profit from this windfall of wisdom which you have just stumbled across." "How nice it would be," replies Socrates, "if wisdom were the kind of thing that could flow from what is more full into what is more empty."[9] This means that knowledge is not a prefabricated object, or a finished content which can be directly transmitted by writing or by just any discourse.

When Socrates claims that he knows only one thing—namely, that he does not know anything—he is repudiating the traditional concept of knowledge. His philosophical method consists not in transmitting knowledge (which would mean *responding* to his disciples' questions) but in *questioning* his disciples, for he himself has nothing to say to them or teach them, so far as the theoretical content of knowledge is concerned. Socratic irony consists in pretending that one wants to learn something from one's interlocutor, in order to bring him to the point of discovering that he knows nothing of the area in which he claims to be wise.

Yet this critique of knowledge, although it seems entirely negative, has a double meaning. On the one hand, it presupposes that knowledge and truth, as we have already seen, cannot be received ready-made, but must be engendered by the individual himself. This is why Socrates says in the *Theaetetus* that when he talks with other people, he contents himself with the role of midwife. He himself knows nothing and teaches nothing,[10] but is content to ask questions; and it is Socrates' questions and interrogations which help his interlocutors to give birth to "their" truth. Such an image shows that knowledge is found within the soul itself and it is up to the individual to discover it, once he has discovered, thanks to Socrates, that his own knowledge was empty. From the point of view of his own thought, Plato expressed this idea mythically, by saying that all knowledge is the remembrance of a vision which the soul has had in a previous existence. We thus have to learn how to remember.

On the other hand, in Socrates the point of view is wholly different. Socrates' questions do not lead his interlocutor to know something, or to wind up with conclusions which could be formulated in the form of propositions on a given subject. Rather, it is *because* the interlocutor discovers the vanity of his knowledge that he will at the same time discover his truth. In other words, by passing from knowledge to himself, he will begin to place himself in question. In the Socratic dialogue, the real question is less what is being talked about than who is doing the talking. This is made explicit by Nicias, one of Plato's characters:

> Don't you know that whoever approaches Socrates closely and be-gins a dialogue with him, even if he begins by talking about some-thing entirely different, nevertheless finds himself forcibly carried around in a circle by this discourse, until he gets to the point of having to give an account of himself—as much with regard to the way he is living now, as to the way he has lived his past existence. When that point is reached, Socrates doesn't let you leave until he has submitted all that to the test of his control, well and thoroughly ... It is a pleasure for me to keep company with him. I see no harm in being reminded that I have acted or am acting in a way that is not good. He who does not run away from this will necessarily be more prudent in the rest of his life.[11]

Thus, Socrates brought his interlocutors to examine and be-come aware of themselves. "Like a gadfly," Socrates harassed his interlocutors with questions which placed them in question, and obliged them to pay attention to themselves and to take care of themselves: "What? Dear friend, you are an Athenian, citizen of a city greater and more famous than any other for its science and its power, and you do not blush at the fact that you give care to your fortune, in order to increase it as much as possible, and to your reputation and your honors; but when it comes to your thought, to your truth, to your soul, which you ought to be improving, you have no care for it, and you don't think of it!" (*Apology*, 29d–e). The point was thus no so much to question the apparent knowledge we think we have, as to question *ourselves* and the val-ues which guide our own lives. In the last analysis, Socrates' interlocutor, after carrying on a dialogue with him, no longer has any idea of why he acts. He becomes aware of the contradictions in his discourse, and of his own internal contradictions. He doubts himself; and, like Socrates, he comes to know that he knows nothing. As he does this, however, he assumes a distance with regard to himself. He splits into two parts, one of which henceforth identifies itself with Socrates, in the mutual accord which Socrates demands from his interlocutor at each stage of the discussion. The interlocutor thus acquires awareness and begins to question himself.

The real problem is therefore not the problem of knowing this or that, but of *being* in this or that way: "I have no concern at all for what most people are concerned about: financial affairs, administration of property, appointments to generalships, oratorical triumphs in public, magistracies, coalitions, political factions. I did not take this path . . . but rather the one where I could do the most good to each one of you in particular, by persuading you to be less concerned with what you *have* than with what you *are*; so that you may make yourselves as excellent and as rational as possible." Socrates practiced this call to being not only by means of his interrogations and his irony, but above all by means of his way of being, by his way of life, and by his very being.

THE CALL FROM "INDIVIDUAL" TO "INDIVIDUAL"

Doing philosophy no longer meant, as the Sophists had it, acquiring knowledge, know-how, or *sophia;* it meant questioning ourselves, because we have the feeling that we are not what we ought to be. This was to be the defining role of the *philosopher*—the person who desires wisdom—in Plato's *Symposium.* In turn, this feeling comes from the fact that, in the person of Socrates, we have encountered a personality which, by its mere presence, obliges those who approach it to question themselves. This is what Alcibiades allows us to understand at the end of the *Symposium*. It is in Alcibiades' speech in praise of Socrates that the representation of the Individual appears, perhaps for the first time in history. This is the Individual dear to Kierkegaard—the Individual as unique and unclassifiable personality. Normally, says Alcibiades, there are different types or classifications of individuals. For instance, there is the "great general, noble and courageous," like Achilles in Homeric times; or, among contemporaries, Brasidas, the Spartan leader. There is also the "clever and eloquent statesman": Nestor in Homeric times, and nowadays Pericles. Socrates, by contrast, is impossible to classify; he cannot be compared with any other man. At most, he could be compared with Silenoi or Satyrs. He is *atopos,* meaning strange, extravagant, absurd, unclassifiable, disturbing. In the *Theaetetus,* Socrates says of himself: "I am utterly disturbing [*atopos*], and I create only perplexity [*aporia*]."[12]

There is something fascinating about this unique personality, which exerts a kind of magical attraction. According to Alcibiades, Socrates' philosophical discourse bites the heart like a viper, and provokes in the soul a state of philosophical possession, delirium, and drunkenness; in other words, the listener's soul is completely bowled over.[13] It is important to emphasize that Socrates acts upon his listeners in an irrational way, by the emotions he provokes and the love he inspires. In a dialogue written by Socrates' disciple Aeschines of Sphettos, Socrates says with regard to Alcibiades that although he (Socrates) is not able to teach Alcibiades anything useful—which is not surprising, since Socrates does not know anything—he nevertheless thinks he can make him a better person, thanks to the love he feels for him, and because he lives with him.[14] In the *Theages*—a dialogue wrongly attributed to Plato but actually written between 369 and 345 B.C., and thus probably during Plato's lifetime[15]—a disciple tells Socrates that, although he has not received any instruction from Socrates, he still makes progress when he is near him and touches him. In the *Symposium*, Alcibiades says again and again that Socrates' incantations have a disturbing effect on him: "I was in such a state that it did not seem possible to live while behaving as I was behaving. . . . He forces me to admit to myself that I do not take care for myself."[16]

It is not that Socrates is more eloquent or more brilliant than others. On the contrary, says Alcibiades, one's first impression is that his discourses seem utterly ridiculous: "He talks about packsaddled asses, blacksmiths, shoemakers, and tanners; he always seems to repeat the same phrases on the same subjects."[17] Here Alcibiades seems to be alluding to Socrates' habitual argument (which we find in the Socratic reminiscences written by Xenophon)[18] according to which he is astonished at the fact that in order to learn the trade of a shoemaker, a carpenter, a blacksmith, or an equerry, or even to learn how to train a horse or an ox, people know where to go to find a master. When it comes to justice, however, they don't know where to go. In Xenophon's text, the Sophist Hippias remarks to Socrates that he always repeats "the same phrases on the same subjects." Socrates admits this willingly, to which his interlocutor replies that he, Hippias, quite to the contrary, always tries to say something new, even if it is about justice. Socrates very much wants to know what Hippias could say that was new on a subject which ought not to change; but Hippias refuses to respond until Socrates gives his opinion on justice: "You have been making fun of others long enough, by always questioning and refuting them, without ever wanting to explain yourself to anybody or to set forth your opinion." Socrates replies: "I never stop showing what I think is just. If not in words, I show it by my actions." This means, in the last analysis, that it is the just person's life and existence which best determine what justice is.

Socrates' powerful individuality was able to awaken the individuality of his interlocutors, yet their reactions vary tremendously. We have seen the joy which Nicias felt when Socrates subjected him to questioning; Alcibiades, for his part, tried to resist his influence. He felt nothing but shame before Socrates, and in order to escape his attraction, he sometimes wished for his death. Socrates could only urge his interlocutor to examine himself and put himself to the test. In order for a dialogue to be established which, as Nicias says, can lead the individual to give an account of himself and of his life, the person who talks with Socrates must submit, along with Socrates, to the demands of rational discourse—that is, to the demands of reason. In other words, caring for ourselves and questioning ourselves occur only when our individuality is transcended and we rise to the level of universality, which is represented by what the two interlocutors have in common.

SOCRATES' KNOWLEDGE, OR THE ABSOLUTE VALUE OF MORAL INTENT

We have glimpsed what Socrates' knowledge can be, over and above his lack of knowledge. Socrates says again and again that he knows nothing, that he has nothing to teach to others, and that others must think for themselves and discover their truth by themselves. Yet we can at least wonder whether there wasn't also knowledge that Socrates himself had discovered, by himself and in himself. A passage from the *Apology*, in which knowledge is opposed to lack of knowledge, allows us to hazard this conjecture.[19] In the passage, Socrates imagines that other people might say to him, "Aren't you ashamed to have lived the kind of life which now is placing you in mortal danger?" Socrates claims he would respond as follows: "You do not speak well, my friend, if you think that a man who is worth something ought to calculate the risks of living and dying, instead of considering only, when he acts, whether he is acting justly or unjustly, and whether his deeds are those of a good man or a bad one." From this point of view, what appears as lack of knowledge is the fear of death: "For to fear death, Gentlemen, is nothing other than to think one is wise when one is not, for it means to think one knows what one does not know. No one knows whether death might not be the greatest of goods for man, but people fear it as if they were perfectly certain it is the greatest of evils. Yet how could it be anything but the most shameful ignorance to think one knows what one does not know?"[20] Socrates, for his part, knows that he knows nothing about death. Nevertheless, he does claim to know something concerning an entirely different subject: "I do, however, know that committing injustice and disobeying my betters, whether God or man, is bad and shameful. Therefore, I shall never fear or flee something whose badness or goodness I am ignorant of, as opposed to those evils which I know are bad."

It is most interesting to note that here knowledge and lack-of-knowledge have to do not with concepts, but with values: on the one hand, the value of death; on the other, the value of moral good and moral evil. Socrates knows nothing about the value which ought to be attributed to death, because it is not in his power, and because the experience of his own death escapes him by definition. Yet he does know the value of moral action and intention, for they do depend upon his choice, his decision, and his engagement. They therefore have their origin within him. Here again, knowledge is not a series of propositions or an abstract theory, but the certainty of choice, decision, and initiative. Knowledge is not just plain knowing, but knowing-what-ought-to-be-preferred, and hence knowing how to live. And it is this knowledge of value which guides him in his discussions with his interlocutors: "And if some one of you objects and claims that he does care (for intelligence, for truth, and for the best state of his soul), then I will not release him on the spot and go away, but I will question him, ex-

amine him, and refute him; and if he does not seem to me to have
acquired virtue, but says that he has, I will reproach him with at-
tributing the least importance to what is worth the most, and the
most importance to what is most base."[21]

This knowledge of value is taken from Socrates' inner experience—the experience of a choice which implicates him entirely.
Here once more, then, the only knowledge consists in a personal
discovery which comes from within. Such interiority is reinforced
in Socrates by the idea of the *daimōn,* that divine voice which, he
says, speaks to him and stops him from doing certain things. Was
this a mystical experience or a mythical image? It is difficult to say.
In any case, we can see in it a kind of figure of what later was called
moral conscience.

Socrates seems to have admitted implicitly that an innate desire
for the good exists in all human beings. This is the sense in which
he presented himself as a simple midwife whose role was limited
to making his interlocutors discover their inner possibilities. We
can now better understand the meaning of the Socratic paradox
according to which no one is evil willingly;[22] or, in another formulation, virtue is knowledge.[23] He means that if human beings commit moral evil, it is because they think they will thereby find good.
If they are virtuous, it is because they know, with all their soul and
all their being, where the true good lies. The philosopher's entire
role will therefore consist in permitting his interlocutor to "realize," in the strongest sense of the word, what the true good is and
what true value is. At the basis of Socratic knowledge is love of the
good.[24]

The content of Socratic knowledge is thus essentially "the absolute value of moral intent," and the certainty provided by the
choice of this value. This expression is, of course, modern, and
Socrates would not have used it. It can, however, help underscore
the entire range of the Socratic message. Indeed, we can say that a
value is absolute for a person when that person is ready to die for

that value. This is Socrates' attitude concerning "that which is best"—meaning justice, duty, and moral purity. As Socrates repeats several times in the *Apology*, he prefers death and danger to renouncing his duty and his mission.[25] In the *Crito*, Plato imagines that Socrates makes the Laws of Athens speak: they make him understand that if he tries to flee and escape his condemnation, he will do wrong to the city by giving an example of disobedience to the laws; he must not place his own life above what is just.[26] As Socrates says in the *Phaedo:* "If I had not thought that it was more just and more beautiful to leave up to the City the penalty which she may decide to impose upon me, rather than to flee and escape, my bones and my muscles would have been in Megara or Boeotia a long time ago, having been carried there by my judgment about what was 'best.'"[27]

This absolute value of moral choice also appears in another perspective, when Socrates declares that "for the good man, there is no evil, neither during his life, nor after he is dead."[28] This means that all those things that seem to people to be evil—death, sickness, poverty—are not evils for him. In his eyes, there is only one evil thing: moral fault. And there is only one good and one value: the will to do good. This implies that we must not avoid constantly and rigorously examining the way we live, in order to see if it is always guided and inspired by this will to do good. To a certain extent, we can say that what interests Socrates is not to define the theoretical and objective contents of morality—that is, what we ought to do—but to know if we really, concretely *want* to do what we consider just and good—in other words, how we must act. In the *Apology*, Socrates gives no theoretical explanation for why he forces himself to examine his own life and that of others. Instead, he contents himself with saying, on the one hand, that this is the mission with which the deity has entrusted him; and on the other hand, that only such lucidity and rigor with regard to ourselves can give meaning to life: "An unexamined life is not livable for man."[29] Here we find a kind of sketch—still confused and indistinct—of an idea which would be developed later, in the context of a wholly different problematic, by Kant: morality hinges on the purity of the intent which guides action. Such purity consists precisely in giving absolute value to the moral good, and totally renouncing one's individual interest.

There is, moreover, every indication that such wisdom is never acquired once and for all. It is not only others that Socrates never stops testing, but also himself. The purity of moral intent must be constantly renewed and reestablished. Self-transformation is never definitive, but demands perpetual reconquest.

CARE OF THE SELF AND CARE OF OTHERS

Speaking of the strangeness of philosophy, Maurice Merleau-Ponty said that philosophy is "never entirely within the world, yet never outside the world."[30] The same holds true of strange, unclassifiable Socrates. He, too, was neither in the world nor outside it.

On the one hand, in the view of his fellow citizens he proposed a complete reversal of values, which seemed incomprehensible to them: "Again, if I say that the greatest good for man happens to be the following: to spend time every day talking about virtue, as well as the other things you hear me discussing when I examine myself and others, and that an unexamined life is not livable for man—then you will believe me even less."[31]

Socrates' fellow citizens could not help perceiving his invitation to question all their values and their entire way of acting, and to take care for themselves, as a radical break with daily life, with the habits and conventions of everyday life, and with the world which they were familiar. What is more, this invitation to take care for themselves seemed like a call to detach themselves from the city, coming from man a who was himself somehow outside the world, who was *atopos*, disturbing, unclassifiable, and unsettling. Might not Socrates be the prototype for that image of the philosopher— so widespread, yet so false—who flees the difficulties of life in order to take refuge within his good conscience?

On the other hand, the portrait of Socrates as sketched by Alcibiades in Plato's *Symposium*—and also by Xenophon—reveals a man who participated fully in the life of the city around him. This Socrates was almost an ordinary or everyday man: he had a wife and children, and he talked with everybody—in the streets, in the shops, in the gymnasiums. He was also a *bon vivant* who could drink more than anyone else without getting drunk, and a brave, tough soldier.

Care for the self is thus not opposed to care for the city. In the *Apology* and the *Crito*, what Socrates proclaims, in a remarkable way, as his duty and that to which he must sacrifice everything, even his life, is obedience to the laws of the city. In the *Crito*, these personified "Laws" exhort Socrates not to give in to the temptation to escape from prison and flee far from Athens, by making him understand that his egoistic salvation would be an injustice with regard to Athens. This attitude is not one of conformity, for Xenophon makes Socrates say that it is quite possible to "obey the laws while hoping that they change, just as one serves in war while hoping for peace." As Merleau-Ponty has emphasized, "Socrates has a way of obeying which is a way of resisting."[32] He submits to the laws in order to prove, from within the city itself, the truth of his philosophical attitude and the absolute value of moral intention. Hegel was thus wrong to say that "Socrates flees within himself, in order to find the just and good there." Instead, we shall agree with Merleau-Ponty, who wrote: "He thought that it was impossible to be just by oneself. If one is just all by oneself, one ceases to be just."[33]

Care for the self is thus, indissolubly, care for the city and care for others. We can see this from the example of Socrates himself, whose entire reason for living was to concern himself with others. Socrates had both a missionary and a popular aspect, which we will encounter again in some philosophies of the Hellenistic period: "I am available both to the poor and to the rich, without distinction. . . . That I happen to be like a being that the deity has given to the city, you might conclude from the following considerations. After all, it does not seem human for me to have neglected all my own affairs and to have kept neglecting my own affairs for so many years now, and always to concern myself with your interests, going up to each one of you individually like a father or an elder brother and persuading you to care for virtue."[34]

Thus, Socrates is simultaneously in the world and outside it. He transcends both people and things by his moral demands and the engagement they require; yet he is involved with people and with things because the only true philosophy lies in the everyday. Throughout antiquity, Socrates was the model of the ideal philosopher, whose philosophical work is none other than his life and his death.[35] As Plutarch wrote at the beginning of the second century A.D.:

> Most people imagine that philosophy consists in delivering discourses from the heights of a chair, and in giving classes based on texts. But what these people utterly miss is the uninterrupted philosophy which we see being practiced every day in a way which is perfectly equal to itself. . . . Socrates did not set up grandstands for his audience and did not sit upon a professorial chair; he had no fixed timetable for talking or walking with his friends. Rather, he did philosophy sometimes by joking with them, or by drinking or going to war or to the market with them, and finally by going to prison and drinking poison. He was the first to show that at all times and in every place, in everything that happens to us, daily life gives us the opportunity to do philosophy.[36]

The Definition of "Philosopher" in Plato's *Symposium*

We do not know if Socrates used the word *philosophia* in his discussions with his interlocutors. If he did, it is likely he would have intended the word in the sense which was current at the time. In other words, he would have used it, as was common in those days, to designate the general culture which the Sophists and others dispensed to their students. This is the meaning we find, for example, in the rare occurrences of the word *philosophia* in the *Memorabilia*—recollections of Socrates which were collected by his disciple Xenophon. Nevertheless, it was under the influence of the personality and teaching of Socrates that Plato, in the *Symposium*, gave new meaning to the word "philosopher," and therefore also to the word "philosophy."

PLATO'S SYMPOSIUM

Like the *Apology*, the *Symposium* is a literary monument erected to the memory of Socrates. It is constructed with wonderful skill, as only Plato could do. Philosophical themes and mythical symbols are artfully woven together. As in the *Apology,* the theoretical element is reduced to a minimum. The *Symposium* contains only a few pages—which are, moreover, extremely important—pertaining to the vision of Beauty. The essential part is devoted to describing the way of life of Socrates, who reveals himself to be the model of the philosopher. The definition of the word "philosopher" proposed in the course of the dialogue thus becomes all the more significant.[1]

The figure of Socrates dominates the entire dialogue, which is presented as the story of a certain Aristodemus. He tells how Socrates asked him to accompany him to a banquet given by the poet Agathon in honor of his victory in the tragedy contest. Socrates arrives late, because he has remained standing still for quite a while, pursuing his meditations. The participants in the banquet produce speeches in honor of Eros, and Socrates' contribution is almost as long as those of the all the other speakers put together. When Alcibiades arrives at the end of the banquet, drunk, crowned with flowers, and accompanied by a flute-player, he gives a long speech in praise of Socrates, in which he enumerates all the aspects of the latter's personality. In the last lines of the work, Socrates, although he has drunk more than the others, is the only one still awake, remaining lucid and serene amid the sleeping guests:

> Only Agathon, Aristophanes, and Socrates had stayed awake, drinking from a great cup which they passed from right to left. Socrates was conversing with them. . . . He was gradually forcing them to admit that one man could compose both comedies and tragedies. . . . Aristophanes fell asleep first, and then Agathon, when the sun had already come up. Socrates . . . got up and left. He headed in the direction of the Lyceum, and after performing his ablutions, he spent the rest of the day just as he would have any other.

The end of this dialogue has inspired poets. One thinks of Hölderlin's verses about the sage who is able to bear the intensity of the happiness offered by the deity: "To each his measure. The weight of misfortune is heavy, but happiness is heavier still. Yet there was one sage who stayed lucid at the banquet, from noon until the heart of the night, and until the first glimmer of dawn."[2] As Nietzsche remarked, Socrates entered into death with the same calm with which he left the banquet: "He went to his death with that calm which Plato's description attributes to him when, last of all the guests, he left the banquet at the first glimmer of dawn to begin a new day, while behind him, on the benches and the floor, the sleepy guests remained behind to dream of Socrates, the true eroticist. For young people of the elite, the dying Socrates became the new ideal, never before encountered."[3]

As Daniel Babut has shown, even the slightest details are important in the construction of this dialogue, which is intended both to portray Socrates and to idealize him.[4] The company of drinkers had drawn up a program for the gathering which determined both the way they would drink and the theme of the speeches that each of the participants would have to give; the subject was to be Love. As the dialogue tells the story of the banquet which Socrates attended, it tells how each guest fulfilled his task, in what order the speeches succeeded one another, and what the various orators said. According to Babut, the first five speeches—those by Phaedrus, Pausanias, Eryximachus, Aristophanes, and Agathon—prepare the way, by a dialectical progression, for the praise of Love by Diotima, the Mantinean priestess, whose words Socrates quotes when it is his turn to speak.

Throughout the dialogue, but especially in the speeches of Diotima and Alcibiades, we notice that the features of the figure of Eros tend to become confused with those of the figure of Socrates. In the last analysis, the reason they become so closely enmeshed is that Eros and Socrates personify—one mythically, the other historically—the figure of the philosopher. This is the profound meaning of the dialogue.

EROS, SOCRATES, AND THE PHILOSOPHER

Socrates' praise of Eros was obviously composed according to the genuine Socratic manner. This means that Socrates does not act like the other guests, making a speech which affirms that Love possesses such-and-such a quality. He himself does not speak, because he knows nothing, but he makes the others speak. First of all comes Agathon, who praises Love just before Socrates, and who declares that Love is beautiful and gracious. Socrates therefore begins by questioning Agathon, asking him if Love is the desire for what one has or for what one does not have. If we must admit that Love is the desire for what we do not have, and if Love is the desire for beauty, must we not conclude that Love cannot be beautiful himself, since he does not possess beauty? After forcing Agathon to admit this view, Socrates does not go on to set forth his own theory of Love; instead, he tells of what Diotima, priestess of Mantinea, made him understand about Love in a conversation he once had with her. Since Love exists relatively to something else, and to something which it lacks, it cannot be a god, as has wrongly been thought by all the other guests who have thus far praised Love. On the contrary, Love is only a *daimōn*—a being that is intermediate between gods and men, immortals and mortals.[5] Not only does Love occupy a position between two opposing orders of reality, but it is in the situation of a mediator. The *daimōn* has a relation both to gods and to men; he plays a role in mystery initiations, in the incantations which cure maladies of the soul and body, and in the communications which come from the gods to men, both while they are awake and while they are asleep. To give Socrates a better understanding of this representation of Eros, Diotima tells him a mythical story of the birth of this *daimōn*.[6] On the day of Aphrodite's birth, the gods had a banquet. At the end of the meal, Penia (the name signifies "Poverty" or "Privation") came to beg. Poros ("Means," "Wealth," "Expedient") was asleep at the time, drunk on nectar, in Zeus' garden. Penia lay down beside him, in order to remedy her own poverty by having a child with him; and thus she conceived Eros. According to Diotima, Love's nature and character can be explained by this origin. Born on Aphrodite's birthday, he is enamored of beauty; but since he is the son of Penia, he is always poor, indigent, and a beggar. At the same time, since he is the son of Poros, he is clever and inventive.

In a way which is both skillful and full of humor, Diotima's mythical description applies simultaneously to Eros, Socrates, and the philosopher. Of needy Eros, Diotima says: "He is always poor, for he is far from being delicate or beautiful, as people think. On the contrary, he is rough, dirty, barefoot, and homeless; he always sleeps on the ground, in the open air, on doorsteps and in roadways." Yet since he is also a worthy son of Poros, this enamored Eros is a "dangerous hunter." "He sets traps for noble souls, for he is hardy, brazen, and tough; he is always trying to come up with some trick; he wants to be clever and resourceful; he 'does philosophy' all his life. He is a fearsome sorcerer, a magician and a Sophist."

This description also applies to Socrates, who is likewise an amorous, barefoot hunter. At the end of the dialogue, Alcibiades describes him as he took part in the military expedition at Potidaea, exposed to the winter cold, barefoot, and covered with a coarse cloak which barely protected him. At the beginning of the dialogue, we learn that in order to come to the banquet, Socrates had—exceptionally—bathed and put on shoes. Socrates' bare feet and old cloak were a favorite theme of the comic poets.[7] The Socrates described by the comic playwright Aristophanes in his *Clouds* was a worthy son of Poros: "Hardy, a smooth talker, brazen, impudent, . . . never at a loss for words—a real fox." In his praise of Socrates, Alcibiades also alludes to his impudence, and Agathon has done the same before him, at the beginning of the dialogue.[8] For Alcibiades, Socrates is also a genuine magician, who bewitches souls with his words.[9] As far as Eros' robustness is concerned, we encounter it in the portrait which Alcibiades sketches of Socrates in the army: he can resist cold, hunger, and fear, while still being capable of handling both wine and privation.[10]

This portrait of Eros-Socrates is at the same time the portrait of the philosopher, insofar as Eros, the son of Poros and Penia, is poor and deficient. Yet he knows how to compensate for his poverty, privation, and deficiency by means of his cleverness. For Diotima, Eros is therefore a *philo-sopher,* since he is halfway between *sophia* and ignorance. Here, Plato does not define what he means by wisdom.[11] He merely hints that it is a transcendent state, since, in his view, only the gods are "wise" in the proper sense of the term.[12] We may suppose that wisdom represents the perfection of knowledge, which is identified with virtue; yet as we have seen, knowledge or *sophia* in the Greek tradition is less a purely theoretical wisdom than know-how, or knowing-how-to-live. We can recognize traces of this know-how not in the theoretical knowledge of Socrates the philosopher, but in his way of life, which is precisely what Plato evokes in the *Symposium.*

There are, says Diotima, two categories of beings which do not do philosophy. The first category comprises gods and sages, because they are wise; the second consists of senseless people, because they *think* they are wise. "No god does philosophy, nor does he wish to become wise [*sophos*], since he already is; and if some other wise being exists, he will not do philosophy either. Moreover, ignorant people do not do philosophy and do not want to become wise, for the misfortune of ignorance is to believe one is beautiful, good, and wise, when one is not. He who is not aware of lacking something does not desire what he does not think he needs."

Socrates then asks, "If that is so, Diotima, then who is it that does philosophy, if it is neither the wise nor the senseless?" Diotima replies, "It is those in the middle, midway between the two;

and Love is one of them. For wisdom is, no doubt, one of the most beautiful things; but Love is love of the beautiful. Love must therefore be a *philo-sopher* [lover of wisdom], and, as a philosopher, he must be midway between the wise and the senseless. The reason for this is his birth: his father is wise [*sophos*] and inventive; his mother, senseless and without resources [*en aporiai*]."

Here again, we recognize beneath the features of Eros not only the philosopher but Socrates, who, like senseless people, seemed not to know anything—but who was nevertheless *aware* of not knowing anything. He was therefore different from senseless people by virtue of the fact that, being conscious of his lack of knowledge, he desired to know (although, as we have seen, his representation of knowledge was profoundly different from the traditional concept). Socrates, or the philosopher, is thus Eros: although deprived of wisdom, beauty, and the good, he desires and loves wisdom, beauty, and the good. He is Eros, which means that he is desire—not a passive and nostalgic desire, but desire which is impetuous, and worthy of Eros, the "dangerous hunter."

Apparently, nothing could be simpler and more natural than the philosopher's intermediate position. He is midway between wisdom and ignorance. We might think that it is enough for him to practice his philosophical activity in order to transcend ignorance and attain wisdom once and for all; but matters are much more complex than this.

In the background of this opposition between sages, philosophers, and senseless people, we can glimpse a logical schema of conceptual division which is highly rigorous and does not allow such an optimistic perspective. Diotima had opposed sages to nonsages, which means that she established a contradictory opposition which admits no intermediaries: either one is a sage or one is not, and there is no middle path. From this point of view, we cannot say that the philosopher is an intermediary between the sage and the nonsage, for if he is not a "sage," he is necessarily and decidedly a "nonsage." Therefore, he is destined never to attain wisdom. Yet Diotima has introduced a division among the nonsages: there are those who are unconscious of their lack of wisdom, and these are senseless people. And there are those who are aware of their lack of wisdom, and these are the philosophers. Now, however, we may consider that within the category of nonsages, senseless people, who are unconscious of their lack of wisdom, are opposed to the sages as contraries. From this point of view—that is, in accordance with this opposition of *contrariety*—philosophers are intermediary between sages and the senseless, insofar as they are nonsages who are conscious of their lack of wisdom. They are thus neither sages nor senseless. This division is parallel to another which was very common in Plato's school: the distinction between "what is good" and "what is not good." Since this is a contradictory opposition, there is no intermediary between these two terms. Within the category of what is not good, however, we can distinguish between that which is neither god nor bad, and that which is bad. Here, the relation of contrariety will be established between the good and the bad, and there will be an intermediary between the good and the bad—namely, the "neither good nor bad."[13] Such logical schemes, which were extremely important in Plato's school,[14] were used to distinguish things which have no "more" or "less" from those which exhibit degrees of intensity. Since the sage and that which is good are absolute, they admit no variation; they cannot be more or less wise or more or less good. By contrast, what is intermediate—the "neither good nor bad" and the "philosopher"—*do* display the degrees of more and less. Thus, the philosopher will never attain wisdom, but he can make progress in its direction. According to the *Symposium*, then, philosophy is not wisdom, but a way of life and discourse determined by the *idea* of wisdom.

With the *Symposium*, the etymology of the word *philosophia*—"the love or desire for wisdom"—thus becomes the very program of philosophy. We can say that with the Socrates of the *Sympo-*

sium, philosophy takes on a definite historical tonality which is ironic and tragic at the same time. It is ironic, in that the true philosopher will always be the person who knows that he does not know, who knows that he is not a sage, and who is therefore neither sage nor nonsage. He is not at home in either the world of senseless people or the world of sages; neither wholly in the world of men and women, nor wholly in the world of the gods. He is unclassifiable, and, like Eros and Socrates, has neither hearth nor home. Philosophy's tonality is also tragic, because the bizarre being called the "philosopher" is tortured and torn by the desire to attain this wisdom which escapes him, yet which he loves. Like Kierkegaard, the Christian who wanted to be a Christian but knew that only Christ is a Christian,[15] the philosopher knows that he cannot reach his model and will never be entirely that which he desires. Plato thus establishes an insurmountable distance between philosophy and wisdom. Philosophy is defined by what it lacks—that is, by a transcendent norm which escapes it, yet which it nevertheless possesses within itself in some way, as in the famous, and very Platonic, words of Pascal: "You would not seek me if you had not already found me."[16] As Plotinus was to say, "If something were totally deprived of the good, it would never seek the good."[17] This is why the Socrates of the *Symposium* appears simultaneously as someone who claims to have no wisdom and as someone whose way of living is admired; for the philosopher is not only an intermediary being, but, like Eros, is also a mediator. He reveals to mankind something of the world of the gods, or the world of wisdom. He is like those statuettes known as *silenoi*—figurines that seem grotesque and ridiculous from the outside but that reveal statues of the gods when they are opened up.[18] Thus Socrates, by the magical and demonic effect of his life and his speech, forces Alcibiades to question himself and admit that his life is not worth living if he continues to behave as he does. Let us note in passing, following Léon Robin, that the *Symposium* itself—meaning the literary work with this title written by Plato—is also similar to Socrates.[19] It, too, is a sculpted silenus which, beneath irony and humor, hides the most profound conceptions.

Eros is not the only figure which is devalued and demystified in this way in the *Symposium*, passing from the rank of god to that of demon. The situation is similar with the philosopher, who ceases to be the recipient of ready-made knowledge from the Sophists. Instead, he becomes someone who is aware both of his deficiency and of the desire within him which attracts him to the beautiful and the good.

Thus, in the *Symposium*, the philosopher who becomes aware of himself resembles Socrates as we have described him above: he is neither quite of this world, nor quite outside the world. As Alcibiades had observed during the Potidaea expedition, Socrates was able to remain happy in any circumstances. During this military expedition, he knew how to profit from abundance when it was there, surpassing everyone else in the art of drinking without getting drunk; yet in times of famine, he bore up courageously under hunger and thirst. He was just as much at ease when there was nothing to eat as when there was abundant food; he easily put up with the cold, feared nothing, and showed remarkable courage during combat. He was indifferent to everything that usually seduces men: beauty, wealth, and every sort of advantage, which all seemed to him without value.

Yet he was also someone who could become totally absorbed in meditation, withdrawing from all his surroundings. During the Potidaea expedition, his companions in arms saw him standing motionless and reflecting for an entire day; this also happens to him at the beginning of *Symposium*, and explains why he arrives late at the banquet. Perhaps Plato wishes to hint that Socrates was initiated into the mysteries of love by the Mantinean priestess, and that he has learned to see true beauty. As Diotima says, he who has attained such a vision will lead the only life worth living, and thus he will acquire excellence *(aretē),* or true virtue.[20] Here philosophy appears as an experience of love. Thus, Socrates reveals himself as a being who, although not a god, since he appears at first sight to be an ordinary man, is nevertheless superior to men. He is a *daimōn*, or mixture of divinity and humanity. Such a mixture is, however, is far from self-evident, but is necessarily linked to a strangeness, and almost to a lack of balance, or inner dissonance.

This definition of "philosopher" in the *Symposium* was to be of capital importance throughout the history of philosophy. For example, the Stoics, like Plato, saw the philosopher as being essentially different from the sage and, from the point of view of this contradictory opposition, no different from the average man. As the Stoics used to say, it matters little whether you are one fathom or five hundred fathoms beneath the surface of the water: you drown just the same.[21] In a sense, there was a basic difference between the sage and the nonsage: only the nonsage could be characterized by "more or less," whereas the sage represented absolute perfection, which admits of no degrees. The fact that the philosopher was a nonsage does not, however, mean that there was no difference between him and other people. The philosopher was aware of his lack of wisdom; he desired wisdom and tried to make progress toward wisdom, which, for the Stoics, was a kind of transcendent state which could be attained only by a sudden, unexpected mutation. Besides, the sage either did not exist, or existed only rarely. The philosopher could therefore make progress, but always within the limits of lack-of-wisdom. He tended toward wisdom, but in an asymptotic way, and without ever being able to reach it.

The other philosophical schools did not have such a precise doctrine on the difference between philosophy and wisdom. In general, however, wisdom appeared as an ideal which guided and attracted the philosopher. Above all, philosophy was viewed as an exercise of wisdom, and therefore as the practice of a way of life. This idea was still alive in Kant, and it is implicit in all those philosophers who define philosophy etymologically as the love of wisdom. What philosophers have least retained from the model presented by Socrates in the *Symposium* are his irony and his humor, which are likewise seen in the dancing Socrates of Xenophon's *Symposium*.[22] Traditionally, philosophers have deprived themselves of what they need the most. Nietzsche was well aware of this: "Socrates' advantage over the founder of Christianity was the smile which inflected his seriousness, and that wisdom full of mischievousness which gives a person the best state of soul."[23]

ISOCRATES

We also encounter the opposition between philosophy and wisdom in the orator Isocrates, one of Plato's contemporaries. His writings show that there had been an evolution in the conception of philosophy since the time of the Sophists: "Philosophy, . . . which has educated us with a view to action, has made us gentle in our mutual relations, has distinguished the misfortunes caused by ignorance from those resulting from necessity, and has taught us to avoid the former and bear the latter courageously—this philosophy was revealed by our city."[24] Philosophy was still Athens' pride and glory, but its content had changed considerably. In Isocrates' description, philosophy is no longer a matter of overall scientific culture; it has become a means of training for life which transforms human relationships and arms us against adversity. Above all, Isocrates introduces a capital distinction between *sophia* (or *epistēmē*) and *philosophia:*

> Since it is not in the nature of human beings to possess knowledge [*epistēmē*] such that, if we possessed it, we would know what we must do and what we must say, I consider wise [*sophoi*], within the limits of what is possible, those who, thanks to their opinions, can most often hit upon what is best. And I consider philosophers

[*philosophoi*] those who spend their time at those exercises from which they will most rapidly acquire such a capacity of judgment [*phronēsis*].[25]

Thus, Isocrates first distinguishes an ideal knowledge (*epistēmē*), conceived of as perfect know-how in the conduct of life, based on a completely infallible capacity of judgment. He then mentions practical wisdom (*sophia*), which is know-how acquired by the solid formation of judgment, which allows its possessor to make rational yet conjectural decisions in whatever situations happen to present themselves. Finally, there is the formation of judgment itself, which is nothing other than philosophy. This, moreover, is a different kind of philosophy from Plato's; in the case of Isocrates, we could speak of humanism is the classical sense of the term. "Isocrates is deeply convinced that one can become better by learning how to speak well," so long as one deals with "subjects which are elevated, beautiful, serve humanity, and concern public welfare."[26] Thus, for Isocrates, philosophy was indissolubly both the art of speaking well and the art of living well.

PART TWO

PHILOSOPHY AS A WAY OF LIFE

∎ ∎ ∎

Plato and the Academy

Plato's *Symposium* thus immortalized the figure of Socrates as a philosopher—that is, as a man who sought, both by his words and by his way of life, to approach and to make others approach the way of being or transcendent ontological state called wisdom. From this perspective, the philosophy of Plato—and, following him, all the philosophies of antiquity, even those which were farthest away from Platonism—all shared the aim of establishing an intimate link between philosophical discourse and way of life.

PHILOSOPHY AS A WAY OF LIFE IN PLATO'S ACADEMY

The Educative Project

We must return to the link between Socrates and Eros, philosophy and love, in Plato's *Symposium*. Here, love appears not only as the desire for what is wise and beautiful, but also as the desire for fecundity—that is, the desire to immortalize oneself by producing. Love, in other words, is creative and fruitful. There are two kinds of fruitfulness, says Diotima: that of the body and that of the soul.[1] Those whose fruitfulness resides in the body try to immortalize themselves by engendering children, but those whose fecundity resides in the soul try to immortalize themselves in a work of the intellect, whether literary or technical. But the highest form of intelligence consists in self-mastery and justice, and these are exercised in the organization of cities or other institutions. Many historians have seen in this mention of "institutions" an allusion to the founding of Plato's school, for in the following lines Plato clearly gives us to understand that the fruitfulness he is talking about is that of an educator, who, like Eros, son of Poros, is "full of resources" (euporei) "in order to speak about virtue—to say what kind of things a good man ought to think about, and with what he ought to busy himself."[2] In the Phaedrus, Plato speaks of "impregnating minds" and of "sowing discourses which themselves contain a seed from which, in other natures, will grow other discourses, capable . . . of leading us to the highest degree of happiness possible for human beings."[3] Robin has summarized these Platonic themes as follows: "The fruitful soul can fecundate and fructify only by its commerce with another soul, in which the necessary qualities have been recognized. This commerce can be instituted only by living words and the daily interchange required by a life in common, organized with a view to spiritual ends and for an indefinite future. In other words, a philosophical school, such as Plato conceived his own, in its present state and for the continuity of tradition."[4]

Here we discover another important aspect of the new definition of philosophy which Plato proposes in the Symposium and which would leave a definitive mark on philosophical life in antiquity. Philosophy could be carried out only by means of a community of life and dialogue between masters and disciples, within the framework of a school. Several centuries later, Seneca still spoke of the philosophical importance of life in common:

> The living word and life in common will benefit you more than written discourse. It is to current reality that you must go, first be-

cause men believe their eyes more than their ears, and then because the path of precepts is long, but that of examples is short and infallible. Cleanthes [the Stoic] would not have imitated his master Zeno if he had been merely his auditor; but he was involved in his life, he penetrated his secret thoughts, and he was able to observe first hand whether Zeno lived in conformity with his own rule of life. Plato, Aristotle, and that whole crowd of sages which ended up going in opposite directions—all derived more profit from Socrates' morals than from his words. It was not Epicurus' school which made great men of Metrodorus, Hermarchus, and Polyaenus, but his companionship.[5]

As we shall see further on, it is true that Plato was not the only person of his time to found a school devoted to philosophical education. Other disciples of Socrates, such as Antisthenes, Euclid of Megara, and Aristippus of Cyrene, did so in the same period, as did Isocrates. Plato's Academy, however, was to have an important influence both in his day and in the following centuries, by the quality of its members as much as by the perfection of its organization. Throughout the subsequent history of philosophy, we will encounter the memory and the imitation of this institution, as well as of the discussions and debates which took place there.[6] Its name derives from the fact that school activities took place in meeting rooms located in a gymnasium called the Academy, on the outskirts of Athens. Plato had acquired a small property near this gymnasium, where the members of the school could meet and even live together.[7]

Socrates and Pythagoras

The ancients used to say that Plato's originality consisted in his synthesis of Socrates, whom he had known at Athens, and Pythagoreanism, which he may have come to know during his first trip to Sicily.[8] From Socrates, he got his dialectic method, his irony, and his interest in the problems of the conduct of life; from

Pythagoras, he inherited the idea of education by mathematics and the possible application of these sciences to the knowledge of nature, as well as the idea of a community of life among philosophers. It is indisputable that Plato knew some Pythagoreans; indeed, he depicts them in his dialogues. Yet given the uncertainty of our knowledge of Old Pythagoreanism, we cannot define with exactitude the extent of the influence of Pythagoreanism on Plato's development. One thing is certain, though: in the *Republic*, Plato praises Pythagoras, claiming that he was loved because he proposed to men and to future generations a "way" or rule of life, called "Pythagorean," which distinguished those who practiced it from other men and which still existed in Plato's time.[9] Pythagorean communities did in fact play an important political role in the cities of southern Italy and of Sicily. We are justified in thinking that the foundation of the Academy was inspired both by the model of the Socratic form of life and by the model of the Pythagorean way of life, even if we cannot define the latter's characteristics with certainty.[10]

Political Intentions

Plato's initial intentions were political. He believed in the possibility of changing political life by means of the philosophical education of those men who were influential in the city. The autobiographical testimony Plato gives us in the *Seventh Letter* deserves our attention; it tells how, in his youth, he, like other young men, wanted to devote himself to the affairs of the city. But as a result of the death of Socrates and his examination of laws and customs, he discovered how difficult it was to administer the affairs of the city correctly. Ultimately, he realized that all the cities which existed in his time possessed a defective political regime. This is why, he says, "I was irresistibly drawn to praise true philosophy and to proclaim that by its light alone can one recognize where justice lies, both in public and in private life." Yet this is no simple matter of abstract talk; for Plato, the "philosopher's task" consists in action. He tried to play a political role in Syracuse precisely so that he might not appear, in his own eyes, as a "big talker," incapable of action.[11] Many students of the Academy did in fact play a political role in many cities, as counselors to rulers, legislators, or opponents of tyranny.[12] The Sophists had claimed to train young people for political life, but Plato wanted to accomplish this by providing them with a knowledge far superior to that which the Sophists could give them. On the one hand, this knowledge was to be founded upon a rigorous rational method; on the other, in accordance with the Socratic concept, it was to be inseparable from the love of the good and from the inner transformation of the person. Plato wanted to train not only skillful statesmen, but also human beings.

In order to realize his political goal, Plato thus had to make an immense detour: he had to create an intellectual and spiritual community whose job it would be to train new human beings, however long this might take. In the course of this detour, moreover, his political goals risked being forgotten, and it is interesting in this regard to hear Plato say that the philosophers will have to be forced to be kings.[13] When Aristotle's disciple Dicearchus came to describe life in Plato's Academy, he emphasized the fact that its members lived as a community of free, equal people, insofar as their aspiration toward virtue equaled their desire to pursue shared research.[14] Plato did not require tuition fees from his students, in line with his principle that equal things ought to be given to equal people. In accordance with Platonic principles, moreover, this was a geometric equality which gave to each person according to his merits and needs.[15] Plato, as we can see here, was convinced that human beings could live as human beings only within a perfect city. While he waited for the latter to be realized, however, he wanted to make his disciples live in the conditions of an ideal city;

and if they could not govern a city, he wanted them at least to be able to govern their own selves in accordance with the norms of the ideal city.[16] This is what most subsequent philosophical schools would attempt to do as well.[17]

While they waited to take part in political activity, the members of the school devoted themselves to a disinterested life of study and of spiritual practices. Like the Sophists, therefore, but for different reasons, Plato created an educational milieu which was relatively separate from the city.

Socrates had a different concept of education. Unlike the Sophists, he considered that education should take place not in an artificial milieu, but by immersing one's self in the life of the city, as was done in ancient tradition. What characterized Socrates' pedagogy was the fact that it attributed capital importance to living contact between human beings; and here Plato agreed. We find this Socratic conception of education by living contact and by love in the works of Plato; but as John Patrick Lynch has pointed out, Plato institutionalized it, so to speak, in his school.[18] Education took place within a community, group, or circle of friends in which an atmosphere of sublimated love prevailed.

Training and Research in the Academy

We know little about the way the Academy functioned as an institution.[19] We must not, as has been done too often, imagine the Academy—or, for that matter, the other Athenian philosophical schools—as religious associations *(thiasoi)* of the Muses. Their founding merely resulted from exercising the right of association which was in force in Athens. There seem to have been two categories of members: the older members, who were researchers and teachers; and the younger ones, who were students. The latter group seems to have played a decisive role in the election of

Xenocrates as second successor to Plato; the story goes that Speusippus, the first successor, was chosen by Plato himself.

In antiquity, it was considered significant that two women, named Axiothea and Lastheneia, had been pupils of Plato and Speusippus. It was said that Axiothea was not ashamed to wear the simple cloak of the philosophers.[20] From this, we can assume that the members of the Academy, like other philosophers of the time, held fast to this outfit, which distinguished them from other people. Judging by later traditions concerning the school, we may infer that, in addition to discussions, classes, and scientific work, group meals were sometimes part of the school's curriculum.[21]

We have mentioned the older members, who were Plato's associates in research and teaching. We know the names of some of them: Speusippus, Xenocrates, Eudoxus of Cnidos, Heraclides of Pontus, and Aristotle. Aristotle remained in the Academy for twenty years, first as a disciple and then as a teacher. Academy members were philosophers and scholars; in particular, they included astronomers and mathematicians of the very first rank, such as Eudoxus and Theaetetus. If the works of Speusippus, Xenocrates, and Eudoxus had been preserved, we would probably have an entirely different view of the Academy, and of the role that Plato played within it.

Geometry and the other mathematical sciences were crucially important in training, but they represented only the first stage in the training of future philosophers. Within Plato's school, they were practiced in a totally disinterested way. Their utility was not considered;[22] instead, since they were intended to purify the mind from sensible representations, their aim was primarily ethical.[23] Geometry was the subject not only of elementary instruction, but also of advanced research; in fact, the Academy was the birthplace of mathematics. Its members were the first to develop mathematical axiomatics, which formulated the presuppositions of reasoning—principles, axioms, definitions, postulates—and placed the theorems in order by deducing them from one another. Half a century later, all this work would result in the famous *Elements* by Euclid.[24]

According to the *Republic,* would-be philosophers should not practice dialectics until they have acquired a certain maturity; once they reach this age, they should study it for five years, from age thirty to thirty-five.[25] We do not know if Plato applied this rule within his school, yet dialectical exercises necessarily had a place in the Academy's curriculum. In Plato's time, dialectics was a debating technique subject to precise rules. A "thesis" was proposed—an interrogative proposition such as: Can virtue be taught? One of the two interlocutors attacked the thesis; the other defended it. The former attacked by interrogating—that is, he asked the defender skillfully chosen questions with the aim of forcing him to admit the contradictory of the thesis he wanted to defend. The interrogator had no thesis, and this was why Socrates was in the habit of playing that role. As Aristotle says, "Socrates always played the part of the interrogator and never that of the respondent, for he admitted he knew nothing."[26] Dialectics taught students not only how to attack—that is, how to lead interrogations judiciously—but also how to respond, by avoiding the interrogator's traps. The discussion of a thesis was to constitute the principal form of teaching until the first century B.C.[27]

Training in dialectics was absolutely necessary, insofar as Plato's disciples were destined to play a role in their city. In a civilization where political discourse was central, young people had to be trained to have a perfect mastery of speech and reasoning. Yet, in Plato's eyes, such mastery was dangerous, for it risked making young people believe that any position could be either defended or attacked. That is why Platonic dialectics was not a purely logical exercise. Instead, it was a spiritual exercise which demanded that the interlocutors undergo an *askēsis,* or self-transformation. It was not a matter of a combat between two individuals, in which the more skillful person imposed his point of view, but a joint effort on the part of two interlocutors in accord with the rational demands of reasonable discourse, or the *logos*. Opposing his method to that of contemporary eristics, which practiced controversy for its own sake, Plato says: "When two friends, like you and me, are in the mood to chat, we have to go about it in a gentler and more dialectical way. By 'more dialectical,' I mean not only that we give real responses, but that we base our responses solely on what the interlocutor admits that he himself knows."[28]

A true dialogue is possible only if the interlocutors *want* to dialogue. Thanks to this agreement between the interlocutors, which is renewed at each stage of the discussion, neither one of the interlocutors imposes his truth upon the other. On the contrary, dialogue teaches them to put themselves in each other's place and thereby transcend their own point of view. By dint of a sincere effort, the interlocutors discover by themselves, and within themselves, a truth which is independent of them, insofar as they submit to the superior authority of the *logos*. Here, as in all ancient philosophy, philosophy consists in the movement by which the individual transcends himself toward something which lies beyond him. For Plato, this something was the *logos:* discourse which implies the demands of rationality and universality. This *logos,* moreover, did not represent a kind of absolute knowledge; instead, it was equivalent to the agreement which is established between interlocutors who are brought to admit certain positions in common, and by this agreement transcend their particular points of view.[29]

The ethics of dialogue did not necessarily translate into a perpetual dialogue. We know, for instance, that some of Aristotle's treatises—those which oppose the Platonic theory of ideas—are preparatory manuscripts for the oral lessons which Aristotle had given at the Academy. They are arranged as continuous discourse, in didactic form.[30] It does seem, however, as though the auditors,

in accordance with a custom which was continued throughout antiquity, could express their opinion after the exposition. There
were certainly many other lectures by Speusippus or by Eudoxus,
each expressing very different points of view. Thus, research was
shared and ideas were exchanged, and this process, too, was a kind
of dialogue. Plato, moreover, conceived of thought itself as a dialogue: "Thought and discourse are the same thing, except that it is
the soul's silent, inner dialogue with itself which we have called
'thought.'"[31]

The Platonic Choice of Life

This ethics of the dialogue explains the freedom of thought which,
as we have seen, reigned in the Academy. Speusippus, Xenocrates,
Eudoxus, and Aristotle professed theories which were by no
means in accord with those of Plato, especially on the subject of
Ideas. They even disagreed about the definition of the good, since
we know that Eudoxus thought the supreme good was pleasure.
Such intense controversies among the members of the school left
traces not only within Plato's dialogues and in Aristotle, but
throughout Hellenistic philosophy,[32] if not throughout the entire
history of philosophy. In any event, we may conclude that the
Academy was a place for free discussion, and that within it there
was neither scholastic orthodoxy nor dogmatism.

If this is true, we may wonder what the school's unity could be
based upon. I think we can say that although Plato and the other
teachers at the Academy disagreed on points of doctrine, they nevertheless all accepted, to various degrees, the choice of the way or
form of life which Plato had proposed. It seems that this choice of
life consisted, first, in adhering to the ethics of dialogue of which
we have just spoken. This was a "form of life" (to use J. Mittelstrass' expression)[33] which was practiced by the interlocutors; for
insofar as, in the act of dialoguing, they posited themselves as sub-

jects but also transcended themselves, they experienced the *logos* which transcends them. Moreover, they also experienced that love of the good which is presupposed by every attempt at dialogue. From this perspective, the object of the discussion and its doctrinal content are of secondary importance. What counts is the practice of dialogue, and the transformation which it brings. Sometimes, the function of dialogue can even be to run into *aporia*, and thus to reveal the limits of language—its occasional inability to communicate moral and existential experience.

Ultimately, to use the expression of Luc Brisson, what mattered was "learning to live in a philosophical way,"[34] with a common will to carry out disinterested research and in deliberate opposition to sophistic mercantilism.[35] This was already a choice of life. To live in a philosophical way meant, above all, to turn toward intellectual and spiritual life, carrying out a conversion which involved "the whole soul"[36]—which is to say, the whole of moral life. For Plato, science and knowledge are never purely theoretical and abstract knowledge, which could be placed "ready-made" within the soul. When Socrates said that virtue is knowledge, he was not using "knowledge" to mean pure, abstract knowledge of the good. Rather, he meant knowledge which chooses and wants the good— in other words, an inner disposition in which thought, will, and desire are one. For Plato, too, if virtue is knowledge, then knowledge itself is virtue.

We can thus assume that the members of the Academy shared a certain conception of knowledge. They saw it as the training of human beings, as the slow and difficult education of the character, as the harmonious development[37] of the entire human person, and finally as a way of life, intended to "ensure . . . a good life and thereby the 'salvation' of the soul."[38]

In Plato's view, what was most essential was the choice of a philosophical way of life. This is confirmed by the story of Er in the *Republic*, which mythically presents this choice as having been made in a previous life: "That is where all the risk lies for man, and it is for this reason that each individual must leave aside all other studies and devote all his care to research, and cultivate this alone. Perhaps he will be able to discover and recognize the man who will impart to him the ability and the knowledge to discern what the good life is, and what the bad life is, and to choose the good life always and everywhere, as far as possible."[39]

Spiritual Exercises

In his *Seventh Letter*, Plato declares that if we do not adopt this way of life, life is not worth living; and this is why we must decide right now to follow this "wonderful path." This kind of life requires, moreover, a considerable effort, which must be renewed every day. It is with regard to this kind of life that those who "really do philosophy" are distinguished from those who "don't really do philosophy," who have only a veneer of superficial opinions.[40] Plato alludes to this kind of life when he evokes the figure of his disciple Dio of Syracuse.[41] It consists in "setting more store by virtue than by pleasure," in renouncing the pleasures of the senses, in observing a specific diet, and in "living every day in such a way as to become master of oneself as much as possible." As Paul Rabbow has shown, it does seem that certain spiritual practices, which have left traces in many passages from the dialogues, were in use in the Academy.[42]

In the final pages of the *Timaeus*, Plato affirms that we must exercise the superior part of the soul—which is none other than the intellect—in such a way that it achieves harmony with the universe and is assimilated to the deity. He does not give details on how to perform these exercises, but we can find interesting specifications in other dialogues.[43]

When Plato mentions the unconscious drives revealed to us by dreams—for instance those "terrible and savage" desires for murder and rape that lie deep within us—one could speak in terms of "preparation for sleep."[44] If we wish to avoid such dreams, we must prepare ourselves every evening by trying to awaken the rational part of the soul through inner discourses and research on elevated subjects. We should also devote ourselves to meditation, which will calm our desire and anger. Plato also advises us not to sleep too much: "As to sleep, people should sleep only as much as is useful for health; but the amount needed is not large, once it has become a habit."[45]

Another exercise consisted in knowing how to maintain one's calm in misfortune, without rebelling.[46] Thus, we must tell ourselves that we do not know what is good and what is bad in such accidents; that it does no good to become upset; that no human matter is worth being considered very important; and that, as in a dice game, we must deal with things as they are, and act appropriately.[47]

The most famous practice is the exercise of death. Plato alludes to it in the *Phaedo*, whose theme is precisely the death of Socrates. Here, Socrates declares that a man who has spent his life in philosophy necessarily has the courage to die, since philosophy is nothing other than an exercise of death [*meletē thanatou*].[48] It is an exercise of death because death is the separation of the soul and the body, and the philosopher spends his time trying to detach his soul from his body. The body causes us no end of trouble, because of the passions which it engenders and the needs it imposes upon us. Thus, the philosopher must purify himself—that is, he must try to concentrate and collect his soul, and deliver it from the dispersion and distraction which the body imposes upon it. Here we think of the passages in the *Symposium* that describe the long periods in which Socrates stood still and reflected upon himself, without moving or eating. This exercise was, indissolubly, an *askēsis* of the body and of thought—a divestment of the passions in order to accede to the purity of the intelligence. In a certain sense, dialogue is already an exercise of death; for as René Schaerer has said, "corporeal individuality ceases to exist the moment it is externalized in the *logos*."[49] This was one of the favorite themes in the thought of the late Brice Parain: "Language develops only upon the death of individuals."[50] From the perspective of the story of Socrates' death in the *Phaedo*, we can thus see that the "I" which must die transcends itself and becomes an "I" which is henceforth a stranger to death, since it has identified itself with the *logos* and with thought. Socrates hints at this at the end of the dialogue: "My friends, I cannot convince Crito that I am Socrates, who is talking with you this very instant, and who is setting all his arguments in order. He thinks that I am that other whom he will soon see as a corpse."[51]

Whereas, in the *Phaedo*, this exercise is presented as an exercise of death which frees the soul from the fear of death, in the *Republic* it appears as something like the soul's flight on high, or a look down upon reality from above: "Small-mindedness is what is most opposed to a soul which must always stretch itself toward the entire totality of the divine and the human. . . . The soul to which elevation of thought and the contemplation of the totality of time and of being belong—do you think human life can seem to be something important to it? . . . Such a man will therefore not look on death as something terrible."[52]

Here again, the exercise which consists in radically changing one's point of view, and in embracing the whole of reality within one universal vision, allows us to defeat the fear of death. Greatness of soul reveals itself to be the fruit of the universality of thought. The philosopher described in the *Theaetetus* casts the same glance from above at the things down here below.[53] His thought directs its flight in every direction, to the stars above and to the earth below. This is why Plato humorously describes him as an alien, lost in a world which is human, all too human; like

Thales the sage, he runs the risk of falling down a well. He is ignorant of fights over magistracies, political debates, and parties with
flute players. He does not know how to plead his case at court, or
how to insult others, or how to flatter them. Even the most enor-
mous estates seem insignificant to him, "since he is used to embracing the entire earth in his vision." He mocks that nobility
which is supposed to be proved by long genealogies. As Rabbow
has noted, Plato is not making a distinction between the contemplative and the active life, but establishing an opposition between
two modes of life. There is the philosophical life, which consists in
"becoming just and holy with intelligence," and is thus simultaneously knowledge and virtue; and there is the way of life of
nonphilosophers, who are at ease within the perverted city only
because they content themselves with false appearances of skillfulness and wisdom, which lead merely to brute force.[54] What this
means is that although philosophers may seem ridiculous outsid-
ers within the city, this is true solely in the eyes of the common
people, who have been corrupted by the city and recognize only
trickery, cleverness, and brutality as values.

To some extent, the ethics of the dialogue, which for Plato is the
spiritual exercise par excellence, is linked to another fundamental
process: the sublimation of love. According to the myth of the
preexistence of souls, the soul, before it came down into the body,
saw the Forms, or transcendent Norms. Once fallen into the sensible world, it forgot them, and now cannot even recognize them in-
tuitively in their images within the sensible world. Only the Form
of beauty still has the privilege of appearing, in those images of itself constituted by beautiful bodies. The amorous emotion which
the soul feels before some beautiful bodies is provoked by the unconscious recollection of the soul's vision of transcendent beauty
during its previous existence.[55] When the soul feels even the humblest earthly love, it is this transcendent beauty which attracts it.

Here we find once again that condition of the philosopher discussed in the *Symposium:* a strange, contradictory condition of inner lack of balance, for the lover is torn between his desire for carnal union with the object of his love and his yearning for the transcendent beauty which attracts him through the beloved object. The philosopher will therefore attempt to sublimate his love, by trying to improve the object of his love.[56] As is said in the *Symposium,* his love will give him spiritual fruitfulness, which will manifest itself in the practice of philosophical discourse.[57] Here we can discern the presence in Plato of an element which is not reducible to discursive rationality. It is the heritage of Socratism, or the educative power of loving presence. "We learn only from people we love."[58]

According to Diotima in the *Symposium,* the experience of love, under the effect of the unconscious attraction of the Form of beauty, rises from the beauty within bodies to that which is in souls.[59] It then proceeds to the beauty within actions and the sciences, until it achieves the sudden vision of a wonderful, eternal beauty. This vision is analogous to that enjoyed by people initiated into the mysteries of Eleusis; it transcends all enunciation and discursivity, but engenders virtue within the soul. Philosophy then becomes the lived experience of a presence. From the experience of the presence of a beloved being, we rise to the experience of a transcendent presence.

We said above that for Plato, knowledge is never purely theoretical. It is the transformation of our being; it is virtue. And now we can say that it is also affectivity. Whitehead's saying could be applied to Plato: "Concepts are always dressed in emotions."[60] Science—even geometry—is knowledge which engages the entire soul and is always linked to Eros, desire, yearning, and choice. "The idea of pure knowledge, or of pure understanding," said Whitehead, "was completely foreign to Plato's thought. The age of the Professors had not yet come."[61]

PLATO'S PHILOSOPHICAL DISCOURSE

Up to now, we have spoken solely of oral dialogue as it must have been practiced within the Academy. We can only imagine what this dialogue must have been like, by means of the examples we find in Plato's written work; and in order to simplify things, we have often quoted them using the phrase "as Plato says." Yet this expression is quite inexact, for Plato, in his written works, never says anything in his own voice. Whereas Xenophanes, Parmenides, Empedocles, the Sophists, and Xenophon had not hesitated to write in the first person, Plato makes fictional characters speak within fictional situations. Only in the *Seventh Letter* does he allude to his philosophy, and when he does he describes it more as a way of life. Above all, he declares that with regard to the object of his concerns, he has not published any written work, nor will he ever do so, for the knowledge in question cannot under any circumstances be formulated like other bodies of knowledge. Instead, it springs forth within the soul, when one has long been familiar with the activity in which it consists and has devoted one's life to it.[62]

We might wonder why Plato wrote dialogues, for, in his view, spoken philosophical discourse is far superior to that which is written. In oral discourse, there is the concrete presence of a living being. There is genuine dialogue, which links two souls together, and an exchange in which, as Plato says, discourse can respond to the questions asked of it and defend itself. Thus, dialogue is personalized: it is addressed to a specific person, and corresponds to his needs and possibilities. Just as, in agriculture, it takes time for a seed to germinate and develop, many conversations are necessary for knowledge to be born in the soul—knowledge which, as we have seen, will be identical to virtue. Dialogue does not transmit ready-made knowledge or information; rather, the interlocutor conquers his knowledge by his own effort. He discovers it by himself, and thinks for himself. Written discourse, by contrast, cannot respond to questions. It is impersonal, and claims immediately to give a knowledge which is ready-made, but lacks the ethical dimension represented by voluntary assent. There is no real knowledge outside the living dialogue.

If, in spite of these considerations, Plato still wrote dialogues, it was perhaps because he wanted above all to address not only the members of his school, but also absent people and strangers; for, as he said, "Written discourse goes rolling around in every direction."[63] His dialogues can be considered as works of propaganda, decked out with all the prestige of literary art but intended to convert people to philosophy. Plato used to read them in the course of those sessions of public reading which, in antiquity, were the way to make oneself known. Yet the dialogues also spread far from Athens. Thus Axiothea, a woman from Phlius, read one of the books of the *Republic* and came to Athens to become Plato's student;[64] ancient historians claimed she was long able to hide the fact that she was a woman. In a life of Plato which dates from the second half of the fourth century B.C., we find the following remark: "By composing his dialogues, he exhorted a mass of people to do philosophy; but he also gave many the opportunity to do philosophy in a superficial way."[65] In order to convert people to this way of life called philosophy, however, some indication had to be given of what philosophy is. For this purpose Plato chose the dialogue form, primarily for two reasons. First, the literary genre of the Socratic dialogue, which presented Socrates himself as the primary interlocutor, was very fashionable at the time; and it was precisely the Socratic dialogue which allowed the ethical value of dialogue, as practiced in Plato's school, to be emphasized. It is reasonable to suppose that some of the dialogues convey an echo of what discussions within the Academy must have been like—though the character of Socrates, which is very vivid in the first dialogues, tends to become more and more abstract in the later dialogues, until it finally vanishes in the *Laws*.[66]

It must be admitted that this ironic, often ludic presence of Socrates makes reading the dialogues rather disconcerting for the modern reader, who reads them looking for Plato's theoretical "system." Compounding this difficulty are the numerous doctrinal inconsistencies which become evident when the reader moves from one dialogue to another.[67] In the last analysis, all historians are obliged to admit—for different reasons—that the dialogues are an imperfect representation of what Plato's doctrine may have been; they "fall short of the Platonic philosophy"[68] and "transmit to us only a particularly limited and impoverished image of Plato's activity within the Academy."[69]

Victor Goldschmidt cannot be suspected of wanting to minimize the systematic aspect of Plato's doctrines; yet he proposed the best explanation of the aforementioned facts by saying that the dialogues were written not to "inform" people but to "form" them.[70] Such was the deepest intention of Plato's philosophy. He did not aim to construct a theoretical system of reality, and then "inform" his readers of it by writing a series of dialogues which methodically set forth this system. Instead, his work consisted in "forming" people—that is to say, in transforming individuals by making them experience, through the example of a dialogue which the reader has the illusion of overhearing, the demands of reason, and eventually the norm of the good.

From this perspective of formation, the role of the written dialogue consists primarily of learning how to practice the methods of reason, both dialectical and geometric, which will enable the student to master the arts of measure and definition in every domain. This is what Plato hints with regard to the long discussion which he introduces in the *Statesman*:

"In classes where people learn to read, when the student is asked which letters go to make up such-and-such a word, do we say that he undertakes this investigation only so that he can be brought to resolve one problem, or in order to make him more apt at solving all possible grammatical questions?"

"All questions, obviously."

"What then shall we say about our investigation on the subject of the 'statesman'? Has it been undertaken out of interest solely in this topic, or rather so that we may become better dialecticians on all possible subjects?"

"Here again, obviously, it is so that we may become better dialecticians on all possible subjects."

"To find the solution to the problem proposed in the easiest and quickest way possible ought to be only a secondary preoccupation and not a primary goal, if we are to believe reason, which orders us to accord our esteem and the first rank to the method itself."[71]

This is not to say that the dialogues may not also have had some doctrinal content, since they usually pose a precise problem and propose, or try to propose, a solution to it.[72] Each one forms a coherent whole, but they do not necessarily cohere with one another. What is remarkable is that several dialogues—the *Parmenides* and the *Sophist*, for instance—deal with the conditions on which dialogue itself is founded. They try to render explicit all the presuppositions implied by the ethics of the true dialogue—that is to say, within the Platonic choice of way of life. In order for the interlocutors to get along—better yet, in order for them to get along while choosing the good—the existence of "normative values" must be supposed. Independent of circumstances, conventions, and individuals, these values underlie the rectitude and rationality of discourse: "Imagine that one refuses to determine for each object of discussion a definite Form or Idea. Then one will not know where to turn one's thought, since one will not have wanted the Idea of each being to be always the same. Then the possibility even of discussion will be annihilated."[73]

The affirmation of the Forms is thus inherent to every dialogue worthy of the name. At this point, however, there arises the problem of how they are known—it cannot be through the senses—and of how they exist, for they cannot be sensible objects. Plato was thus brought to propose his theory of intelligible, or nonsensible, forms;[74] and he was consequently dragged into the problems posed by their existence and their relations with sensible things. Plato's philosophical discourse was based on a willing choice to engage in dialogue, and therefore on the concrete, lived experience of spoken, living dialogue. It bears essentially upon the existence of immutable objects, or nonsensible Forms, which guarantee the rectitude of discourse and action; but also upon the existence within human beings of a soul, which, more than the body, ensures the individual's identity.[75] As we see from most of the dialogues, moreover, these Forms are first and foremost moral values, which serve as the foundation for our judgments on things concerning human life. Above all, what is important is to try to determine, thanks to a study of the measure proper to each thing, the triad of values within the life of the city and the individual. This triad appears throughout the dialogues: that which is beautiful, that which is just, and that which is good.[76] Like Socratic knowledge, Platonic knowledge is, above all, a knowledge of values.

René Schaerer wrote that "the Essence of Platonism is and remains supradiscursive."[77] What he meant was that the Platonic dialogue does not say everything. It does not say what the Norms are, or the Forms, or Reason, or the Good, or Beauty; for all these things are inexpressible in language and inaccessible to any definition. One experiences them, or shows them in dialogue and in desire; but nothing can be said about them.

This Socratic-Platonic model of philosophy has played a role of capital importance. Throughout the history of ancient philosophy, we will encounter the two poles of philosophical activity which we have just distinguished: one the one hand, the choice and practice of a way of life; on the other, a philosophical discourse which is at the same time an integral part of this way of life, and renders explicit the theoretical presuppositions implicated in this way of life. In the last analysis, however, this philosophical discourse seems incapable of expressing that which is essential. For Plato, this meant the Forms and the Good, which we experience in a nondiscursive way, in desire and in dialogue.

Aristotle and His School

THE "THEORETICAL" FORM OF LIFE

The usual idea of Aristotle's philosophy seems a complete contradiction of the fundamental thesis we wish to defend—namely, that the ancients conceived of philosophy as a way of life. Certainly, Aristotle strongly asserts that the highest knowledge is knowledge which is chosen for itself and which therefore seems to bear no relation to the knower's way of life.[1]

Yet this affirmation must be placed within the general framework of Aristotle's idea of ways of life, as revealed in the goals he assigned to the school he founded. We have seen that Aristotle had been a member of Plato's Academy for twenty years, which means he had been a long-time participant in the Platonic way of life. When, in 355 B.C., he founded his own philosophical school in an Athenian gymnasium called the Lyceum, he was probably influenced by the model of the Academy, even if the goals he proposed for his school were different from those of Plato's school.

At the origins of Aristotle's school, as at the origins of the Academy, we can discern the same will to create a lasting institution.[2] Aristotle's successor was chosen by election, and we also know that one of the members of the school was responsible for the material administration of the institution, which implies some form of life in common.[3] As in the Academy, there were two kinds of members: the older ones, who took part in the teaching, and the younger ones. Also as in the Academy, there was a certain equality between such older members as Aristotle, Theophrastus, Aristoxenus, and Dicearchus. Admission to the school was likewise entirely free.

Yet there was a profound difference between the project aimed at by Aristotle's school and the Platonic project. Plato's school had an essentially political aim, even though it was the site of intense activity in mathematical research and philosophical discussion. Plato believed it was enough to be a philosopher in order to lead the city; in his eyes, there was a unity between philosophy and politics. But Aristotle's school, as Richard Bodéüs has shown, trained people only for the philosophical life.[4] Practical and political teaching was addressed to a wider public, made up of politicians, who, although outside the school, sought instruction on the best way to organize the city. Aristotle distinguishes between the happiness man can find in political life, in active life (this is the happiness that can be procured by practicing virtue in the city), and philosophical happiness, which corresponds to *theōria*—a kind of life devoted entirely to the activity of the mind.[5] Political and practical happiness, in Aristotle's view, is happiness only in a secondary way.[6] Philosophical happiness is found in "life according to the mind," which is situated in man's highest excellence and virtue.[7] This virtue corresponds to the mind, the highest part of man, and is free of the inconveniences brought by the active life. It is not subject to the intermittent nature of action, and does not produce fatigue. It brings marvelous pleasures, which are unmixed with pain or impurity and are stable and solid. These pleasures, moreover, are greater for those who reach reality and truth than for those who are still searching for them. It ensures independence from others, says Aristotle, insofar as we are otherwise assured of independence with regard to material things. A person who devotes himself to the activity of the mind depends only on himself. Perhaps his intellectual activity will be of higher quality if he has collaborators; but the more a sage he is, the more he will be able to be alone. Life in accordance with the mind does not seek any result other than itself, and is therefore loved for itself. It is its own goal and its own reward.

The life of the mind also eliminates worry. By practicing the moral virtues, we find ourselves involved in a struggle against the passions and also mired in material cares. In order to act within the city, we must become involved in political struggles; in order to help others, we must have money; in order to practice courage, we must go to war. The philosophical life, by contrast, can be lived only in leisure and in detachment from material worries.

This form of life represents the highest form of human happiness. Yet it can also be said that such happiness is superhuman: "Then, man no longer lives *qua* man, but insofar as there is something divine about him."[8] This paradox corresponds to Aristotle's paradoxical and enigmatic view of the mind and the intellect: the intellect is what is most essential in man, yet at the same time it is something divine which enters into him; what transcends man constitutes his true personality. It is as if man's true essence consisted in being above himself: "The mind *is* our self, insofar as it represents that which decides and which is best."[9] As in Plato, then, philosophical choice leads the individual self to go beyond its limits to a superior self, and to raise itself up to a universal, transcendent point of view.

In a sense, this paradox, which is inherent in the life of the mind according to Aristotle, corresponds to the paradox inherent in the notion of wisdom as opposed to philosophy, in Plato's *Symposium*. There, wisdom was described as a divine state, inaccessible to man, yet a state that the *philo-sopher* ("he who loves wisdom") desires. To be sure, Aristotle does not claim that the life of the mind is inaccessible and that we must be content to make progress toward it; but he does admit that we can attain it only "insofar as is possible."[10] This means that we must take into consideration the distance which separates man from the deity (as well as, we might add, the philosopher from the sage); and Aristotle also admits that we can attain it only in infrequent moments. When Aristotle wants to make us understand the mode of life of Thought—the first principle, upon which the world of the stars and sublunary nature depend—he declares: "Its way of life is comparable to what, for us, is the best way of life, which we can live only for short periods of time. For it always remains in this state, whereas for us this is impossible."[11] For the deity, the act of contemplation is sovereign beatitude: "If, then, the deity is perpetually in a state of joy comparable to that in which we sometimes find ourselves, that is admirable. If, however, he is in a state of still greater joy, then that is still more marvelous." Thus, the summit of philosophical happiness and of the activity of the mind—that is, the contemplation of the divine Intellect—is accessible to man only in rare moments, for the *proprium* of the human condition is that it cannot be continuously in actuality.[12] This implies that for the rest of the time, the philosopher must be content with the inferior grade of happiness which consists in searching. There are different degrees of the activity designated by the word *theōria*.

It appears, then, that for Aristotle philosophy consists in a "theoretical" way of life. We must not, however, confuse the term "theoretical" with "theoretic."[13] "Theoretic" is a word of Greek origin but does not appear in Aristotle. In a nonphilosophical context, it meant "referring to processions." In modern parlance, "the theoretic" is opposed to "the practical" the way the abstract and speculative is opposed to the concrete. From this perspective, then, we may oppose a purely theoretic philosophical discourse to a practical, lived philosophical life. Aristotle himself, however, uses only the word "theoretical" [*theōrētikos*], and he uses it to designate, on the one hand, the mode of knowledge whose goal is knowledge for knowledge's sake, and not some goal outside itself; and on the other, the way of life which consists in devoting one's life to this mode of knowledge. In this latter meaning, "theoretical" is not opposed to "practical." In other words, "theoretical" can be applied to a philosophy which is practiced, lived, and active, and which brings happiness. Aristotle says as much explicitly: "Practical life is not necessarily directed toward other people, as some think; and it is not the case that practical thoughts are only those which result from action for the sake of what ensues. On the contrary, much more practical are those mental activities [*theōriai*] and reflections which have their goal in themselves and take place for their own sake."[14] In the lines following this passage, Aristotle hints that the model for this contemplative action is the deity and the universe, which exert no action directed toward the outside but take themselves as the object of their action. Here again, it appears that the model of a knowledge which does not seek any goal other than itself is the divine Intellect—or Thought which thinks, which has no object or goal other than itself, which and has no interest in anything else.

From this perspective, "theoretical" philosophy is at the same time ethics. Just as virtuous praxis consists in choosing no other goal than virtue and in wanting to be a good person without seeking any particular interest, so theoretical praxis (it is Aristotle himself who inspires us to hazard this apparently paradoxical phrase) consists in choosing no goal other than knowledge. It means wanting knowledge for its own sake, without pursuing any other particular, egoistic interest which would be alien to knowledge. This is an ethics of disinterestedness and of objectivity.

THE DIFFERENT LEVELS OF THE "THEORETICAL" LIFE

How should we conceive of this life according to the mind? Should we follow Ingemar Düring, and define it as the life of a scholar?[15] If we consider the activities which were honored in Aristotle's school, it is evident that philosophical life there had the features of what we could call a great scientific undertaking. From this perspective, Aristotle reveals himself as a superb research administrator.[16] His school engaged in an immense hunt for information in every area. His students and colleagues gathered all kinds of data, from historical (for instance, the list of the winners at the Pythian games) to sociological (the constitutions of the different cities), psychological, and philosophical (the opinions of ancient thinkers). Innumerable zoological and botanical observations were also collected. This tradition was to remain in force throughout the lifespan of the Aristotelian school. The material gathered was not, however, intended to satisfy vain curiosity. The Aristotelian researcher was no simple collector of facts.[17] Rather, facts were amassed to make possible comparisons and analogies, to establish a classification of phenomena, and to enable an investigation into their causes. All this was accomplished with close collaboration between observation and reasoning—an alliance in which, says Aristotle, one must have more trust in observation of facts than in reasoning; the latter is to be trusted only insofar as it accords with the observed facts.[18]

It is thus indisputable that for Aristotle the life of the mind consists, to a large degree, in observing, doing research, and reflecting on one's observations. Yet this activity is carried out in a certain spirit, which we might go so far as to describe as an almost religious passion for reality in all its aspects, be they humble or sublime, for we find traces of the divine in all things. Nothing could be more instructive in this regard than the first pages of Aristotle's treatise *On the Parts of Animals,* in which he presents both the domains and the motivations of research. After distinguishing, within the realm of natural things, between those which, unengendered and incorruptible, exist for all eternity and those which are subject to generation and destruction, Aristotle points out the contrast in the means we have to know them. So far as the eternal substances are concerned—that is, the stars and the celestial spheres—our knowledge is very scanty, despite the great desire we have to know them. But in the case of perishable substances, which are within our reach, we have a great deal of information. Aristotle invites us to devote ourselves to the study of these two domains of reality because knowledge of them is a source of pleasure:

> The two studies each have their charm. Knowledge of the eternal beings, although we touch them only slightly, is nevertheless, because of its excellence, sweeter than the knowledge of things within our grasp, just as the partial, fleeting glance of people we love is sweeter than the precise observation of many other things, however great they may be. Yet insofar as the certainty and extent of knowledge is concerned, it is the knowledge of earthly things that has the advantage.[19]

Some people, Aristotle continues, will perhaps say that in order to study living nature, we must concern ourselves with contemptible things. Aristotle responds to this objection by evoking the pleasures of contemplation:

> In truth, some of these beings do not present a pleasant appearance; yet Nature, which has created them, affords incredible pleasure to those who, when they contemplate them, are able to know their causes and are of a philosophical nature. Besides, it would be unreasonable and absurd if we derived pleasure from contemplating images of these beings because we also saw them as embodiments of art (for example, that of the sculptor or the painter) but did not, when we considered them as creations of nature, feel a still greater joy from this contemplation, at least if we observed their causes. We must therefore not let ourselves succumb to childish repugnance for the investigation of the less noble animals, for there is something wonderful in all the works of Nature. We must recall the words they say were spoken by Heraclitus to some foreign visitors

who, on the point of entering, stopped when they saw him warm-
ing himself in front of his stove: he urged them to enter without
fear, saying that there were gods there as well. Likewise, we must approach the inquiry concerning each animal with the belief that
there is something natural and beautiful in each one.[20]

In this text, we glimpse the deep-seated tendencies which animate the life of the mind and the theoretical way of life. If we feel
joy in knowing the stars as well as the beings of sublunary nature,
it is because we find in them, directly or indirectly, a trace of that
reality which attracts us irresistibly. That reality is the first principle, which, as Aristotle says, moves all things as the beloved moves
the lover.[21] This is why the stars and the celestial spheres, which are
themselves principles of attraction, give us so much pleasure when
we observe them, like the vague and fleeting vision of a beloved
person. As for the study of nature, it gives us pleasure insofar as we
discover divine art in it. Artists merely imitate the art of nature,
and human art, in a sense, is merely a particular case of the fundamental, original art of nature. This is why natural beauty is superior to all artistic beauty. Yet there are repulsive things, it may be
objected. Perhaps; but do they not become beautiful to us when
imitated by our art? If we derive pleasure from seeing artistic representations of ugly and repulsive things, it is because we admire
the art with which the artist has imitated them. We may note in
passing that it was precisely in the Hellenistic period, which began
in Aristotle's time, that Greek art became realistic, representing
commonplace subjects, people from the lower classes, and all
kinds of animals.[22] If, however, we derive pleasure from observing
the artist's skillfulness in these works of art, why should we not admire Nature's skillfulness in creating *her* works, especially since
she makes beings grow from within, and practices, as it were, an
immanent art? If we seek Nature's intention and the finality she
pursues in her action, we will find pleasure in studying all of her
works.

According to Aristotle, we sense a divine presence in the natural world; this is the meaning of the his anecdote about Heraclitus. Strangers who have come to visit the philosopher wait to be greeted in the main room, which contains the dwelling's hearth where the fire in honor of Hestia burns. Yet Heraclitus invites them to come as far as the kitchen stove, for all fire is divine.[23] This means that the sacred is no longer restricted to certain places such as the altar of Hestia: all physical reality and the entire universe are sacred. There is something marvelous and divine about even the most humble beings.

In the philosophy of Plato, as we have seen, knowledge is always linked to desire and to affectivity; and we could say the same thing about Aristotle. The pleasure we feel when contemplating beings is the same pleasure we feel when contemplating people we love. For the philosopher, each being is beautiful because he knows how to situate it within the perspective of Nature's plan and of the general, hierarchical movement of the entire universe toward that principle which is supremely desirable. This intimate link between knowledge and affectivity is expressed in the following phrase from the *Metaphysics:* "The supreme desirable is one with the supreme intelligible."[24] Once again, the theoretical way of life reveals its ethical dimension. If the philosopher derives pleasure from the knowledge of beings, it is because, in the last analysis, he desires nothing other than what leads him to what is supremely desirable. This idea could be expressed by means of a remark by Kant: "To take an immediate interest in the beauties of nature . . . is always the sign of a good soul."[25] The reason, says Kant, is that the good-souled person derives pleasure not only from the form of a natural being, but also from its existence, "without the intervention of sensual attraction or an end he himself attaches to it." The pleasure we derive from the beauties of nature is, paradoxically, somehow a disinterested interest. From an Aristotelian perspective, this disinterestedness corresponds to the detachment from the self that enables the individual to raise himself up to the level of the mind and the intellect, which is his true self, and become aware of the attraction exerted on him by the supreme principle—both supreme desirable and supreme intelligible.

Can the "theoretical" life really and definitively be characterized as a scholar's life? I think that the notion of "scholar" in its modern sense is too limited to comprise such diverse activities as making up a list of the winners at the Pythian games, reflecting on being *qua* being, observing animals, and demonstrating the existence of a first principle in the movement of the universe. It would be difficult to say that the activities of a "scholar" include the activity of the mind which, according to Aristotle, is analogous, in certain privileged moments, to the activity of that first principle which is the Thought of Thought. We saw above how Aristotle tries to make us understand the beatitude of divine thought by comparing it with what the human intellect experiences in rare moments. It certainly seems that the beatitude of the human intellect attains its highest point when, at certain moments of indivisible intuition, it thinks the indivisibility of divine beatitude.[26] Nothing is farther from theory than the theoretical, or contemplation.

Rather than referring to the life of a scholar, then, we should speak of "life exercising itself for wisdom," or the "philo-sophical" life, since for Aristotle wisdom represents the perfection of *theōria*. For him, the human intellect is far from possessing this perfection, and approaches it only at certain moments. Theoretical life contains numerous hierarchical levels, from the humblest to the highest. As we have seen, Aristotle himself, when he speaks of the happiness of *theōria*, says that the happiness of one who searches is inferior to the happiness of one who knows. Aristotle's praise of life of the mind is simultaneously the description of a way of life actually practiced by Aristotle and the members of his school, and an ideal program or project: that is, an invitation to rise up by degrees toward wisdom—a state which is more divine than human, for "only God can enjoy this privilege."[27]

THE LIMITS OF PHILOSOPHICAL DISCOURSE

Aristotle's works are the fruit of the philosophical activity of the philosopher and his school. Yet Aristotelian philosophical discourse unnerves modern readers, not only by its sometimes frustrating concision, but especially by the uncertainty of his thought on points concerning his most important doctrines—for instance, his theory of the intellect. We do not find an exhaustive, coherent exposition of the theories constituting the different parts of Aristotle's system.[28]

In order to explain this phenomenon, we must first resituate his teaching within the framework of the school from which it was inseparable. Like Socrates and Plato, Aristotle wanted above all to train disciples. His oral teaching and his written work were always addressed to a specific audience. Most of his treatises, with the possible exception of those on ethics and politics, which were probably intended for a wider public, are the echo of oral classes Aristotle gave in his school. Many of these works, moreover, like the *Metaphysics* and *De Caelo*, do not form true unities but are the artificial union of writings which correspond to classes given at very different moments. It was Aristotle's successors, and especially his commentators,[29] who carried out this grouping and interpreted his work as if it were the theoretical exposition of a system aimed at explaining the whole of reality.

When Aristotle taught a course, it was not, as Bodéüs has pointed out, "a 'course' in the modern sense of the term, with students intent on writing down the master's thoughts, in view of God-knows-what kind of subsequent study."[30] The goal was not to "inform," or to transplant specific theoretical contents into the auditors' minds; rather, it was to "form" them. The goal was also to carry out collaborative research, for that was the meaning of the theoretical life. Aristotle expected discussion, reaction, judgment, and criticism from his listeners; teaching was still, fundamentally, a dialogue.[31] Aristotle's texts, as they have come down to us, are preparatory lecture notes supplemented with corrections and modifications that derive either from Aristotle himself, or else from his discussions with other members of the school. First and foremost, these lectures were intended to familiarize the disciples with methods of thought. For Plato, the exercise of dialogue was more important than the results obtained from the exercise. Similarly, for Aristotle the discussion of problems was ultimately more formative than their solution. In his lectures, Aristotle shows in an exemplary way the movement of thought and the method by which the causes of phenomena in all areas of reality should be sought. He liked to approach the same problem from different angles, starting from different points of departure.

No one was more conscious than Aristotle of the limits of philosophical discourse as an instrument of knowledge.[32] First of all, its limits come from reality itself. Everything simple is inexpressible in language. Language's discursivity can express only what is composite and what is divisible successively into parts. It cannot say anything about such indivisible things as the point in the domain of quantity; at most, it can say something negative, by denying the contrary. In the case of simple substances like the first Intellect—the principle of movement for all things—discourse cannot express its essence but merely describe its effects, or else proceed by comparison with our own intellect. It is only in rare moments that the human intellect can rise to the nondiscursive, instantaneous intuition of this reality, insofar as it can imitate the divine Intellect in some way.[33]

The limits of discourse also stem from its inability to transmit knowledge to the auditor all by itself. This is even more true of persuasion: discourse cannot act on the auditor without the latter's collaboration.

On the theoretical plane, it is not enough just to hear a discourse, or even to repeat it, in order to know or to have access to truth and reality. To understand discourse, the auditor must first have had some experience with what the discourse is about, and some degree of familiarity with its object.[34] Slow assimilation is then required, capable of creating within the soul a permanent disposition, or *habitus:* "Those who have begun to learn link words together but do not yet know their meaning; for the words must be integral parts of our nature [word for word: they must grow with us]. But this takes time."[35] Just as it had been for Plato,[36] so for Aristotle true knowledge is born only from long familiarity with concepts and methods, and also with observed facts. We must have lengthy experience with things in order to know them, and to familiarize ourselves with the general laws of nature, as well as with the processes and rational necessities of the intellect. Without this personal effort, the auditor cannot assimilate discourse; it will remain useless to him.

This is even more the case in the area of practice, where it is a matter not of knowing things but of practicing and exercising virtue. Philosophical discourse is not enough to make a person virtuous.[37] There are two categories of auditors: the first are already predisposed to virtue or have received a good education. For such people, moral discourse can be useful, for it could help them transform their natural virtues—those acquired by habit—into conscious virtues, accompanied by prudence.[38] In such cases, we might say, the lecturer is preaching to the converted. The second category consists of people who are slaves to their passions, and in this case moral discourse will have no effect: "He who is inclined to obey his passions will listen in vain and without profit, since the goal is not knowledge but practice."[39] Auditors of this type will therefore need something other than discourse to form them to virtue: "The auditor's soul must be worked on for a long time, in order that it make good use of attractions and repulsions, just as we turn over the earth which will nourish the seeds."[40]

Aristotle believed it was up to the city to undertake this educative work, by coercion and by the constraint of its laws. The politician and the legislator were thus responsible for assuring their citizens' virtue—and thereby their happiness—by organizing a city where the citizens really could be educated so as to become virtuous. They had also to ensure that people within the city had the chance to enjoy the leisure which would permit philosophers to accede to the theoretical life. This is why it does not occur to Aristotle to found an individual ethics with no relation to the city.[41] Instead, in the *Nicomachean Ethics,* he addresses politicians and legislators in order to form their judgment, by describing to them the various aspects of man's virtue and happiness and thus teaching them to legislate in such a way as to give the citizens the possibility of practicing the virtuous life, or (in the case of a few privileged people) the philosophical life. As Bodéüs perceptively notes,[42] the *Ethics* and the *Politics* ultimately aim at "an objective which is beyond knowledge." The goal is not to "set forth in a discourse the truth on some specific questions," but rather, by doing so, to contribute to the perfection of human becoming.

When it came to the need for changing both the city and human beings, Aristotle—like Plato—founded his hopes on politicians. Plato, however, thought that philosophers themselves ought to be the politicians who would carry out such work; and so he proposed to philosophers a choice of life and a course of training which would make them simultaneously contemplatives and men of action—since knowledge and virtue imply each other. Aristotle, by contrast, believed that the philosopher's activity within the city should be limited to forming politicians' judgment, and that it is the politicians' task to act personally by their legislation to ensure citizens' moral virtue. The philosopher, for his part, should choose a life devoted to disinterested research, study, and contemplation—a life which will ultimately be independent of political worries. Thus, for Aristotle, as for Plato, philosophy was both a way of life and a way of discourse.

CHAPTER SEVEN

The Hellenistic Schools

GENERAL CHARACTERISTICS

The Hellenistic Period

The word "Hellenistic" traditionally designates the period in Greek history which extends from the time of the Macedonian king Alexander the Great to the age of Roman domination; thus, it stretches from the end of the fourth century B.C. to the end of the first century B.C. Thanks to Alexander's extraordinary expedition, which spread Greek influence from Egypt to Samarkand and Tashkent and as far as the Indus, a new period in world history was inaugurated. We might say that it was then that Greece began to discover the immensity of the world. This was the beginning of intense commercial exchange, not only with central Asia but also with China, Africa, and western Europe. Traditions, religions, ideas, and cultures were mixed, in an encounter was to mark the culture of the West indelibly. After Alexander's death, his generals fought each other over his immense empire, and these conflicts led to the formation of three great kingdoms centered around three capitals: Pella in Macedonia, which ruled over Macedonia and Greece; Alexandria in Egypt; and Antioch in Syria, the home of the Seleucid dynasty, which reigned not only over Asia Minor but also over Babylonia. We must add the kingdom of Pergamum and the Greek kingdom of Bactriana, which stretched as far as the Indus.

The end of the Hellenistic era is usually thought to be marked by the suicide of Cleopatra, queen of Egypt, after the victory at Actium of the future emperor Augustus in 30 b.c. The Romans had been in contact with the Greek world since the end of the third century b.c., and they had gradually discovered philosophy. In the course of our exposition, we will sometimes have to allude to philosophers who lived under the Roman Empire (that is, after 30 b.c.), since they bring to our attention documents concerning Hellenistic philosophy. As we shall see, however, the characteristics of philosophy in the Imperial age were very different from those in the Hellenistic era.

The Hellenistic period of Greek philosophy has often been presented as a phase of decadence in Greek civilization, which was supposedly bastardized by contact with the Orient. There are many causes for this severe judgment. First is the classical prejudice which fixes a priori an ideal model of classical culture and decides that only Greece of the Presocratics, the tragic poets, and perhaps Plato deserves to be studied. Second, there is the idea that with the transition from a democratic to a monarchic regime and the end of political liberty, the public life of Greek cities was extinguished. Philosophers abandoned the great speculative effort of Plato and Aristotle, along with the hope of training politicians capable of transforming the city, and resigned themselves to providing a refuge in inner life for those who had been deprived of political freedom. This representation of the Hellenistic age, which probably goes back to the beginning of the twentieth century, often continues to falsify our idea of the philosophy of this period.[1]

In fact, it is quite erroneous to think of this period as one of decadence. By carefully studying the inscriptions found in the ruins of the Greek towns of antiquity, the epigraphist Louis Robert has shown throughout his work that all these cities continued to engage in intense cultural, political, religious, and even athletic activity, both under the Hellenistic monarchies and later under the Roman Empire. Moreover, technology and the exact sciences expanded enormously at this time. Under the influence of the Ptolemies, who reigned in Alexandria, this city became a kind of living center of Hellenistic civilization.[2] The museum of Alexandria was organized by Demetrius of Phalerum, who was faithful to the Aristotelian tradition which privileged scientific studies. It became a Mecca for research in every science, from astronomy to medicine. The library of Alexandria gathered together the entire corpus of philosophical and scientific literature, and provided a fertile environment for great scholars—the physician Herophilus and the astronomer Aristarchus of Samos, for example. It is enough to cite the name of Archimedes of Syracuse, mathematician and engineer, in order to glimpse the extraordinary scientific activity which developed throughout this period.

Neither did the cities' purported loss of freedom cause a decline in philosophical activity. Besides, can we really say that the democratic regime had been more favorable to it? Wasn't it democratic Athens that prosecuted Anaxagoras and Socrates for impiety?

Nor was the change in the orientation of philosophical activity quite so radical as has been suggested. It is often claimed that in the face of their inability to act within the city, the philosophers of the Hellenistic period developed an ethics of the individual and advocated interiority. Things are, however, rather more complex. On the one hand, although Plato and Aristotle both had political concerns, it is nevertheless true that for them the philosophical life was a means to free themselves from political corruption. Life according to the mind, which was the way of life of the Aristotelian school, avoided the compromises of life within the city. For all philosophers of antiquity, Plato gave definitive formulation to the attitude which the philosopher must adopt in a corrupt city:

Thus, there remain very few people who are worthy of taking up philosophy. . . . Now, regarding an individual who is a member of this small group and who has tasted the sweetness and happiness of such a good: when he has become sufficiently aware of the madness of the multitude, aware that there is, as it were, nothing sensible in the conduct of any politician, and that there is no ally with whom he can go to the assistance of justice without risking death; when, like a man who has fallen among wild animals and refuses to be as unjust as they are but cannot stand up to this savage mob alone, he is sure to perish before he can benefit the city or his friends, being unprofitable to both—when he reflects on all this, he keeps quiet and concerns himself only with his own affairs, and, just as a traveler caught by a storm takes shelter behind a wall against the cloud of dust and rain kicked up by the wind, in the same way, when he sees others filled to the bursting point with lawlessness, he considers himself happy if he can live his earthly existence free of injustice and impiety and leave this life with a fine hope, in serenity and peace of mind.[3]

When the philosopher realizes that he is completely incapable of helping to remedy the corruption of the city, what can he do except practice philosophy, either alone or with others? Unfortunately, this was the position in which most of the philosophers of antiquity found themselves with regard to the world of politics.[4] Even though he was emperor, Marcus Aurelius also expressed feelings of impotence in the face of his subjects' inertia and lack of understanding.[5]

Yet the philosophers of the Hellenistic period—even the Epicureans[6]—never lost their interest in politics and often served as royal counselors or ambassadors for cities, as is shown by the inscriptions often erected in their honor. Stoic philosophers played an important role in the elaboration of social and political reforms in several states; for instance, the Stoic Sphaerus had an important influence on the Spartan kings Agis and Cleomenes, and the Stoic Blossius influenced the Roman reformer Tiberius Gracchus.[7] They often opposed the Roman emperors, with exemplary courage. In general, the philosophers never renounced their hope of changing society, even if only by the examples of their lives.

Philosophical life was extremely rich and diverse in the Hellenistic period; unfortunately, however, we know it only imperfectly, and we would have a very different idea of it if all the philosophical works written during that period had been preserved for us. In those days, philosophical writings were not printed by the thousands and widely distributed, as they are today. They were hand-copied many times; and this was the source of numerous errors, which oblige modern scholars to undertake tremendous critical work when they wish to study these texts. Philosophical writings were sometimes sold in bookstores, but the more technical works were simply preserved in the libraries of the various philosophical schools. In the course of the centuries, much of this precious material was lost—particularly at Athens, during Sulla's sack of the city in March 86 B.C., but also at Alexandria, during successive destructions of the library. Thousands of works disappeared in this way, and the other cataclysms which put an end to the Hellenistic period also annihilated treasuries of poetry and art, which we know about only from the copies made of them by the Romans. To cite but one example: the philosopher Chrysippus, a founder of Stoicism, wrote at least seven hundred treatises, but not one has been preserved and only a few rare fragments have come down to us, from the papyri discovered at Herculaneum and through the quotations furnished by authors of the Roman period. Our image of the history of philosophy has thus been irredeemably falsified by the contingencies of history. If the works of Plato and Aristotle had disappeared and those of the Stoics Zeno and Chrysippus had been preserved, we would perhaps have a wholly different view of things. Be this as it may, it is thanks to authors who lived in the

Roman world—either in the time of the Republic (as in the case of Cicero, Lucretius, and Horace) or in the time of the Empire (Seneca, Plutarch, Epictetus, Marcus Aurelius)—that precious information on the Hellenistic philosophical tradition has been preserved. This is why we will sometimes cite these authors, although they belong to a later period.

Oriental Influences?

Did Alexander's expedition have an influence on the evolution of Greek philosophy? It certainly benefited scientific and technical development, thanks to the geographic and ethnographic observations it allowed. We know, moreover, that Alexander's expedition brought about meetings between Greek and Hindu sages. In particular, a philosopher of the Abderan school named Anaxarchus, together with his student Pyrrho of Elis, accompanied the conqueror as far as India. Pyrrho supposedly lived in retreat from the world ever afterward, because he had heard an Indian tell Anaxarchus that, as a result of frequenting royal courts, he was incapable of teaching.[8] There does not seem to have been any real exchange of ideas or confrontations of theories in these contacts; at least, we have no obvious trace of any. The Greeks were, however, impressed by the way of life of those people they called the "gymnosophists," or "naked sages."[9] The historian and philosopher Onesicritus, who also participated in the expedition and wrote an account of it shortly after the death of Alexander, gives many details of their customs and their practice of committing suicide by fire. In the gymnosophists, Greek philosophers had the impression of finding the same way of life they themselves recommended: a life free of conventions, in accordance with pure nature, and completely indifferent to what other people considered desirable or undesirable, good or bad—a life which led to perfect inner peace and lack of worries. Anaxarchus' teacher Democritus had preached the same method for attaining peace of mind.

The Cynics also affected to despise all human conventions; and in the gymnosophists they found this attitude developed to an extreme degree. In the words of the Stoic Zeno, probably with regard to the suicide of the Hindu sage Calanus, who had been in contact with Alexander: "I'd rather see one single Indian roasted over a slow fire than learn in the abstract all the theses and arguments people have developed about suffering."[10] Without going as far as such dramatic situations, what the ancients tell us about Pyrrho's life points to such a degree of indifference to everything that one cannot help thinking he was trying to imitate what he had seen in India. We might note in passing the extreme subjectivism of Anaxarchus, who said that existing things were no more real than stage sets and that they resembled the images which appear to dreamers or madmen.[11] One might think here of some oriental source; but we ought not to forget that Democritus,[12] founder of the Abderan school, already taught that there was a radical opposition between reality in itself—in other words, atoms—and the subjective perceptions of the senses.

Alexander's expedition thus does not seem to have provoked much of a stir in the philosophical tradition. In fact, Hellenistic philosophy seems to have developed naturally out of the movement which preceded it. It often revisits Presocratic themes, and above all is deeply marked by the Socratic spirit. Perhaps the experience of the encounter between peoples played a role in the development of the idea of cosmopolitanism—the idea that man is a citizen of the world.[13]

The Philosophical Schools

We have already described the ways of life which characterized the schools of Plato and Aristotle. Now we must return to the highly singular phenomenon of the philosophical schools of antiquity, not forgetting that the conditions of the teaching of philosophy were very different then from what they are now. Modern students study philosophy only because it is a required course; at the most, a student may become interested by an initial contact with the discipline and may wish to take exams in the subject. In any case, it is chance that decides whether the student will encounter a professor who belongs to some particular "school," be it phenomenological, existentialist, deconstructionist, structuralist, or Marxist. Perhaps, someday, he will pledge intellectual allegiance to one of these "isms"; in any case, his adherence will be intellectual and will not engage his way of life, with the possible exception of Marxism. For us moderns, the notion of a philosophical school evokes only the idea of a doctrinal tendency or theoretical position.

Things were very different in antiquity. No university obligations oriented the future philosopher toward a specific school; instead, the future philosopher came to attend classes in the school *(skholē)* of his choice as a function of the way of life practiced there.[14] Once led into a classroom by chance, however, the student might unexpectedly became converted as he heard a master speak. This was the story of Polemo, who, after a night of debauchery, entered Xenocrates' school one morning on a dare with a band of drunken comrades. Seduced by the master's discourse, Polemo decided to become a philosopher, and later became head of the school. No doubt this is an edifying fiction; nevertheless, it could appear to be completely believable.[15]

Toward the end of the fourth century, almost all philosophical activity was concentrated in Athens, in the four schools founded by Plato (the Academy), Aristotle (the Lyceum), Epicurus (the Garden), and Zeno (the Stoa). These institutions were to remain alive for nearly three centuries. In contrast to the transitory groups which formed around the Sophists, these were permanent institutions not only during their founders' lifetimes but long after their death. The various heads of the schools who succeeded the founders were most often chosen by the vote of the members of the school, or designated by their immediate predecessors. These institutions depended on the head of the school, and, under the law, schools had no judicial standing.[16] This is clearly evident from the philosophers' wills (we possess those of Plato, Aristotle, Theophrastus, Strato, Lycon, and Epicurus),[17] none of which contains any mention of school property as such. Instead, books and real estate were considered the property of the head of the school. It is thus unnecessary to suppose, as has been done, that in order to acquire judicial standing the philosophical schools were forced to organize themselves as religious brotherhoods dedicated to the Muses. In fact, Athenian legislation concerning the right to association did not stipulate any particular status for educational institutions.

Usually, these schools were located in multi-use facilities called gymnasiums (this was the case with the Academy and the Lyceum), or in other public places (as with the Stoa Poikilē, or "Portico") where people could meet to hear lectures or debates. In these cases, the school took its name from its meeting place.

At least until the end of the Hellenistic period, then, almost every school existed not only as a doctrinal tendency, but also as a locus of teaching and as a permanent institution organized by a founder who was at the origin of the way of life practiced by the school and the doctrinal tendency linked to it. The destruction of most of the Athenian educational institutions changed this situation.

These schools were open to the public. Most philosophers, but not all, took pride in teaching without a salary; this was what distinguished them from the Sophists. Financial resources were either personal, or else provided by benefactors—for example, Idomeneus in the case of Epicurus. The needs of the school were covered by a daily fee of two obols, which was "the wage of a slave who worked by the day. As Menander said, it was barely enough to pay for a cup of tea."[18] In general, a distinction was made between the auditors—those who simply attended the school—and the

group of true disciples, called "familiars," "friends," or "companions." The latter were divided into juniors and seniors, and sometimes lived with the master in his house or nearby. It was said that
the disciples of Polemo (the student of Xenocrates mentioned
above) built huts in order to live close to him.[19] The same custom
of taking meals in common at regular intervals held sway in the
Academy, the Lyceum, and Epicurus' school; perhaps it was with a
view to the organization of such gatherings that both the Academy
and the Lyceum had a position called "magistrate," which all
members of the school had to take up in turn for several days at a
time.[20]

We possess fewer details on the Stoic school, founded around
300 B.C. by Zeno of Citium, who taught in the portico called the
Stoa Poikilē. Ancient historians say that he had many students; in
particular, Antigonus Gonatas, king of Macedonia, came to hear
him while visiting Athens. In Zeno's school, as in the other
schools, there was a distinction between mere auditors and true
disciples such as Perseus, who lived in his house and whom he sent
to the court of Antigonus Gonatas.[21] The evolution of Athens' attitude toward philosophy since its condemnation of Anaxagoras
and Socrates is apparent in the text of a decree promulgated (under pressure of Antigonus) in honor of Zeno by the Athenians in
261 B.C. This decree honored Zeno with a golden crown and provided for the construction of a tomb for him, at the city's expense.[22] The reason for this was remarkable: "because Zeno, son of
Mnaseas, of Citium, who for many years has lived in the city in accordance with philosophy, not only has shown himself to be a
good man on every occasion, but in particular, by his encourage-
ment to practice virtue and temperance, has inspired the young
people attending his school to follow the most admirable conduct,
and has offered to all the model of a life which was always in accordance with the principles he taught." Here Zeno is praised not
for his theories but for the education he gave to young people, the

kind of life he led, and the harmony between his life and his discourse. Contemporary comedies alluded to the austerity of his life:
"Bread, figs, and a bit of water. That one is 'philosophizing' a new
philosophy: he teaches hunger, and finds disciples."[23] Note that the
word "philosophy" here designates a way of living. Stoic scholastic
institutions were much less monolithic than the Epicurean school.
The places of instruction varied, and, above all, different doctrinal
tendencies came to the surface after Zeno's death. On many
points, Ariston of Chios, Cleanthes, and Chrysippus professed dif-
fering opinions. These oppositions between tendencies were to
continue throughout the duration of the Stoic school—that is, up
until the second and third centuries A.D. We have very few details
on the atmosphere which prevailed in these various Stoic schools.

In Athens, then, from the fourth to the first centuries B.C., there
were four philosophical schools, all of which, in one way or another, took on institutional form and in general had analogous
teaching methods. This is not to say that there were no philosophical schools in other cities, but only that they lacked the prestige of
the Athenian schools. Two other currents must be added which
seem very different from the four schools: in the first place Skepticism (or rather Pyrrhonism, for the idea of "skepticism" developed relatively late) and Cynicism. These schools had no scholastic organization or dogmas; but they were ways of life, the first
proposed by Pyrrho, and the latter by Diogenes the Cynic. In this
sense they were indeed two *haireseis,* or attitudes of thought and
life. In the words of the Skeptic physician Sextus Empiricus: "If it
is said that a school [*hairesis*] is the adhesion to numerous dogmas
which are mutually coherent, . . . we will say that the Skeptic has
no school. If, however, it is said that a school is a way of life which
follows a specific rational principle, in conformity with what appears to us, . . . then we say he has a school."[24]

The Skeptics developed arguments to show that we must suspend our judgment and refuse adherence to all dogmas, in the be-

lief that we would thereby achieve peace of mind. The Cynics, for their part, did not argue and gave no instruction. It was their very life that bore meaning within itself and implied an entire doctrine.

Identities and Differences: The Priority of Choosing a Way of Life

In fact, as we have already seen with regard to Socrates, Plato, and Aristotle, and as we will see again with in the case of the Hellenistic schools, each school was defined by a specific existential choice. Philosophy was the love of and search for wisdom, and wisdom was, precisely, a certain way of life. This initial choice, proper to each school, was thus the choice of a certain type of wisdom.

At first glance, in fact, one might wonder if the conceptions of wisdom were really all that different among the schools. All Hellenistic schools seem to define it in approximately the same terms: first and foremost, as a state of perfect peace of mind. From this viewpoint, philosophy appears as a remedy for human worries, anguish, and misery brought about, for the Cynics, by social constraints and conventions; for the Epicureans, by the quest for false pleasures; for the Stoics, by the pursuit of pleasure and egoistic self-interest; and for the Skeptics, by false opinions. Whether or not they laid claim to the Socratic heritage, all Hellenistic philosophers agreed with Socrates that human beings are plunged in misery, anguish, and evil because they exist in ignorance. Evil is to be found not within things, but in the value judgments which people bring to bear *upon* things. People can therefore be cured of their ills only if they are persuaded to change their value judgments, and in this sense all these philosophies wanted to be therapeutic.[25] In order to change our value judgments, however, we must make a radical choice to change our entire way of thinking and way of being. This choice is the choice of philosophy, and it is thanks to it that we may obtain inner tranquillity and peace of mind.

Yet despite these apparent similarities, deep differences may be discerned. First, we must distinguish between the dogmatic schools, for whom therapeutics consisted in transforming value judgments, and the Skeptics, who only wished to suspend them. Above all, although the dogmatic schools agreed that the fundamental philosophical choice must correspond to an innate human tendency, some distinctions must be made: for Epicureanism, it was the search for pleasure which motivated all human activity; whereas for Platonism, Aristotelianism, and Stoicism, in accordance with the Socratic tradition, the love of the good was the primordial instinct of human beings. Despite this fundamental identity in intention, however, these three schools were still founded upon existential choices which were radically different from one another.

Identities and Differences: Teaching Methods

We also find points of identity and of difference in teaching methods. In Platonism, Aristotelianism, and Stoicism—the three schools which, as we have just said, followed the Socratic tradition—teaching retained the double finality it had had in the time of Plato and of Aristotle, despite the transformations in political condition. Directly or indirectly, the goal was to mold citizens— political leaders, if possible, but also philosophers. Training for life in the city aimed for mastery of speech by means of a number of rhetorical and, especially, dialectical exercises, and sought the principles of the science of government in philosophers' instruction. This is why many students came to Athens from Greece, the near East, Africa, and Italy, in order to receive training which would then permit them to carry out political activity in their own countries. Many Roman statesmen, such as Cicero, later did the same. They learned not only to govern others but to govern *themselves*, since philosophical training, or the exercise of wisdom, was intended to bring about full realization of the existential option we mentioned, thanks to the intellectual and spiritual assimilation of the principles of thought and life that it implied. In order to achieve this, living dialogue and discussion between master and disciple were indispensable, in accordance with the Socratic-Platonic tradition. Under the influence of this double finality, instruction always tended to take on a dialogic and dialectical form. Even in the case of *ex cathedra* expositions, it maintained the appearance of a dialogue, or a rapid succession of questions and answers, which constantly presupposed at least a potential relation to specific individuals to whom the philosopher's discourse was addressed. To ask a question called a "thesis" (for instance, "Is death an evil?" "Is pleasure the supreme good?") and to discuss it—this was the fundamental schema of all philosophical instruction at that time. This feature distinguishes it radically from the instruction in vogue during the subsequent Imperial period, from the first and especially second century A.D. on, when the master's task was to comment upon texts. Farther on, we will look at the historical reasons for this change; for the moment, however, let us cite a text from this later period of the commentators. It comes from the commentary on Aristotle's *Topics* by the Aristotelian Alexander of Aphrodisias (second century A.D.), and it gives a good description of the difference between the discussion of theses, which was a method peculiar to the period we are studying, and the commentary, which was peculiar to the subsequent period: "This form of discourse [the discussion of 'theses'] was customary among the ancients, and this was how they gave most of their classes: not by commenting on books, as is done now (at that time, there were no books of this kind), but by arguing for or against a thesis once it was proposed, in order to exercise their faculty of inventing arguments, basing themselves on premises admitted by everyone."[26]

The argumentation mentioned by Alexander was a purely dialectical exercise, in the Aristotelian sense of the term. The discussion of theses, however, could take on dialectical or rhetorical form, and could also be dogmatic or aporetic. In dialectical argumentation, discussion of the thesis took place by question and answer, and therefore in a dialogue. Arcesilaus, for instance, who considered philosophical discourse to be purely critical, used to ask an auditor to propose a thesis; he then refuted it by asking questions which gradually brought the interlocutor to admit the contradictory of the thesis he had proposed.[27] Yet the Stoics, although they were dogmatics, also practiced the dialectical method of question-and-answer in their instruction. Cicero reproaches them with not leaving enough room for oratorical and rhetorical developments, which he viewed as the only thing capable of moving and persuading people: "They prick you as if with darts, with short, pointed questions. Those who answer them affirmatively, however [in dialectical argumentation, the person who has set forth the thesis had to content himself with answering yes or no], are not transformed in their soul and go away as they had come. For although the thoughts which the Stoics express may be true and sublime, they do not treat them as they should, but do so in a rather dry manner."[28]

Argumentation could also be rhetorical: an auditor would ask a question, thereby furnishing the thesis or the theme for discussion, and the master would reply in a continuous, fully developed discourse. Either he successively proved the *pro* and the *contra* (in which case it was either a purely scholastic exercise, or an attempt to prove the impossibility of any dogmatic assertion) or he proved or refuted the thesis, depending on whether or not it corresponded to his doctrine (in which case it was a dogmatic exposition, setting forth the dogmas of the school). Insofar, then, as philosophical instruction practiced the exercise of the "thesis"—a pedagogical method based on the question-and-answer schema—it could not consist in developing theories for their own sake, independently of the needs of the audience. Discourse was developed within the limited domain of a question asked by a particular auditor. The usual intellectual method thus consisted in going back to the general logical or metaphysical principles, which served as the starting point from which the specific question could be resolved.

In Epicureanism and Stoicism, however, there was another approach, which was deductive and systematic. In the Epicurean school, the technical exercise of dialectics played no role. Here, philosophical discourse took on a resolutely deductive form: it started out from principles, and went as far as the consequences of those principles—as we can see, for instance, in the *Letter to Herodotus*. Some of these discourses were made available in written form to the disciple, so that he could learn them by heart. As I. Hadot has shown, Epicurean instruction began with the reading and memorization of short summaries of Epicurean doctrine, presented in the form of very brief sayings.[29] The student then became familiar with more developed summaries, like the *Letter to Herodotus*; and finally, if he so desired, he could tackle Epicurus' great work *On Nature*, in thirty-seven books. He always had to return to the summaries, however, to avoid becoming lost in details, and had to keep a sense of the whole constantly in his mind. There was thus a give-and-take between the expansion of knowledge and concentration on the essential nucleus.

Although, as we have seen, the Stoics used the dialectical method in their instruction, they, too, nevertheless tried to present their doctrine in accordance with a rigorously systematic logical sequence, for which the ancients admired them. The Stoics required their students to keep the school's essential dogmas present in their minds, by dint of a constant effort of memory.

This was not an instance of conceptual construction as an end in itself which just happened to have ethical consequences for the Stoic or Epicurean way of life. On the contrary, the goal of these systems was to gather the fundamental dogmas together in condensed form, and link them together by rigorous argumentation, in order to form a systematic, highly concentrated nucleus, sometimes reduced to one brief saying, which would thus have greater persuasive force and mnemonic efficacy. Above all, such sayings had a psychagogic value: they were intended to produce an effect on the soul of the auditor or reader. This does not mean that such theoretical discourse did not respond to the demands of logical coherence; on the contrary, such coherence was its strong suit. But just as it gave expression to a vital choice, it was intended to lead to a vital choice.

The modern reader will certainly be astonished by the extraordinary stability of the methodological principles and dogmas in most of the philosophical schools of antiquity, from the fourth century B.C. to the second or third century A.D. This was because philosophy meant choosing a specific way of life—a way of life that corresponded either to a critical method (like that of the Skeptics or the Academics, which we shall discuss below) or to dogmas which justified the way of life. For the dogmatic philosophies like Epicureanism or Stoicism, the system or coherent ensemble of fundamental dogmas was inviolable, since it was intimately linked to the Epicurean or Stoic way of life. This does not mean that all discussion was abolished in these two schools; the Stoic school, in particular, quickly became fragmented into different tendencies. Yet these divergences and polemics allowed the original option and the dogmas which expressed it to persist, for they bore only upon secondary points, such as theories concerning celestial or terrestrial phenomena, the mode of demonstration and systematization of the dogmas, and teaching methods. Besides, such discussions were reserved for students who were making progress and who had already assimilated the essential dogmas.[30]

This was why dogmatic philosophies like Stoicism and Epicureanism had a popular and missionary character: since technical and theoretical discussions were matters for specialists, they could be summed up—for the benefit of beginners and students who were making progress—in a small number of formulas which were tightly linked together and which were essentially rules for practical life. In this respect, such philosophies coincided with the "missionary" and "popular" spirit of Socrates. Whereas Platonism and Aristotelianism were reserved for an elite which had the "leisure" to study, carry out research, and contemplate, Epicureanism and Stoicism were addressed to everyone: rich and poor, male and female, free citizens and slaves.[31] Whoever adopted the Epicurean or Stoic way of life and put it into practice would be considered a philosopher, even if he or she did not develop a philosophical discourse, either written or oral.

In a sense, Cynicism was also a popular, missionary philosophy. From the time of Diogenes, the Cynics had been ardent propagandists who addressed themselves to all social classes. They preached by example, denouncing social conventions and urging a return to a simple life in conformity with nature.

CYNICISM

There is still no consensus as to whether Antisthenes, a disciple of Socrates, was the founder of the Cynic movement. It is agreed, at any rate, that his disciple Diogenes was the leading figure in this movement, which, although it never took on an institutional character, remained alive until the end of antiquity.

The Cynic way of life was spectacularly opposed not only to the life of nonphilosophers but even to the lives of other philosophers.[32] Other philosophers differentiated themselves from their fellow citizens only within certain limits; the Aristotelians, for instance, devoted their lives to scientific research, while the Epicureans led a simple, retiring life. The Cynics' break with the world, by contrast, was radical. They rejected what most people considered the elementary rules and indispensable conditions for life in society: cleanliness, pleasant appearance, and courtesy. They practiced deliberate shamelessness—masturbating in public, like Diogenes, or making love in public, like Crates and Hipparchia.[33] The Cynics were absolutely unconcerned with social proprieties and opinion; they despised money, did not hesitate to beg, and avoided seeking stable positions within the city. They were "without a city, without a home, without a country, miserable, wandering, living from day to day."[34] Their bags contained only what was strictly necessary for survival. They did not fear the powerful, and always expressed themselves with provocative freedom of speech [*parrhēsia*].[35]

From the perspective of the problem which interests us—namely, the exact nature of philosophy in the ancient world—Cynicism supplies us with a highly revelatory example, since it represents a limit case. In antiquity, one historian wondered whether Cynicism could be called a philosophical school—whether it mightn't be, instead, only a way of life.[36] It is true that Cynics such as Diogenes, Crates, and Hipparchia gave no scholarly instruction, even though they eventually may perhaps have engaged in some literary activity, especially the writing of poetry. Nevertheless, they did form a school, insofar as a master-disciple relationship can be discerned among the various Cynics.[37] Throughout antiquity, moreover, Cynicism was generally considered a philosophy; but it was a philosophy in which philosophical discourse was reduced to a minimum. Take, for instance, the following symbolic anecdote: when someone declared that movement did not exist, Diogenes simply got up and began to walk.[38]

Cynic philosophy was exclusively a choice of life: it was the choice of freedom—complete independence *(autarkeia)* from useless needs—and the refusal of luxury and vanity *(tuphos)*. Such a choice obviously implied a certain conception of life; but this conception, which was probably defined in conversations between the master and disciple or in public speeches, was never directly justified in theoretical philosophical treatises. There are many typically Cynic philosophical concepts, but they are not used in logical argumentation. Instead, they serve to designate concrete attitudes which correspond to the choice of life: *askēsis, ataraxia* (lack of worry), *autarkeia* (independence), effort, adaptation to circumstances, impassiveness, simplicity or the absence of vanity *(atuphia)*, lack of modesty. The Cynic chose his way of life because he believed that the state of nature *(phusis)*, as seen in the behavior of animals or children, was superior to the conventions *(nomos)* of civilization. Diogenes threw away his bowl and his cup when he saw children do without such utensils, and he drew comfort regarding his way of life when he saw a mouse eat a few crumbs in the dark.

The opposition between nature and culture was the object of long theoretical discussions in the Sophistic period; for the Cynics, however, what was at stake was not speculation but a decision which engaged the whole of life. Thus, their philosophy was entirely exercise *(askēsis)* and effort. The artifices, conventions, and commodities of civilization, luxury and vanity—all soften the body and mind. For this reason, the Cynic way of life consisted in an almost athletic, yet reasoned training to endure hunger, thirst, and foul weather, so that the individual could acquire freedom, independence, inner strength, relief from worry, and a peace of mind which would be able to adapt itself to all circumstances.[39]

Plato is supposed to have said of Diogenes that he was "Socrates gone mad."[40] Whether or not this is true, it gives us cause for reflection. In a sense, Socrates was the precursor of the Cynics. The comic poets also mocked Socrates' external appearance—his bare feet and old cloak. If, as we have seen, the figure of Socrates is conflated in the *Symposium* with that of Eros the beggar, wasn't Diogenes, that homeless wanderer with his poor traveling bag, a second Socrates, heroic figure of the unclassifiable philosopher and a stranger to the world? Like Socrates, Diogenes thought he had been entrusted with the mission of making people reflect, and of denouncing their vices and errors with his caustic attacks and his way of life. His care for himself was, indissolubly, care for others. And although Socratic care of the self, by making people attain inner freedom, dissolved the illusions of the appearances and phantoms linked to social conventions, it nevertheless retained a kind of smiling urbanity, which disappeared with Diogenes and the Cynics.

PYRRHO

Pyrrho, a contemporary of Diogenes and Alexander, followed the latter in his expedition to India, where he some met oriental sages.[41] He, too, can be considered a somewhat extravagant Socrates. In any case, he deserves our attention, because we are once again in the presence of a philosopher who did not devote himself to teaching, (although he was skilled in the art of dialogue) and who did not even write; instead, he simply lived, thereby attracting disciples who imitated his way of life.

His behavior was completely unpredictable. Sometimes he retired into complete solitude; at other times he went off traveling without telling anyone, taking whomever he met on the way as traveling and conversation partners. He confronted all kinds of risks and dangers, defying prudence, and kept talking even when his audience had gone. One day he saw his master Anaxarchus, who had fallen into a swamp; he continued on his way without helping him, and Anaxarchus congratulated him for his indifference and insensitivity. Unlike the Cynics, however, he seems to have behaved in a simple manner, in perfect conformity with the lifestyle of other people. This is suggested by an ancient historian:

"He lived piously with his sister, who was a midwife. Sometimes he went to the market to sell chickens or pigs. He did housekeeping with indifference, and it is said he bathed a pig with indifference, too."[42] Let us note in passing that this anecdote reminds us of what Chuang-tzu reports about Lao-tzu, though there was no historical connection: "For three years he locked himself up, performing household tasks for his wife and serving food to the pigs as he would have served it to men; he made himself indifferent to everything, and eliminated all ornamentation, in order to rediscover simplicity."[43]

Pyrrho's behavior thus corresponds to a choice of life which can be perfectly summed up in one word: indifference. Pyrrho was completely indifferent to everything. He therefore always remained in the same state;[44] in other words, he felt no emotions or change in his dispositions under the influence of external things. He attached no importance to the fact that he was present at such-and-such a place or meeting such-and-such a person. He made no distinction between what is usually considered dangerous and what is harmless; between tasks judged to be superior and those considered inferior; between what is called suffering and what is called pleasure; between life and death. For the judgments people make about the value of such things are based on mere conventions. In fact, it is impossible to know whether a given thing is good or bad in itself. People's unhappiness comes from the fact that they want to obtain what they think is good, or to escape what they think is bad. If we refuse to make this kind of distinction between things, and refrain from making value judgments about them or from preferring one thing above another—if we say to ourselves, "This is no better than that"—we will achieve peace and inner tranquillity, and will no longer feel the need to talk about such things. It doesn't matter what we do, so long as we do it with an attitude of indifference. Thus, according to Pyrrho's philosophy our goal should be to seek stability in a state of perfect equality with ourselves, in complete indifference, inner freedom, and impassiveness, a state he considered divine.[45] In other words, everything was indifferent for him except the indifference we have for indifferent things—which was ultimately, therefore, virtue,[46] and hence absolute value. To acquire such indifference is no easy task; as Pyrrho said, it required "stripping off man completely," or liberating oneself entirely from the human point of view.[47] This formula can be very revealing. Doesn't "stripping off man" mean that the philosopher completely transforms his vision of the universe, transcending the limited viewpoint of what is human, all-too-human, in order to elevate himself to a superior point of view? Such a perspective is in a way inhuman; it reveals the nudity of existence, beyond the partial oppositions and false values which human beings add to it, in order, perhaps, to attain a state of simplicity prior to all distinctions.

If we fail to achieve this total divestiture, we must train ourselves by inner discourse. In other words, we must recall the principle of "This is no better than that" and the arguments that can justify it. Pyrrho and his disciples thus practiced methods of meditation. It was said that Pyrrho himself sought solitude, and spoke aloud to himself; when asked why he behaved in this way, he replied, "I am training to become useful."[48] His disciple Philo of Athens was described as follows: "Living far from men in solitude, being his own master, talking to himself, with no care for glory or disputes."[49] The philosophy of Pyrrho—like that of Socrates, like that of the Cynics—was thus a lived philosophy, and an exercise of transforming one's way of life.

EPICUREANISM

In 306 B.C., Epicurus (ca. 342–271) founded a school in Athens which remained alive in that city at least until the second century

A.D.[50] Lucretius' poem *On Nature,* and the gigantic inscription that the Epicurean Diogenes had engraved in the town of Oinoanda at an uncertain date (first century B.C. or second century A.D.) to make the writings and doctrines of Epicurus known to his fellow citizens, are evidence of the missionary fervor with which his disciples tried to disseminate his message, even if they lived in distant lands.

An Experience and a Choice

Epicureanism originated in an experience and a choice. The experience was that of the "flesh": "The voice of the flesh: not to be hungry, not to be thirsty, not to be cold. He who possesses this state, and hopes to possess it in the future, can rival Zeus for happiness."[51] The "flesh" here is of course not an anatomical part of the body, but—in a sense which is phenomenological and apparently wholly new in philosophy—it is the subject of pleasure and pain, or the individual. As Carlo Diano has expertly shown, Epicurus had to speak of "suffering," of "pleasure," and of "flesh" to express his experience, for

> there was no other way to reach and to point out the man in the street in the pure and simple historicity of his being-in-the-world, and finally to discover what we call the "individual"—that individual without which we cannot speak of a human person. . . . For it is only in the "flesh," which experiences pain and relief from pain, that our "self"—our soul—emerges and becomes apparent to itself and to others. . . . This is why the greatest works of charity . . . are those which have the flesh as their object—satisfying its hunger and quenching its thirst.[52]

Moreover, the "flesh" cannot be separated from the "soul," if it is true that there is no pleasure or suffering without our being conscious of them, and that the state of our consciousness in turn has repercussions upon the "flesh."

An experience, then; but also a choice. What is most important is to deliver the "flesh" from its suffering and thus allow it to experience pleasure. For Epicurus, the Socratic and Platonic choice in favor of love of the good is an illusion: in reality, individuals are moved only by their search to gratify their own pleasures and interests. Yet philosophy consists in knowing how to seek pleasure in a reasonable way. In fact, this means seeking the only genuine pleasure: the pure pleasure of existing. For all people's misfortune and suffering comes from the fact that they are unaware of genuine pleasure. When they seek pleasure, they are unable to find it, because they cannot be satisfied with what they have; or because they seek what is beyond their reach; or because they spoil their pleasure by constantly fearing they will lose it. In a sense, one could say that people's suffering comes primarily from their empty opinions, and hence from their souls.[53] The mission of philosophy and of Epicurus was therefore above all therapeutic: the philosopher must tend to the sickness of the soul, and teach mankind how to experience pleasure.

Ethics

The fundamental choice was justified, in the first place, by a theoretical discourse on ethics, which aimed to set forth a definition of genuine pleasure and an ascetics of desire. In the Epicurean theory of pleasure, historians of philosophy correctly discern an echo of the discussions of pleasure which had taken place in Plato's Academy,[54] and which are exemplified by Plato's dialogue *Philebus* and the tenth book of Aristotle's *Nicomachean Ethics*. According to Epicurus, there are "sweet and flattering" pleasures which are found "in motion." Propagating in the flesh, they provoke a violent but ephemeral excitement. People who seek only such pleasures will find dissatisfaction and pain, because such pleasures are insatiable, and when they reach a certain level of intensity, they become suffering once again. These mobile pleasures must be strictly distinguished from stable pleasure, which is pleasure in repose as a "state of equilibrium." This is the state of the body when it is appeased and free of suffering; it consists in not being hungry, not being thirsty, and not being cold:

> We do what we do in order to avoid suffering and fear. When once we have succeeded in this, the tempest of the soul is entirely dissipated, for the living being now no longer needs to move toward anything as if he lacked it, or to seek something else by which the good of the soul and body might be achieved. For we have need of pleasure precisely when we are suffering from the absence of pleasure. When we are not suffering from this lack, we do not need pleasure.[55]

From this perspective, pleasure as the suppression of suffering is the absolute good. It cannot be increased, and no new pleasure can be added to it, "just as a clear sky cannot get any brighter."[56] Such stable pleasure is different in nature from mobile pleasures. It is opposed to them as being is to becoming; as the determinate is to the indeterminate and the infinite; as rest is to movement; and as the supratemporal is to what is temporal.[57] It is perhaps surprising to see such transcendence attributed to the simple suppression of hunger or thirst, and the satisfaction of vital needs. Yet this suppression of the body's suffering—the state of equilibrium—makes the individual conscious of a global, coenesthetic feeling of his own existence. It is as though, by suppressing the state of dissatisfaction which had absorbed him in the search for a particular object, he was finally free to become aware of something extraordinary, already present in him unconsciously: the pleasure of his own existence, or (in Diano's words) of "the identity of pure existence."[58] This state is not unlike the "sufficient, perfect, and full happiness" of which Rousseau speaks in *Les rêveries du promeneur solitaire:* "What does one enjoy in such a situation? Nothing external to oneself; nothing except oneself and one's own existence. So long as this state lasts, one is sufficient unto oneself, like God." Let us add that this state of stable pleasure also corresponds to a state of peace of mind and absence of worry.

The method for achieving this stable pleasure consists in an *askēsis* of desire. The reason people are unhappy is that they are tortured by "immense, hollow" desires, such as those for wealth, luxury, and domination.[59] The *askēsis* of desire should be based on a tripartite distinction: there are desires which are natural and necessary; desires which are natural and not necessary; and empty desires, which are neither natural nor necessary.[60] This distinction was already outlined in Plato's *Republic*.[61]

Natural and necessary desires are those whose satisfaction delivers people from pain, and which correspond to the elementary needs or vital necessities. Natural but not necessary are, for example, desires for sumptuous foods and for sexual gratification. Neither natural nor necessary, but produced by empty opinions, are the limitless desires for wealth, glory, and immortality. An Epicurean saying aptly sums up this division of desires: "Thanks be to blessed Nature, who has made necessary things easy to obtain, and who has made things difficult to obtain unnecessary."

The *askēsis* of desire consists in limiting one's appetites—suppressing those desires which are neither natural nor necessary, and limiting as much as possible those which are natural but not necessary. The latter do not suppress any real suffering, but aim only at variations in pleasure; and they may result in violent and excessive passions.[62] This *askēsis* of pleasure thus determined a specific way of life, which we shall now describe.

Physics and Canonics

A grave threat impairs human happiness. Can pleasure be perfect if it is disturbed by the fear of death, and by divine decisions in this world and the next? As is shown with great force by Lucretius, it is the fear of death which is, in the last analysis, at the base of all the passions which make people unhappy.[63] It was in order to free people from these terrors that Epicurus proposed his theoretical discourse on physics. Above all, we must not imagine Epicurean physics as a scientific theory, intended to reply to objective, disinterested questions. The ancients knew that the Epicureans were hostile to the idea of a science studied for its own sake.[64] Indeed, philosophical theory is here merely the expression and consequence of the original choice of life, and a means of obtaining peace of mind and pure pleasure. Epicurus never tires of repeating this:

> If we were not disturbed by our worries about celestial phenomena and death, fearing (because of our ignorance of the limits of pain and desire) that the latter is something dire for us, we would have no need of the study of nature.
>
> We cannot free ourselves of fear about the most essential things if we do not know exactly what the nature of the universe is, but attribute some hint of truth to mythological stories, so that without the study of nature it is impossible to obtain pleasure in its state of purity.
>
> . . . There is no profit to be derived from the knowledge of celestial phenomena other than peace of mind and firm assurance, just as this is the goal of all other research.[65]

As is clearly shown in the *Letter to Pythocles*,[66] for Epicurus there are two very different areas of research on physical phenomena. On the one hand, there is the indisputable systematic core, which justifies the existential option. For instance, there is the representation of an eternal universe constituted by atoms and the void, in which the gods do not intervene. On the other hand, there are investigations on questions of secondary importance—on celestial or meteorological phenomena, for instance, which do not involve the same rigor and which allow for multiple explanations. In both areas, research is carried out only to ensure peace of mind, either thanks to the fundamental dogmas which eliminate the fear of the gods and of death; or, in the case of secondary problems, thanks to one or more explanations which will suppress the mind's worries by showing that such phenomena are merely physical.

Epicurus' goal, then, is to suppress our fear of the gods and of death. Especially in his letters to Herodotus and to Pythocles, he shows, on the one hand, that the gods have nothing to do with the creation of the universe, and do not care about the conduct of the world or of human beings; and, on the other hand, that death is nothing for us. Epicurus proposes a theory of the world that is heavily indebted to the "naturalistic" theories of the Presocratics, in particular Democritus. The All has no need to be created by a divine power, for it is eternal: being can no more come from not-being than not-being can come from being. This eternal universe is constituted by bodies and space, or the void, in which they move. The bodies which we see—the bodies of living beings, but also of the earth and the stars—are made up of indivisible, immutable bodies, infinite in number. These are the atoms, which fall at equal speed in a straight line, as a result of their weight, in the infinite void. They collide and engender composite bodies as soon as they deviate infinitesimally from their trajectory. In this way bodies and worlds are born, and also disintegrate, as a result of the continuous movement of atoms. In the infinity of time and of the void, there is an infinity of worlds which appear and disappear, and our world is only one among them. The idea of the deviation of atoms had a twofold purpose. On the one hand, it explained the formation of bodies, which could not be constituted if the atoms merely fell in a straight line at equal speed.[67] On the other hand, by introducing "chance" into "necessity," it provided the foundation for human freedom.[68] Here again, it is obvious that physics is elaborated as a function of the Epicurean choice of life. People must be masters of their desires. In order to obtain stable pleasure, they must be free; but if their mind and intellect are formed by material atoms, which move in an always predictable way, how can people be free? The solution consists precisely in admitting that it is within the atoms themselves that the principle of internal spontaneity is situated. This is none other than the possibility that they may deviate from their trajectory, which provides a foundation for freedom of the will and makes it possible. In the words of Lucretius: "If the spirit is not ruled by necessity in all its acts, if it escapes domination and is not reduced to total passivity, it is because of this slight deviation of atoms, in a place and a time determined by nothing."[69] It need scarcely be added that, from antiquity right up to the present, this uncaused deviation and abandonment of determinism has seemed scandalous to historians of philosophy.[70]

Thus, human beings need not fear the gods, for the gods have no effect on the world or the people in it. Nor do people need to fear death, for the soul is made up of atoms, and, like the body, it disintegrates at death and loses all sensory capacity. "Thus, death is nothing for us. So long as we are here, death is not, and when death is here, we are not."[71]

This is how Diano sums up the affirmations of the *Letter to Menoecus:* We ourselves cease to exist as soon as death appears. Why, then, should we be afraid of that which has nothing to do with us?

The Epicurean theory of knowledge, called canonics, derives from this materialistic physics. All material objects emit a flux of particles which strike our senses. The continuity of this flux gives us the impression of the solidity and resistance of bodies. From the multiple sensations reaching us from bodies which resemble one another, general images or notions are produced which permit us to recognize and identify forms; this is especially true because words and language are linked to these notions. With language, however, the possibility of error also appears. In order to recognize the truth of a statement, we will therefore have to see if it is in agreement with the criteria of truth—that is, with our general notions and sensations. The Epicureans thus used to say that thought can "project itself" forward in order to seize that which is not present. For instance, this is true of the affirmation of the existence of the void, which by definition is invisible but whose existence is necessary in order to explain that of movement. Such projection must always be verified by experience, and therefore by sensation.[72]

Delivering people from the fear of the gods and of death was not the only goal of this theoretical edifice of physics. It also afforded access to the pleasure of contemplating the gods. For the knowledge we have of the gods is clear evidence that they exist—evidence which manifests itself in the general preconception of the gods that is present in all humanity.[73] Reason also necessarily demands the existence of a nature superior to all others, and supremely perfect. Thus, the gods exist, although they exert no action upon the world, for this is the condition of their perfection: "That which is blessed and immortal has no troubles itself, nor does it cause any to others; so that it is not subject either to anger or to benevolence. For everything of this kind is found only in that which is weak."[74]

This is one of Epicurus' great intuitions. He does not imagine divinity as the power of creating, dominating, or imposing one's will upon the less powerful. Instead, it is the perfection of the supreme being: happiness, indestructibility, beauty, pleasure, and tranquillity. In representations of the gods, the philosopher finds both the amazed pleasure we may feel when admiring beauty, and the comfort that can be provided by contemplating the model of wisdom. From this point of view, Epicurus' gods are the projection and incarnation of the Epicurean ideal of life. The gods spend their lives enjoying their own perfection and the pure pleasure of existing, with no needs and no worries, in the most pleasant company. Their physical beauty is identical to the beauty of the human figure.[75] We might think—not without reason—that such ideal gods are merely representations imagined by human beings and owe their existence only to human beings. Nevertheless, Epicurus seems to conceive of them as independent realities who maintain their eternal existence because they know how to ward off what could destroy them and what is alien to them. The gods are friends of the wise, and the wise are friends of the gods. For the wise, the highest good is to contemplate the splendor of the gods. They have nothing to ask of them, yet they pray to them, in prayers of praise.[76] Their homage is addressed to the gods' perfection. In this regard, scholars have spoken of "pure love"—a love that demands nothing in return.[77]

With this representation of the gods—as deities who embody the Epicurean way of life—physics becomes an exhortation to practice concretely the initial option of which it was the expression. It thus leads to peace of mind, and to the joy of participating in the life of contemplation which the gods themselves lead. Like the gods, the wise man gazes into the infinity of innumerable worlds. The closed universe expands into infinity.

Exercises

In order to obtain a cure for the soul's distress and a life in conformity with the fundamental choice, it is not enough for us to become acquainted with Epicurean philosophical discourse; we must also exercise constantly. In the first place, we must meditate—that is, become intensely aware of, and assimilate within ourselves, the fundamental dogmas: "All these teachings—meditate upon them night and day, alone and also with a companion similar to yourself. Thus, you will feel no worries either asleep or awake, but will live like a god among men. Accustom yourself to living with the thought that death is nothing for us."[78]

The systematization of dogmas and their concentration into summaries and sayings is intended to make them more persuasive, more striking, and easier to remember. For instance, consider the famous "fourfold remedy" intended to ensure psychic health—a formula that summarizes everything essential in Epicurean philosophical discourse:

> The gods are not to be feared,
> Death is not to be dreaded;
> What is good is easy to acquire
> What is bad is easy to bear.[79]

Reading dogmatic treatises by Epicurus and other masters of the school could also be food for meditation, and could impregnate the soul with the fundamental intuition.

Above all, Epicureans believed that it is necessary to practice the discipline of desire. We must learn to be content with what is easy to obtain and what satisfies the organism's fundamental needs, while renouncing what is superfluous. A simple formula, but one that cannot but imply a radical upheaval of our lives. It means being content with simple foods and simple clothes; renouncing wealth, honors, and public positions; and living in retreat.

Such meditations and such *askēsis* cannot be practiced in solitude. As in the Platonic school, friendship, in the Epicurean school, was the privileged path toward and means for the transformation of one's self. Masters and disciples helped one another closely, in order to obtain a cure for their souls.[80] In this atmosphere of friendship, Epicurus himself assumed the role of a director of conscience. Like Socrates and Plato, he was well aware of the therapeutic role of the word. Such spiritual direction can have meaning only if it is conducted individual to individual: "It is not to the crowd that I say these things, but to you. Each of us is a big enough audience for the other."[81]

In particular, Epicurus knew that our moral conscience is tortured by guilt,[82] and that we can free ourselves from this guilt by admitting our faults and accepting reprimands, even if these sometimes provoke a state of "contrition." Examination of one's conscience, confession, and fraternal correction are indispensable exercises for obtaining a cure for the soul. We possess some fragments of a work by the Epicurean Philodemus entitled *On Freedom of Speech*, which deals with the confidence and openness that was considered indispensable between master and disciples, as well as among disciples. For the master, free self-expression meant not being afraid to hand out reproaches; for the disciple, it meant not hesitating to admit one's faults, and even not being afraid to tell friends about their own faults. One of the school's primary activities thus consisted in corrective and formative dialogue.

The personality of Epicurus also played a role of the first importance. He himself had established the precedent for this: "Act as though Epicurus were watching you."[83] And the Epicureans echoed him: "We will obey Epicurus, whose way of life we have chosen."[84] This is perhaps why the Epicureans attached so much importance to portraits of their founder, which figured not only in paintings but also on rings.[85] To his disciples, Epicurus appeared "like a god among men."[86] He was the incarnation of wisdom, and the model they had to imitate.

In all this, however, effort and tension had to be avoided. On the contrary: the Epicureans' fundamental exercise consisted in relaxation, serenity, and the art of enjoying the pleasures of the soul and the stable pleasures of the body.

The pleasures of knowledge: "In the exercise of wisdom [philosophy], pleasure goes hand in hand with knowledge; for we do not obtain enjoyment *after* we learn, but learn and enjoy simultaneously."[87]

The supreme pleasure was contemplating the infinity of the universe and the majesty of the gods.

The pleasure of discussion. As is said in a letter sent to Idomeneus while Epicurus was dying: "To these pains, I have opposed
the joy I feel in my soul when I recall our philosophical conversations."[88]

The pleasures of friendship, as well. On this subject, we have the
testimony of Cicero: "Epicurus says that of all the things which
wisdom provides in order for us to live happily, there is nothing
better, more fruitful, or more pleasant than friendship. Nor did he
merely declare this; he confirmed it in his actions and habits. In
Epicurus' one little house, what a troop of friends there was, all
gathered together by him! What a conspiracy of love united their
feelings!"[89]

The pleasure of a life in common, which did not disdain to allow slaves and women to participate in it. A true revolution, which
denoted a complete change in atmosphere compared to the sublimated homosexuality of Plato's school. Women, who in exceptional cases had already been admitted to Plato's school, were now
part of the community. Among them were not only married
women like Themista, wife of Leonteus of Lampsacus, but also
courtesans like Leontion ("the Lioness") who was portrayed in
meditation by the painter Theorus.[90]

Finally, the pleasure of becoming aware of what is wonderful
about existence. First of all, we must know how to master our
thought, in order to represent mainly pleasurable things to ourselves, to resuscitate the memory of pleasures of the past, and to
enjoy the pleasures of the present. We must recognize how intense
and gratifying such immediate pleasures are, and deliberately
choose relaxation and serenity. We should live in profound gratitude toward nature and life, which constantly offer us pleasure
and joy—if only we know how to find them.

Meditating on death can awaken in our souls an immense gratitude for the marvelous gift of existence: "Persuade yourself that
each new day that dawns will be your last; then you will receive

each unexpected hour with gratitude. Recognize all the value of each moment of time which is added on as if it were happening by an incredible stroke of luck."[91]

Ernst Hoffmann has given an admirable account of the Epicurean choice of life: "Existence must, first of all, be considered as pure chance, in order to be lived completely as a unique wonder. We must realize that, inevitably, it occurs only once; not until then can we celebrate it in its irreplaceability and uniqueness."[92]

STOICISM

The Stoic school was founded by Zeno at the end of the fourth century B.C.[93] It got a new start near the middle of the third century, under the leadership of Chrysippus. Although the school maintained a remarkable degree of unity with regard to its fundamental dogmas, it soon split into opposing camps which continued to divide the Stoics throughout the centuries.[94] We have little information about the history of the school from the first century B.C. onward, but it is certain that Stoic doctrine continued to flourish in the Roman Empire until the second century A.D. We need only mention the names of Seneca, Musonius, Epictetus, and Marcus Aurelius.

The Fundamental Choice

When discussing Epicureanism, we spoke of an experience—that of the "flesh"; and of a choice—that of pleasure and individual interest, transfigured into the pure pleasure of existing. We must also talk about experience and choice with regard to Stoicism. Here the choice is fundamentally that made by Socrates, who in Plato's *Apology of Socrates* declared: "For the good person, no evil is possible, whether he is dead or alive."[95] The good person believes that the only evil is moral evil and that there is no good but moral good—namely, what we call duty or virtue. This is the supreme value, for which we must not hesitate to face death. The Stoic choice is thus situated in the direct line of the Socratic choice, and is diametrically opposed to the Epicurean choice: happiness consists not in pleasure or in individual interest but in the demands of the good, which are dictated by reason and transcend the individual. The Stoic choice is also opposed to the Platonic choice, insofar as it holds that happiness—that is, the moral good—is accessible to all, within this life.

The Stoic experience consists in becoming sharply aware of the tragic situation of human beings, who are conditioned by fate. It would seem that we are not free at all, for it is not up to us to be beautiful, strong, healthy, or rich, to feel pleasure, or to escape suffering. All these things depend on causes which are external to us. A necessity which is inexorable and indifferent to our individual interest breaks our aspirations and our hopes; we are helpless and defenseless in the face of the accidents of life, the setbacks of fortune, illness, and death. Everything in our life escapes us. The result of this is that people are unhappy, because they passionately seek to acquire things which they cannot obtain and to flee evils which are inevitable. There is one thing, and only one, which does depend on us and which nothing can tear away from us: the will to do good and to act in conformity with reason. There is thus a radical opposition between what depends on us and can therefore be either good or bad, since it is the object of our decision, and what depends not on us[96] but on external causes and fate and which is therefore indifferent. The will to do good is an unbreachable fortress which everyone can construct within themselves. It is there that we can find freedom, independence, invulnerability, and that eminently Stoic value, coherence with ourselves. Seneca summed up this attitude in the following saying: "Always want the same thing; always refuse the same thing. For the same thing can please people universally and constantly only if it is morally right."[97]

Such self-coherence is the domain of reason. Rational discourse cannot but be self-coherent; and living according to reason means submitting to this demand for coherence. Zeno defined the Stoic choice of life as follows: "To live coherently—that is, according to a rule of life which is unique and harmonious. For those who live in incoherence are unhappy."[98]

Physics

Stoic philosophical discourse contained three parts: physics, logic, and ethics. Philosophical discourse about physics aimed to justify the choice of life we have just mentioned, and to make explicit the way of being-in-the-world which it implies. For the Stoics, as for the Epicureans, physics was not developed for its own sake but had an ethical finality: "One teaches physics only so that one can teach the distinction which must be established with regard to goods and evils."[99] In the first instance, we can say that Stoic physics was indispensable for ethics, because it showed people that there are some things which are not in their power but depend on causes external to them—causes which are linked in a necessary, rational manner.

It also has an ethical finality, insofar as the rationality of human action is based on the rationality of nature. From the point of view of physics, the will for self-coherence, which is the basis of the Stoic choice, appears as a fundamental law within material reality, internal to each being and to the totality of beings.[100] From the first moment of their existence, living beings are instinctively in tune with themselves; they strive to preserve themselves, and they love their own existence and everything that can preserve it. Yet the world itself is also one single living being which is likewise in tune with itself and self-coherent. Just as within a systematic, organized unity, everything in the world is related to everything else, all is in all, and everything needs everything else.

The Stoic choice of life both postulates and demands, simultaneously, that the universe be rational. "Is it possible that there could be order in us, but that disorder should reign in the All?"[101] Human reason, which seeks logical and dialectical coherence with itself and posits morality, must be based upon a Reason possessed by the All, of which it is only a portion. Living in conformity with reason thus means living in conformity with nature, or the universal Law, which causes the evolution of the world from within. It is a rational universe, but at the same time totally material: Stoic Reason was identical to Heraclitean Fire. According to Georges Rodier and Victor Goldschmidt, it is material because of the Stoic choice of life.[102] Stoic materialism is explained by the desire to make happiness available to all, within this world, which is not opposed to any superior world.

Just as they rationally justified their radically different options, Stoics and Epicureans posited radically opposing physics. For the Epicureans, although bodies consist of aggregates of atoms, they do not form a true unity, and the universe is merely a juxtaposition of elements which do not blend together. Each being is an individuality—atomized, as it were, and isolated with regard to the others. Everything is external to everything else, and everything happens by chance; within the infinite void, an infinity of worlds is formed. For the Stoics, on the contrary, everything is within everything else, bodies are organic wholes, and everything happens by rational necessity. Within infinite time, there is only one cosmos, which repeats itself endlessly. These two schemes of physics were mutually contradictory yet analogous, for both schools sought to base the possibility of their existential choice upon nature itself. The Epicureans believed that the spontaneity of atomic particles which could deviate from their trajectory made human freedom possible, as well as the *askēsis* of desire, whereas the Stoics based human reason upon nature conceived as universal Reason. Their explanation of human freedom was, however, much more complex.

Indeed, in order to explain the possibility of freedom, it is not enough simply to base human reason upon cosmic Reason; for cosmic Reason corresponds to rigorous necessity. This is particularly so because the Stoics imagined cosmic Reason according to the Heraclitean model of a force called Fire—a kind of breath and vital heat which mixed itself totally with matter and engendered all beings. It was like a seed in which all seeds are contained, and from which they develop. The cosmos is in tune with itself and self-coherent; as Reason, it necessarily wills itself to be just what it is—so much so, that it repeats itself in an eternally identical cycle in which fire, as it transforms itself into the other elements, finally returns to itself. The reason the cosmos repeats itself, eternally identical, is that it is rational—that is to say, "logical." It is the only cosmos, both possible and necessary, that Reason can produce. It cannot produce one which is either better or worse. In such a cosmos, everything is necessarily linked together, in conformity with the principle of causality: "There is no movement without a cause. If this is so, everything happens by the causes which give impulses. If this is so, everything happens by fate."[103] The slightest event implies the entire series of causes, the linkage of all preceding events, and finally the whole universe. Whether people like it or not, then, things necessarily happen the way they happen. Universal Reason cannot act otherwise, precisely because it is perfectly rational.

How, then, is moral choice possible? The price that must be paid in order for morality to be possible is freedom of choice. It is the possibility that human beings, by refusing to accept fate, can revolt against universal order and act or think against universal Reason or against nature—in other words, separate themselves from the universe and become strangers and exiles from the great city of the world.[104] Such a refusal would not change anything about the order of the world. According to a saying of the Stoic Cleanthes, taken up by Seneca: "The Fates guide the person who accepts them, and hinder the person who resists them."[105] Reason includes all resistance, opposition, and obstacles within its plan for the world, and makes them contribute to its success.[106]

Once more, however, it will be asked how such freedom of choice is possible. The answer is that the form of reason proper to human beings is not universal Reason—the substantial, formative reason which is immediately immanent within things. Instead, it is a discursive reason, which has the power, in judgments and in the discourses it enunciates about reality, to give meaning to the events which Fate imposes upon it and the actions it produces. Human passions, as well as morality, are situated within this universe of meaning. In the words of Epictetus: "It is not things [in their materiality] which trouble us, but the judgments we bring to bear upon things [that is, the meaning we give them]."[107]

The Theory of Knowledge

The Stoic theory of knowledge has two aspects. On the one hand, it affirms that perceptible objects mark our sensory faculties with their imprint, and that we absolutely cannot doubt certain presentations which bear the mark of this indisputable obviousness. These are the so-called "objective" or "comprehensive" presentations. They do not depend on our will; rather, our inner discourse enunciates and describes their content, and we either give or withhold our consent from this enunciation. It is here that the possibility of error—and therefore freedom—is located.[108] In order to help us understand this subjective, voluntary aspect of presentations, Chrysippus used the comparison of a cylinder.[109] The entire network of causes and events—in other words, Fate—can set a cylinder in motion; but the cylinder will still roll in accordance with its particular cylindrical form. In the same way, the linked network of causes can bring about a specific sensation within us, thereby giving us the opportunity to utter a judgment upon this sensation, and accord or deny our assent to this judgment. Such assent, however, even if it is set in motion by Fate, still has its own proper form, and is free and independent.

To gain a clearer understanding of what the Stoics meant, we might develop an example suggested by Epictetus. If I am out on the high seas and perceive a peal of thunder and the whistling winds of a storm, I cannot deny that I perceive these terrifying sounds, for that is a comprehensive and objective presentation. My perception is the result of the entire linked network of causes, and therefore of Fate. If I merely note within myself that Fate has confronted me with a storm, then my inner discourse corresponds exactly to the objective presentation, and I am in the domain of truth. In fact, however, my perception of these sounds will no doubt cause in me a state of terror, which is a passion. Under the sway of emotion, I will say to myself: "Here I am in a state of misery. I may die, and death is an evil." If I give my assent to this inner discourse which is caused by terror, I will be in error as a Stoic, since my fundamental existential option is precisely that there is no other evil than moral evil.[110] In general, it seems that error—but at the same time freedom—is situated in the value judgments which I bring to bear upon events. The right moral attitude consists in recognizing as good or evil only that which is morally good or evil, and in considering as neither good nor bad, and therefore indifferent, that which is morally neither good nor bad.

Moral Theory

The opposition between the domain of the "moral" and that of the "indifferent" can be defined in still another way: that which is moral (in other words, good or bad) depends on us, and that which does not depend on us is indifferent. The only thing that depends on us is our moral intention, or the meaning we give to events. That which does not depend on us corresponds to the necessary linkage of cause and effect—in other words, to Fate, the course of nature, or the actions of other human beings. Thus, life and death, health and sickness, pleasure and suffering, beauty and ugliness, strength and weakness, wealth and poverty, nobility and baseness, political careers—all are indifferent, because they do not depend on us. In principle, all this must be indifferent to us. In other words, we should not introduce differences among them, but accept what happens as willed by Fate: "Do not try to make things happen the way you want, but want what happens to happen the way it happens, and you will be happy."[111]

This is a complete reversal of the usual way of looking at things. We move from a "human" vision of reality, in which our value judgments depend on social conventions and on our passions, to a "natural" or "physical" vision of things, which resituates each event within the perspective of nature and universal Reason.[112] Stoic indifference is profoundly different from Skeptic indifference. For the Pyrrhonist, everything is indifferent because we cannot know, with regard to any particular thing, whether it is good or bad. There is only one thing which is not indifferent, and that is indifference itself. For the Stoics, too, there is only one thing which is not indifferent; but here it is moral intention, which is good and engages human beings to modify themselves and their attitude with regard to the world. Indifference consists in making no differences, but in equally wanting—and even equally loving—everything that is willed by Fate.

We may well ask, however, how the Stoic can orient himself in life if everything outside of moral intention is indifferent. Will he marry, take part in politics, practice a trade, serve his country? This is where an essential part of Stoic moral doctrine steps in: the theory of "duties" (as opposed to duty in general), or of "appropriate actions."[113] This theory permits the beneficent will to find material on which it can practice, to be guided by a code of practical conduct, and to attribute a relative value to indifferent things, which in principle are without value.

To find a basis for this theory of "duties," the Stoics return to their fundamental intuition: that of the living being's instinctive, original accord with itself, which expresses the deepest will of nature. Living beings have an innate tendency to preserve themselves and to repel that which threatens their integrity. When human reason appears, natural instinct becomes reflective, reasoned choice: something is chosen because it responds to the natural tendencies, such as the love of life and of children, or love for one's fellow citizens, which is based on the instinct of sociability. To marry, to be active politically, to serve one's country—all these actions are appropriate to human nature, and therefore have value. What characterizes "appropriate actions" is the fact that they partly depend on us, since they are actions which presuppose a moral intention, and partly do not depend on us, since their success hinges not our will alone but also on other people or on circumstances, external events, and ultimately Fate. This theory of duties or appropriate actions allows philosophers to orient themselves in the uncertainty of everyday life by proposing probable choices which our reason can approve, although it is never absolutely certain that it is acting correctly. What counts, after all, is not the result of our actions, for this is always uncertain; nor is it effectiveness. Instead, it is the *intention* of doing good.[114] The Stoic always acts "under reserve": he tells himself, "I want to do X, if Fate permits." If Fate does not permit it, he will try to succeed in some other way, or else he will accept Fate by "willing what happens."

The Stoic always acts "under reserve"—but he does act, taking part in social and political life. This is another important point which separates him from the Epicureans, who in principle retire from everything that may cause worry. The Stoic does not act in his own material or even spiritual interest, but acts in a way which is always disinterested and in the service of the human community: "No school has more goodness and gentleness; none has more love for mankind or is more devoted to the common good. The goal it assigns for us is to be useful, to help others, and to take care not only of ourselves but of everyone in general and of each person in particular."[115]

Exercises

Because we have lost most of the writings of Zeno and Chrysippus, the founders of the sect, we have far fewer testimonies on the spiritual exercises practiced in the Stoic school than on the exercises practiced by the Epicureans. The most interesting reports are those of Cicero, Philo of Alexandria, Seneca, Epictetus, and Marcus Aurelius; they are relatively late but probably draw on a previous tradition, which we can see traces of in some fragments by Chrysippus and even by Zeno. It thus seems that in Stoicism the parts of philosophy were not only theoretical discourses but exercise themes, which had to be practiced concretely if one wanted to live as a philosopher.

Logic, for instance, was not limited to an abstract theory of reasoning, nor even to school exercises in syllogistics; rather, there was a daily practice of logic applied to the problems of everyday life. Logic was thus the mastery of inner discourse. This was all the more necessary since, in conformity with Socratic intellectualism, the Stoics believed that the human passions correspond to a misuse of human discourse. In other words, they are the result of errors in judgment and in reasoning. We must therefore monitor our inner discourse to see whether erroneous value judgments have crept into it, for this would add something foreign to the comprehensive representation. Marcus Aurelius advises us to construct a definition of objects that present themselves (in other words, things or events that provoke our passion) which is, as it were, "physical": "Look at the object itself as it is in its essence, in its nudity, and tell yourself the name which is peculiar to it."[116] This exercise consists in focusing on reality as it is, without adding to it value judgments inspired by conventions, prejudices, or the passions: "This [Imperial] purple is sheepskin soaked in the blood of a shellfish. Sexual union is the rubbing together of abdomens, with the spasmodic ejaculation of a sticky fluid."[117] Here, logical practice meets the domain of physics, for a definition such as this is formulated from the point of view of nature, without any subjective or anthropomorphic considerations. The reason for this is that Stoic physics, like Stoic logic, was no merely abstract theory but a theme for spiritual exercises.

Putting theory into practice begins with an exercise that consists in recognizing oneself as a part of the Whole, elevating oneself to cosmic consciousness, or immersing oneself within the totality of the cosmos. While meditating on Stoic physics, we are to try to see all things within the perspective of universal Reason. To achieve this, we must practice the imaginative exercise which consists in seeing all human things from above.[118]

From the same perspective, we are to practice seeing things as being in a constant state of metamorphosis: "Acquire a method for contemplating how all things transform themselves into one another. Concentrate your attention on this without ceasing, and exercise yourself on this point. Observe every object, and imagine that it is dissolving and in full transformation; it is rotting and wasting away."[119] This vision of universal metamorphosis leads to the meditation on death, which is always imminent but which we should accept as a fundamental law of universal order. In the last analysis, physics as a spiritual exercise leads the philosopher to give loving consent to the events which have been willed by that Reason which is immanent to the cosmos.[120]

It is not, moreover, simply a matter of consenting to events once they have happened; we must also prepare ourselves for them. One of the best-known Stoic spiritual exercises consisted in the "pre-exercise" *(praemeditatio)* of "evils," which we could gloss as an exercise which prepares us for facing trials.[121] Here, we imagine in advance various difficulties, reversals of fortune, sufferings, and death. Philo of Alexandria says that those who practice *praemeditatio* "do not flinch beneath the blows of Fate, because they have calculated its attacks in advance; for of those things which happen against our will, even the most painful are lessened by foresight, when our thought no longer encounters anything unexpected in events but dulls the perception of them, as if they were old, worn-out things."[122]

Yet the exercise was more complex than this description might lead us to think. When practicing it, philosophers not only wished to dull the shock of reality; they also wanted to steep themselves thoroughly in the truths of Stoicism and restore their inner tranquillity and peace of mind. We must not be afraid to think in advance about events which other people consider unfortunate. On the contrary, we are to think of them often, in order to tell ourselves, above all, that future evils are not evils, because they do not depend on us, and do not pertain to morality. The thought of imminent death also transforms our way of acting in a radical way, by forcing us to become aware of the infinite value of each instant: "We must accomplish each of life's actions as if it were the last."[123] With the exercises of foreseeing evils and foreseeing death, we shift almost unnoticeably from practiced philosophy to practiced ethics. Such foresight is intimately linked to action, as practiced by Stoic philosophers. When they act, they foresee all obstacles, and nothing happens contrary to their expectations. Their moral intention remains whole, even if obstacles arise.[124]

We have seen how, in a philosophy that is put into practice, the limits between the parts of philosophy become indistinct. The exercise of definition is both logical and physical; the thought of death, or the exercise of foreseeing difficulties, is both physical and ethical. By mixing the parts of philosophy in this way, the Stoics probably wanted to respond to Ariston of Chios, a first-generation Stoic who strove to eliminate the physical and logical parts of philosophy and allowed only ethics to remain.[125] According to these Stoics, Ariston was right to consider philosophy as a practice, but the logical and physical parts of philosophy were not purely theoretical. Rather, they too corresponded to a lived philosophy. For them, philosophy was a unique act which had to be practiced at each instant, with constantly renewed attention *(prosokhē)* to oneself and to the present moment. The Stoic's fundamental attitude is this continuous attention, which means constant tension and consciousness, as well as vigilance exercised at every moment. Thanks to this attention, the philosopher is always perfectly aware not only of what he is doing, but also of what he is thinking (this is the task of lived logic) and of what he is—in other words, of his place within the cosmos. This is lived physics. Such self-consciousness is, above all, moral consciousness, which seeks at every moment to purify and rectify our intentions. At every instant, it is careful to allow no other motive for action than the will to do good. Yet such self-consciousness is not merely moral; it is also a cosmic and rational consciousness. Attentive people live in the constant presence of the universal Reason which is immanent within the cosmos. They see all things from the perspective of this Reason, and consent joyfully to its will.

To this lived philosophy—the exercise, simultaneously unique and complex, of wisdom—the Stoics opposed theoretical philosophical discourse. Made up of propositions, this discourse comprises logic, physics, and ethics as distinct parts. By this they meant that when we wish to teach philosophy and invite people to practice it, we are obliged to use discourse; that is, we must set forth physical theory, logical theory, and ethical theory in a series of propositions. When we strive to train *ourselves* for wisdom—

that is, to live philosophically—everything enunciated separately in teaching must now be lived and practiced inseparably.[126]

For the Stoics, the same Reason was at work in nature (and physics), in the human community (and ethics), and in individual thought (and logic). The single act of the philosopher in training for wisdom thus came to coincide with the unique act of universal Reason, which is present within all things and in tune with itself.

ARISTOTELIANISM

The Aristotelians of the Hellenistic Age were, above all, scholars.[127] Only Theophrastus, Aristotle's first successor, seems to have been, like his master, both a contemplative and an organizer of research, particularly in the field of natural history. After Theophrastus, the school seems to have specialized in encyclopedic research, especially on topics in historical and literary fields such as biography, ethnology, and characterology. They also did research in physics, the elaboration of logic, and rhetorical exercises. Unfortunately, only small fragments of this immense amount of work have been preserved. The astronomer Aristarchus of Samos (third century B.C.) came up with the hypothesis that the sun and the stars were immobile and the earth revolved around the sun, while each rotated on its own axis.[128] In the works of Strato of Lampsacus, who professed a materialist physics, we find some attempts at experimental physics, particularly with regard to the void. We have only a few fragments on the ethics of moderating the passions (a doctrine preached by the Aristotelians of this period) and on their attitude concerning the proper way to conduct our lives.[129]

THE PLATONIC ACADEMY

Toward the middle of the third century B.C., when Arcesilaus became head of the Platonic Academy, the school witnessed a kind of return to the Socratic choice of life.[130] Philosophical discourse once again became critical, questioning, and aporetic. This, moreover, explains why Arcesilaus wrote nothing. His teaching method consisted in using argumentation to refute the theses that his auditors were invited to suggest.[131] When a specific thesis was proposed, he set about demonstrating that the opposite could just as well be proved, and he thus showed the impossibility of making affirmations that are capable of attaining absolute certainty and truth. We must therefore suspend all judgment—but this does not mean we must suspend all our research and critical activity. Such reasoning was a return to Socratism, for Socrates said in the *Apology* that, in his eyes, the supreme good was to examine everything, and that a life which was not devoted to such research would not be worth living. Happiness would thus consist in this neverending quest.[132] Ultimately, however, it is also a return to the Platonic definition of philosophy: the consciousness of knowing nothing and of lacking wisdom, which belongs only to the gods.[133] According to Arcesilaus, Plato had seen that human beings cannot accede to absolute knowledge. Like Socrates, Arcesilaus taught nothing, but, also like Socrates, he troubled and fascinated his auditors. He educated them by teaching them to free themselves from their prejudices, developing their critical sense, and inviting them, as Socrates did, to question themselves.[134]

Nevertheless, it seems that we can detect a difference with regard to Socratism. Socrates and Arcesilaus both denounced false knowledge and false certainty, but Socrates criticized the opinions and prejudices of "philosophers" (who for him were the Sophists) and nonphilosophers. Arcesilaus, by contrast, criticized primarily the false knowledge and false certainties of the dogmatic philosophers. For him, philosophy consisted in pointing out the contradictions of a philosophical discourse like that of the Stoics or the Epicureans, which claimed to achieve certainty in things both divine and human. Moral life has no need to be based on principles and justified by philosophical discourse; instead, Arcesilaus, like Socrates and Plato, accepts that human beings have within them a fundamental, innate desire for the good and a natural tendency to act in a way which is good.[135] By purifying themselves of all opinion and completely suspending their judgment, philosophers can thus rediscover their natural tendencies, which precede all speculation. If we follow these tendencies—and it is reasonable to yield to them[136]—then moral action will be justified. Ancient writers generally agreed in recognizing Arcesilaus' extraordinary goodness, and the delicacy with which he practiced benevolence.[137]

With Arcesilaus' successors Carneades and Philo of Larissa, the Academy evolved in the direction of probabilism. It was accepted that if the truth could not be attained, at least it was possible to reach what was probable—that is, solutions which could reasonably be accepted, in the domain of science as well as (most importantly) in the field of moral practice.[138] This philosophical tendency had an immense influence on modern philosophy, thanks to the great success of the philosophical works of Cicero, both in the Renaissance and in modern times. In his writings we can observe Academic philosophy at work. It left to the individual the freedom to choose, in each concrete case, the attitude which he judged to be best according to the circumstances—whether this attitude was inspired by Stoicism, Epicureanism, or another philosophy—and refrained from imposing a mode of conduct dictated by principles fixed in advance. Cicero often boasts of the freedom of the Academic, who is not bound by any system: "We Academics live from day to day (that is, we make our judgments according to each particular case), . . . and that is why we are free. We enjoy greater liberty and are more independent; our power of judgment knows no obstacles; we do not have to obey any prescriptions or orders. I would almost say that we are under no obligation to defend any cause whatsoever."[139] Here, philosophy appears as essentially an activity of choice and decision, the responsibility for which is assumed only by the individual.[140] It is the individual who judges what is suitable to his way of living in the various philosophical discourses which are offered to him. Moral options find their justification in themselves, independently of the metaphysical hypotheses constructed by philosophical discourse—just as the human will is independent of external causes, and finds its cause within itself.[141]

Within the Academy of Arcesilaus and Carneades, which included Cicero and even later philosophers like Plutarch[142] and Favorinus (second century A.D.), the distinction between discourse about philosophy and philosophy itself was particularly clear. Philosophy was, above all, an art of living;[143] but two views on the subject were current in the Academy. Either, as Arcesilaus thought, theoretical philosophical discourses are incapable of grounding or justifying this art of living, and only critical discourse can introduce us to it; or else, as Carneades and Cicero held, theoretical and dogmatic philosophical discourses are only fragmentary, ephemeral means, used on a case-by-case basis, depending on their greater or lesser effectiveness in the concrete practice of philosophical life.

SKEPTICISM

With Skepticism,[144] the distinction between philosophy and philosophical discourse reaches an extreme point. As A.-J. Voelke has shown, skeptical philosophical discourse leads to its own suppression: it abandons the field in favor of a way of life.[145]

Skeptic philosophy—that is, the Skeptic way or choice of life—was the choice of tranquillity and peace of mind. Like all other philosophers of the Hellenistic period, the Skeptic put forth, "out of love for human beings,"[146] his diagnostic of the causes of human unhappiness, and he proposed a remedy and curative therapy for this suffering:

> He who thinks that a thing is beautiful or ugly by nature never stops worrying. When he finds he lacks something he considers good, he imagines he is enduring the worst torments, and he hurls himself into the search for what he thinks is good. No sooner does he come to possess it, however, than he is plunged into myriad worries brought about by his being excited excessively and beyond reason. Fearing that his luck will not last, he does everything possible so that what he thinks is good will not be taken away from him. By contrast, he who utters no opinion on what is naturally good or on what is naturally bad flees nothing, and does not exhaust himself in vain pursuits. In this way, he is free of troubles.
>
> Thus, what happens to the Skeptic is the same as what they say happened to the painter Apelles. One day he was painting a horse, and wanted to represent the foam from the horse's mouth on his canvas. He gave up in a fury, and hurled at the canvas the sponge with which he wiped his brushes; this left a trace of color which imitated the horse's foam. Similarly, the Skeptics hoped to obtain freedom from trouble by using their judgment to resolve the contradiction between what appears to us and what is conceived of; when they did not achieve this, they suspended their judgment. Happily, freedom from trouble accompanied the suspension of their judgment, as shadows accompany bodies.[147]

Just as Apelles was able to achieve perfection in art by renouncing art, so the Skeptic was able to realize the philosophical work of art—that is, peace of mind—by renouncing philosophy, in the sense of philosophical discourse.

Yet philosophical discourse is required in order to eliminate philosophical discourse. We know this Skeptical philosophical discourse thanks to Sextus Empiricus, a physician who wrote at the end of the second century A.D. Sextus also gives us precious information on the history of the Skeptic movement. The Skeptics considered Pyrrho the model of the Skeptic way of life. It seems, however, that the technical argumentation of Skeptic philosophical discourse was not formulated until much later, perhaps in the first century B.C., when Aenesidemus[148] enumerated ten types of argument that justified the suspension of all judgment. They were based on the diversity and contradictions among sense perceptions and beliefs; the diversity of customs and religious practices; the diversity of reactions to rare or frequent phenomena; the diversity of perceptions according to the organs of perception in animals and in human beings; the diversity of perceptions according to the circumstances and inner dispositions of individuals; and the diversity of perceptions according to whether one considers things on a large or a small scale, from near or from afar, or from such-and-such an angle. Aenesidemus also taught that everything is mixed with and related to everything else, which made it impossible to perceive things all by themselves, and finally that the senses are the source of illusion. Agrippa,[149] another Skeptic later than Aenesidemus, proposed five other arguments against the dogmatic logicians: philosophers contradict one another; in order to prove something, it is necessary to continue to infinity, construct a vicious circle, or postulate undemonstrable principles in an unfounded way; ultimately, all things are relative; all things presuppose everything else; and it is impossible to know them either separately or in their totality.

This philosophical discourse leads to *epokhē,* or the suspension of our adherence to dogmatic philosophical discourse, including Skeptical discourse, which, like a purgative, evacuates itself along with the humors whose evacuation it provokes.[150] André-Jean Voelke rightly compares this attitude to that of Wittgenstein, who, at the end of the *Tractatus,* rejects the propositions of the *Tractatus* like a ladder which has become useless. Likewise, Wittgenstein opposes philosophy as pathology to philosophy as a cure.[151]

What is left after this elimination of philosophical discourse by philosophical discourse? Only a way of life. Life itself, everyday life as everyone leads it.[152] This is to be the Skeptic's rule of life: simply to utilize his natural resources—his senses and intelligence—just as lay people do. We are to conform to the customs, laws, and institutions of our country, and follow our natural tendencies and dispositions—eat when we are hungry, drink when we are thirsty. Was this a naive return to simplicity? Perhaps; but the philosopher in question was anything but naive. Since the Skeptic was convinced that it is impossible to know whether one thing or event is better than another thing or event, he would enjoy firmly established peace of mind, thanks to his suspension of all value judgments on things. Such suspension would diminish his pain and suffering, should he ever have to face them, because it would prevent him from adding to his suffering or setbacks the agonizing thought that what he is experiencing is an evil. In everything he did, he was to limit himself to describing what he experienced, without adding anything about what things are or what they are worth. He was to be content to describe the sensory representations he had, and to enunciate the state of his sensory apparatus, without adding to it his opinion.[153] Like the Epicureans and the Stoics, moreover, the Skeptics used short, striking sayings to renew their choice of life at each moment. Some examples are: "This is no better than that," "Perhaps," "All is indeterminate," "Everything escapes comprehension," "Every argument is opposed by an equal argument," "I suspend my judgment." As we can see, the Skeptic way of life also required exercises of thought and the will; and it was a choice of life based on the elimination of philosophical discourse.

CHAPTER EIGHT

Philosophical Schools in the Imperial Period

GENERAL CHARACTERISTICS

The New Schools

During the Hellenistic period and at the beginning of the Roman conquest, philosophical educational institutions were, as we have seen, concentrated primarily in Athens. All of them, it seems, except the school of the Epicureans, disappeared at the end of the Roman Republic or the beginning of the Empire. This was the result of a highly complex set of historical circumstances, of which Sulla's destruction of Athens in 87 B.C. was perhaps not the most important. Beginning with the first century B.C., we find philosophical schools opening up in many cities of the Roman Empire, particularly in Asia, Alexandria, and Rome.[1] The result was a profound transformation of the methods of teaching philosophy. There were still only four great schools (here we are justified in taking the word "school" to mean "doctrinal tendency"): Platonism, Aristotelianism, Stoicism, and Epicureanism, together with two more complex phenomena, Skepticism and Cynicism. From the third and fourth centuries on, Epicureanism and Skepticism gradually disappeared almost completely with the advent of Neoplatonism, which was, in a sense, a fusion of Aristotelianism and Platonism. This tendency had first been sketched as early as the beginning of the first century, with the Platonic Academy under Antiochus of Ascalon.[2] Its definitive acceptance, however, took place only in the third century A.D., first with Porphyry and then in post-Plotinian Neoplatonism.[3]

In this period, philosophical education was no longer given in educational institutions which had maintained continuity with their founders. Each important town had institutions in which one could learn about Platonism, Aristotelianism, Stoicism, or Epicureanism. We can thus observe the culmination of a process which had begun at the end of the Hellenistic period: the teaching of philosophy was taken over by the government.[4] This movement had begun in the Athens of the second century B.C., when the official curriculum for the Athenian ephebes included lessons by philosophers; the latter were probably chosen as representatives of one or another of the four great sects.[5] The city probably gave its philosophers some remuneration for such participation in a public service. Be this as it may, municipal philosophical education, paid for by the cities, tends to become more and more generalized in the Imperial period. This movement reached its apogee and its consecration when, in 176 A.D., the emperor Marcus Aurelius founded four Imperial chairs of philosophy for the teaching of the four traditional doctrines (Platonism, Aristotelianism, Epicureanism, and Stoicism). These chairs had no continuity with the ancient Athenian institutions; instead, they were an attempt on the emperor's part to reestablish Athens as a center of philosophical culture. Indeed, students thronged once again to the ancient city. It is likely that the Aristotelian chair at Athens had a famous occupant at the end of the second century A.D.: the great Aristotelian commentator Alexander of Aphrodisias.[6]

In addition to these municipal and Imperial civil servants, there were always private philosophy professors who opened schools—

which sometimes had no successor—in one of the various cities of the Empire. Examples of this trend were Ammonius Saccas in Alexandria, Plotinus in Rome, and Iamblichus in Syria. We must bear in mind that from the fourth to the sixth centuries, the Neoplatonic school of Athens under the leadership of Plutarch of Athens, Syrianus, and Proclus was a private institution, kept afloat by subsidies from wealthy pagans. It had nothing to do with the Imperial chair in Platonism founded by Marcus Aurelius.[7] The Platonic school in Athens succeeded in artificially resuscitating the organization of the Old Academy and reestablishing properties analogous to those of the school of Plato, which the scholarchs bequeathed to one another. As in ancient times, the scholarchs called themselves "diadochs" (successors); and the members of the schools tried to live in the Pythagorean and Platonic way, which, they thought, had been that of the Old Academics. All this was, however, not the continuation but the re-creation of a tradition they supposed to be alive and uninterrupted.

The dispersal of the philosophical schools had consequences for teaching, as well. We can probably speak of a kind of democratization, with all the risks and advantages such a situation can entail. No matter where one lived within the Empire, it was not necessary to travel great distances to initiate oneself into a specific philosophy. Yet these numerous schools were, for the most part, no longer in living continuity with their great ancestors. Their libraries no longer contained the texts of the lessons and discussions of the various heads of the school—texts which were communicated only to adepts—and there was no longer an uninterrupted chain of heads of the schools.

The situation called for a return to the sources. From this point on, instruction would consist in explaining the texts of the "authorities"—for instance, the dialogues of Plato, the treatises of Aristotle, or the works of Chrysippus and his successors. During the preceding period, by contrast, scholarly activity had consisted above all in training students in methods of thought and argumentation, and the important members of a school often had very different opinions; but during the period we are now examining, the teaching of a school orthodoxy became essential. Freedom of discussion had always existed, but it became much more restricted. There were many reasons for this transformation. In the first place, Skeptics and Academics like Arcesilaus and Carneades had devoted most of their teaching to criticizing the ideas, and often the texts, of the dogmatic schools. Thus, discussion of texts had become a part of teaching. Second, as the years went by, the texts written by the schools' founders had become difficult for apprentice philosophers to understand. Above all, the truth was now conceived as faithfulness to a tradition, which originated in "authorities."

In such a scholarly, professorial atmosphere, there was often a tendency to be satisfied with knowing the dogmas of the four great schools, without worrying about strictly personal training. Apprentice philosophers were more often interested in improving their overall culture than in the existential choice of life which philosophy demands. Nevertheless, many testimonies indicate that throughout this period, philosophy continued to be conceived as an attempt at spiritual progress and a means of inner transformation.

Teaching Methods: The Era of the Commentator

A large body of evidence reveals a radical change in the manner of teaching, which seems to have begun as early as the end of the second century B.C. We know, for instance, that the Roman statesman Crassus had read Plato's *Gorgias* in Athens under the direction of the Academic philosopher Charmadas in 110 B.C.[8] We must note, moreover, that the literary genre of the philosophical commentary was very old. Around 300 B.C., the Platonist Crantor had composed a commentary on Plato's *Timaeus*.[9] The radical change that took place around the first century B.C. consisted in the fact that from this point on, philosophical teaching itself essentially took on the form of textual commentary.

On this point, we possess precious evidence from a Latin author of the second century A.D. He tells us that the Platonist Taurus, who was teaching in Athens at the time, used to recall nostalgically the discipline which prevailed in primitive Pythagorean communities. He opposed this discipline to the attitude of modern disciples, who, he said, "want to decide for themselves the order in which they will learn philosophy." "This one here is burning to begin with Plato's *Symposium* because of the orgy of Alcibiades; this other one, with the *Phaedrus,* because of the speech by Lysias. There are even some who want to read Plato—not in order to make their lives better, but in order to adorn their language and their style; not in order to become more temperate, but in order to acquire more charm."[10] For Platonists, learning philosophy meant reading Plato. We can add that for the Aristotelians, it meant reading Aristotle; for the Stoics, reading Chrysippus; and for the Epicureans, reading Epicurus. This anecdote also shows that in Taurus' school, Plato was read in a specific order, which corresponded to a teaching program—or, in other words, to the stages of spiritual progress. Thanks to this reading, said Taurus, we are to become better and more temperate. This viewpoint did not seem to inspire the enthusiasm of his auditors.

A great deal of other evidence confirms that philosophy classes were henceforth devoted primarily to the reading and exegesis of texts. The students of the Stoic Epictetus, for instance, commented on Chrysippus.[11] In classes taught by the Neoplatonist Plotinus, the session began with the reading of the Aristotelian commentators and Plato; then Plotinus offered his own exegesis of the text being commented upon.[12]

Throughout the preceding period, teaching had been almost

entirely oral. Master and disciple engaged in dialogue; the philosopher spoke, the disciples spoke, and they trained themselves for speaking. In a sense, we can say that they learned to live as they learned to speak. From now on, however, students learned philosophy by reading texts—but this was no solitary reading. Philosophy classes consisted of oral exercises in the explication of written texts. Characteristic was the fact that, especially from the third century A.D. onward, almost all philosophical works had their origin in oral commentaries on texts, which were subsequently written down either by the master or by a disciple. Alternatively, like many of Plotinus' treatises, they were dissertations on "questions" posed by the texts of Plato.

Henceforth, philosophers and their students did not talk about the problems themselves, or about things themselves; instead, they talked about what Plato, Aristotle, or Chrysippus had said about such problems or things. The question "Is the world eternal?" was replaced by the question, "Can we admit that Plato considered the world to be eternal, if he allows for an Artisan of the world in the *Timaeus?*" In fact, as they discussed this latter question, phrased in exegetical form, teachers and students eventually discussed the fundamental question itself, by making the Platonic, Aristotelian, or other texts say what they wanted them to say.

What was essential henceforth was that one's starting point should always be in a text. M.-D. Chenu has given an excellent definition of medieval scholastics as "a rational form of thought which is elaborated consciously and voluntarily from a text considered authoritative."[13] If we accept this definition, we can say that from the first century B.C. on, philosophical discourse starts to change into scholastics, which would be inherited by medieval scholasticism. As we have already seen, from a certain point of view it was this period which saw the birth of the Age of the Professors.

It was also the age of handbooks and summaries, intended either as the basis for a scholarly oral exposition or else to initiate students, and perhaps the wider public as well, into the doctrines of a particular philosopher. For instance, we possess a book entitled *Plato and His Doctrine,* by the famous Latin rhetorician Apuleius; the *Teaching of the Doctrines of Plato,* by Alcinoos; and a *Summary* (of the dogmas of the various schools), composed by Arius Didymus.

In a sense, we can say that in this period, philosophical discourse, especially in the form it adopted in Neoplatonism, considered truth to be revealed. On the one hand, the Stoics already thought that all human beings possess a certain number of common notions which are placed in them by universal Nature or Reason.[14] These sparks of the *logos* permitted an initial knowledge of the fundamental truths which philosophical discourse would then attempt to develop and raise to a scientific level. Yet this natural revelation was augmented by what the Greeks have always believed: revelations made by the gods to a few inspired mortals, preferably at the origins of the various human communities, whether those mortals be legislators, poets, or philosophers like Pythagoras. In his *Theogony,* Hesiod reported what the Muses had told him. In the beginning, according to Plato's *Timaeus,* Athena had revealed to the first Athenians the divine sciences of divination and medicine.[15] There was a constant effort to return to the origins of tradition: from Plato to Pythagoras; from Pythagoras to Orpheus. In addition to these revelations, we must also take into consideration the oracles of the gods, proclaimed in various ways in various sanctuaries. Those of Delphi, in particular, were the source of ancient wisdom, but there were also more recent oracles, like those of Didymus and Claros.[16] Also sought-after were revelations made to the barbarians: Jews, Egyptians, Assyrians, and inhabitants of India. The Chaldean Oracles seem to have been written and presented as a revelation in the second century A.D.; the Neoplatonists considered them as a kind of sacred writ. The older a philosophical or religious doctrine was, the more true and venerable it was. Historical tradition was thus the norm for truth; truth and tradition, reason and authority were identified with each other. Celsus, an anti-Christian polemicist, entitled his work *The True Logos*, by which he meant "The Ancient Norm," or "The True Tradition." The search for truth could consist only in the exegesis of a preexistent, revealed given. The scholastics of this period attempted to reconcile all these traditions and derive from them a kind of general system of philosophy.[17]

Choice of Life

Students thus learned philosophy by commenting on texts, in a way which was both highly technical and highly allegorical. In the final analysis, however, they did this "in order to become better and more temperate" (in the words of the philosopher Taurus), and here we encounter once again the traditional conception of philosophy. To learn philosophy, even by reading and commenting upon texts, meant both to learn a way of life and to practice it. Considered formally and in itself, the exercise of commentary is already formative, just as the exercise of dialectics had been—for it is an exercise of reason, an invitation to modesty, and an element of the contemplative life. Moreover, the content of the texts commented upon, whether they were by Plato, Aristotle, Chrysippus, or Epicurus, invited readers to transform their lives. The Stoic Epictetus reproached his students for using the explication of texts merely to show off: "When I'm asked to comment on Chrysippus, I do not brag; rather, I blush if I cannot display conduct which resembles his teachings and is in accord with them."[18]

According to Plutarch, Plato and Aristotle brought philosophy to its culmination in "epoptics"—that is, in the supreme revelation of transcendent reality, as in the Mysteries. Several testimonies show that from the beginning of the second century A.D., philosophy was conceived of as an ascending spiritual itinerary which corresponded to a hierarchy of the parts of philosophy.[19] Ethics ensured the soul's initial purification; physics revealed that the world has a transcendent cause and thus encouraged philosophers to search for incorporeal realities; metaphysics, or theology (also called "epoptics," because, as in the Mysteries, it is the endpoint of initiation), ultimately entails the contemplation of God. From the viewpoint of the exercise of commentary, it was necessary, in order to travel this spiritual itinerary, to follow a specific order when reading the texts that were to be commented upon.

In the case of Plato, one began with the moral dialogues—in particular the *Alcibiades,* which deals with knowing oneself, and the *Phaedo,* which encourages us to detach ourselves from the body. The student then continued with the physical dialogues, such as the *Timaeus,* in order to learn how to transcend the sensible world; finally, he rose to such theological dialogues as the *Parmenides* or the *Philebus,* in order to discover the One and the good. This is why when Plotinus' student Porphyry edited his master's treatises, which until then had been accessible only to confirmed disciples, he presented them not according to the chronological order of their appearance but according to the stages of spiritual progress. The first *Ennead*—that is, the corpus consisting of the first nine treatises—collects the writings of an ethical nature. The second and third *Enneads* deal with the sensible world and its contents, and they correspond to the physical part. The fourth, fifth, and sixth *Enneads* discuss divine things—the soul, the intellect, and the One—and they correspond to epoptics. The questions of Platonic exegesis that Plotinus deals with in the various *Enneads* correspond rather well to the reading order of the Platonic dialogues as it was put forward in the Platonic schools. This idea of spiritual progress meant that disciples could not undertake the study of a work until they had reached the intellectual and spiritual level which allowed them to profit from it. Certain works were reserved for beginners; others for those making progress. Thus, the complex questions reserved for students making progress were not raised in works intended for beginners.[20]

Moreover, each commentary was considered a spiritual exercise—not only because the search for the meaning of a text really does demand the moral qualities of modesty and love for the truth, but also because the reading of each philosophical text was supposed to produce a transformation in the person reading or listening to the commentary. This is attested, for instance, in the final prayers which Simplicius, the Neoplatonic exegete of Aristotle and Epictetus, placed at the end of some of his commentaries. On each occasion, they announce the spiritual benefit which can be derived from the exegesis of each writing. For instance, one could acquire greatness of soul by reading Aristotle's *On the Heavens,* or rectify one's reason by reading the *Manual* of Epictetus.

According to an ancient custom, masters and pupils engaged in dialogues with one another throughout the course of instruction. This usage persisted in the Platonic school as well as in the Aristotelian, and it seems to have been maintained in the philosophical schools of late antiquity, on the margins of that primary exercise, commentary. For example, the texts which we know as the *Discourses* of Epictetus are nothing other than the notes taken by his student Arrian during the discussions which followed the class proper—that is to say, the textual explications. Aulus Gellius tells us that his master, the Platonist Taurus, allowed his auditors to ask him whatever questions they wished after class. Gellius himself had asked Taurus if the Sage could become angry, and the philosopher had replied to him at length.[21] We know from Plotinus' disciple Porphyry that Plotinus encouraged his auditors to ask him questions; Porphyry adds that this led to much idle chitchat.[22] We can see from Epictetus' *Discourses,* and glimpse from Plotinus' writings, that the master's responses were usually intended to urge his disciples to change their lives or to make spiritual progress.

In general, philosophy professors continued, as in the preceding centuries, to animate the groups of disciples which gathered around them; under certain circumstances, the disciples took meals in common with the master[23] and often lived in close proximity to him. In addition, the master watched over each one of them. Community of life was one of the most important elements in education. Professors did not merely teach, but played the role of genuine directors of conscience who cared for their students' spiritual problems.

In this context, we must note that during this period the Pythagorean tradition was revived. Since the time of Pythagoras, there had always been communities which allied themselves with him; they distinguished themselves from the common run of mortals by a specific lifestyle. The adepts ate no meat, and practiced an ascetic way of living, in the hope of a better fate in the next life.[24] Their attire and their abstinence were favorite targets of the comic poets:

> They are vegetarians; they drink only water;
> Wear an eternal cloak which swarms with vermin;
> And fear the bath. No one in this day and age
> Could stand a routine such as this.[25]

The lifestyle of these Pythagoreans seems to have consisted in practicing the *akousmata:* a collection of maxims which provided a mixture of dietary prohibitions, taboos, moral advice, theoretical definitions, and ritual prescriptions.[26] Beginning approximately with the Christian period, there was a renewal of Pythagoreanism analogous to that of the other schools. An entire apocryphal Pythagorean literature developed; this was the period in which the famous *Golden Verses* were composed.[27] In several *Lives of Pythagoras*—in particular, those by Porphyry and Iamblichus—the idyllic philosophical life led in the master's school was described, as well as the way in which the primitive Pythagorean community was organized.[28] They described the choice of candidates, the novitiate (which consisted in keeping silent for several years), the sharing of possessions among members of the group, their *askēsis,* and their contemplative life.[29] Pythagorean communities were re-created; numerical speculations were developed; and Platonists—adhering to the principle of continuity in the tradition of truth—tended to consider Platonism an extension of Pythagoreanism.

PLOTINUS AND PORPHYRY

Choice of Life

We have just spoken of a renewal of Pythagoreanism. We encounter this phenomenon if we turn to the treatise entitled *On Abstinence,* which Porphyry, the disciple of Plotinus, wrote in order to bring Castricius, another member of the school, back to the practice of vegetarianism. Porphyry reproaches Castricius with being disloyal to the ancestral laws of philosophy—meaning the philosophy of Pythagoras and Empedocles, of which he had been an adept.[30] Here, Porphyry means simply to designate Platonism, conceived as the philosophy which had been revealed since the origins of humanity; but it was precisely that philosophy which presented itself as a way of life encompassing every aspect of existence. Porphyry was perfectly aware that such a way of life was radically different from that of the rest of humanity. He is addressing, he says, not people "who practice manual trades or who are athletes, soldiers, sailors, orators, or politicians, . . . but people who have reflected on the questions, 'Who am I? Where do I come from? Where must I go?' and who, in their diet and in other areas, have established for themselves principles different from those which rule other ways of life."[31]

The way of life which Porphyry recommends is that of the school of Plotinus. Like Aristotle's school, it consisted in "living according to the mind"—that is, in accordance with the highest part of ourselves, namely the intellect. Here, Platonism and Aristotelianism are fused together. At the same time, the viewpoint of philosophers' political action, which had existed in the Academy as well as in primitive Pythagoreanism, disappears, or at least fades into the background. Life according to the mind was not, however, reduced to a purely rational and discursive activity: "*Theōria*, or the contemplation which leads us to happiness, does not consist in an accumulation of ratiocinations or in the volume of acquired knowledge, as might be supposed. It is not built up piece by piece in that way. It does not progress by the quantity of ratiocinations."[32]

Here, Porphyry takes up an Aristotelian theme: it is not enough to acquire knowledge; our knowledge must "become nature within us" and "grow with us." There can be contemplation, says Porphyry, only when our knowledge becomes "life" and "nature" within us. He finds this notion in the *Timaeus,* which affirmed that those who contemplate must render themselves similar to what they contemplate, and thus return to their previous state.[33] It is by this assimilation, said Plato, that we can attain the goal of life. Thus, contemplation is not abstract knowledge but self-transformation: "If happiness could be achieved by writing down discourse, it would be possible to attain this goal without having any concern for choosing our food or carrying out specific actions. Since, however, we must exchange our current life for a different one, purifying ourselves both by discourses and by actions, let us examine what discourses and what actions dispose us toward this other life."[34]

As was also the view of Aristotle, such self-transformation is a return to the true self, which is nothing other than the spirit, or what is divine within us: "The return is not to anything other than to our true self; and the assimilation [literally, the 'connaturality,' *sumphusis*] does not assimilate us to anything other than to our true self. Our true self is the spirit;[35] and the goal we seek is to live in accordance with the spirit."[36] Here, we encounter the same transition from a lower self to the genuine, transcendent self that we have found throughout the history of ancient philosophy.

Porphyry now proceeds to describe the kind of life appropriate to philosophers: they must detach themselves from sensation, imagination, and passions; give the body only what is strictly necessary; and withdraw from the frenzied crowd, like the Pythagoreans and the philosophers described by Plato in the *Theaetetus*. Thus, the contemplative life implies an ascetic lifestyle. Yet such asceticism has value in itself: in the last analysis, it is good for the health, as we see from the story of the conversion of Plotinus' disciple Rogatianus.[37] Rogatianus was a member of the Roman Senate who renounced his position, his house, and his servants; he ate only once every two days, and thereby cured himself of an acute case of gout.[38]

Such asceticism was intended, above all, to stop the lower part of the soul from diverting toward itself the attention which should be oriented toward the spirit. For "we exercise our attention with the totality of our being."[39] The ascetic way of life was thus intended to enable the practitioner to discipline his attention—a type of discipline which was just as strict for Plotinus as it was for the Stoics. As Porphyry remarks in his *Life of Plotinus:* "The attention he devoted to himself was never relaxed, except during sleep; but he was prevented from sleeping, because he ate so little (often he did not even eat bread) and because he constantly oriented his thought toward the spirit."[40] Yet this did not stop Plotinus from taking care of others. He was the tutor of a number of children who were entrusted to him by members of the Roman aristocracy after their death, and he assumed responsibility for their education and their property.

Here we can see that the contemplative life does not abolish care for others, and that such care can also be reconciled with life according to the spirit. Plotinus was available to all: "Never, while he was awake, did he relax his tension toward the intellect. He was simultaneously present to himself and to others."[41] Here, "to himself" means in fact "to his true self"—in other words, to the intellect.

In his treatise On Abstinence, Porphyry affirmed that the goal sought by philosophers was to live in accordance with the spirit or Intellect—this last word can be written either with a capital or without, for it signifies both our intelligence and the divine Intelligence in which ours participates. In the Life of Plotinus, however, we read that "for Plotinus, the goal and the end consisted of union with the supreme deity and the process of growing closer to him."[42] The supreme deity is superior to the Intellect, because, as Porphyry says, he is established above the Intellect and the intelligible. We might therefore think that there are two kinds of contemplative life, and two different goals of life. Yet Plotinian philosophical discourse can explain this difference in divine level, and enable us to see that the two goals are fundamentally identical. Porphyry asserts that Plotinus achieved the "goal" of union with the supreme deity four times during the six years in which he attended Plotinus' school; Porphyry himself, writing at the age of sixty-eight, tells us he attained it once in his life. Such experiences, which we could call "mystical" or "unitive," were thus very rare. These privileged, exceptional moments stand out, as it were, from the background of activity that is constantly turned toward the Intellect. Although they are rare, they nevertheless give the Plotinian way of life its fundamental tonality. This life now appears to us to consist in waiting for the unpredictable emergence of such privileged moments, which give life all its meaning.

Plotinus describes these experiences several times in his writings. Let us take only one example:

And when the soul has the good luck to meet Him, and He comes to her—better yet, when He appears to her as present; when she turns away from all other things present, having prepared herself in order to be as beautiful as possible; and when she has thus achieved resemblance with Him (this preparation and this setting in order are well known to those who practice them), seeing Him *suddenly* appear within her (for there is no longer anything between them, and they are not two but one—indeed, so long as He is present you can no longer distinguish them; the image of this is the lovers and beloved of this world who wish to be fused together)—then the soul is no longer conscious of her body, nor that she is in this body, and she no longer says that she is something other than Him: not man, nor animal, nor being, nor all. (For to look at such things would somehow be to introduce a difference, yet she does not have the leisure to turn toward herself, nor does she desire to do so. Rather, once she has searched for Him, she goes to meet Him and looks at Him instead of herself, and she has no leisure even to see who she is, she who is looking). Then, to be sure, she would not exchange Him for any other thing, even if she were offered all the heavens, for she knows that there is nothing more precious or better than Him (for she cannot run higher, and all other things, even if they are above, are a descent for her). So at that moment she is able to judge and to know perfectly well that "it is He" whom she desired, and to affirm that there is nothing preferable to Him. (For there, no deceit is possible. Where could something more true than the true be found? Thus, what she says—"It is He!"—she also utters later on. Now it is her silence which says it; and, full of joy, she is not wrong, precisely because she is filled with joy. And she says it not because some pleasure is tickling her body but because she has become that which she was before, when she was happy.) . . . If all things around her happened to be destroyed, this would be entirely in accordance with her wishes, so long as she was with Him alone—so great is the joy which she has attained.[43]

The tone and atmosphere here are relatively new in the history of ancient philosophy. Here, philosophical discourse is used only to indicate, without expressing it, that which transcends it—that is to say, an experience in which all discourse is annihilated and in which there is no longer any individual self-consciousness but only a feeling of joy and of presence. Such an experience is, however, inscribed within a tradition which goes back at least as far as Plato's *Symposium*, which speaks of a sudden vision of "the beauty of a wonderful nature," which is nothing other than the good itself.[44] Plato assimilates this vision to that which appears to initiates in the Mysteries of Eleusis. Besides, the "mystical" experience is called "mystical" precisely because of its "mysteries": the secret visions of Eleusis, which likewise appeared as a sudden vision. Plato states that such a vision constitutes the point at which life is worth living; if love for human beauty can overwhelm us, what shall the power be of the love caused by transcendent Beauty?[45] We find traces of this tradition in Philo of Alexandria, as in the following text, where the transitory nature of the experience is strongly emphasized: "When a person's intellect is seized by divine love, when it strives with all its might to arrive at the most secret sanctuary, when the person surges ahead with all his force and with all his zeal, transported by the deity, he forgets everything, and forgets himself; he remembers only the deity, and is suspended from Him. . . . But when this enthusiasm fades, and desire loses its fervor, he becomes a human being once again. He leaves divine things behind, and then encounters the human things which wait for him in the vestibule of the temple."[46]

We must not forget that a similar tendency is not foreign to Aristotelianism, which teaches that human happiness consists in contemplation whose supreme object is the Thought of Thought. Although we have not mentioned the great Aristotelian commentator Alexander of Aphrodisias in this context, because we know very little about his life and teachings, scholars have referred to his "mystical Aristotelianism" because of his concept of the union of our intellect with the divine Intellect.[47]

The mystical experience demonstrates another aspect of the philosophical life. It is no longer a decision for or choice of a way of life; instead, it is an ineffable experience, beyond all discourse, which invades the individual and overthrows all self-consciousness by means of an inexpressible sensation of presence.

Levels of the Self and the Limits of Philosophical Discourse

From Plotinus' fifty-four treatises, we can extract a theory which explains the genesis of reality from a primordial unity—the One, or the good—by means of the appearance of levels of reality that reach ever lower and become more tarnished by multiplicity: first Intellect, then the soul, then sensible things. In fact, like Aristotle and Plato, Plotinus wrote not in order to set forth a system but to resolve particular questions which his listeners raised during his teaching.[48] This does not mean that Plotinus did not have a unified vision of reality; it means that his works are writings of circumstance. To some degree, their goal is also to exhort, since they invite the listener or reader to adopt a certain attitude or way of life. At all levels of reality, Plotinus' philosophical discourse leads solely to an inner *askēsis* and experience which are true knowledge, and which enable the philosopher to rise toward the supreme reality by progressively attaining levels of self-consciousness that are ever higher and more inward. Plotinus adopts the old saying, "Like is known only by like."[49] This means, however, that he believes we can seize the reality we wish to know only by becoming spiritually similar to it. Plotinus' philosophy thus reveals the spirit of Platonism—that is, the indissoluble unity of knowledge and virtue. There can be knowledge only in and through existential progression in the direction of the good.

The first stage of ascent is when the rational soul becomes

aware that it is not intermingled with the irrational soul. The latter, whose job it is to animate the body, is disturbed by the pains and pleasures which come as a result of life within the body. Philosophical discourse can set forth arguments regarding the distinction between the rational and the irrational soul, but the essential thing is not the conclusion that there *is* a rational soul; rather, what is important is that we ourselves *live* as rational souls. Philosophical discourse can try to think of the soul "by considering it in its pure state, because every addition to a thing is an obstacle to the knowledge of that thing."[50] Yet only *askēsis* enables the self to truly know itself as a soul which is separate from what is not it—in other words, to become, consciously and concretely, what it already was without knowing it: "Cut things off and examine yourself. . . . Take away what is superfluous. . . . Do not stop sculpting your own statue."[51] In order to achieve this goal, we must separate ourselves from that which has added itself to the rational soul, and then see ourselves such as we have become.

Yet neither philosophical discourse nor the inner itinerary can stop with the rational soul. Philosophical discourse is constrained to admit, as Aristotle had done, that the soul cannot reason or think unless it is preceded by a substantial Thought, which founds the possibility of reasoning and of knowing. The soul recognizes within itself the traces of this Thought, or transcendent Intellect, in the form of principles which allow it to reason.[52] For Plotinus, as for Aristotle, life according to the spirit is situated at several hierarchical levels. It begins with the level of the rational soul, illuminated by the Intellect, and it then consists in the activity of philosophical reasoning and the reason-guided practice of the virtues. Yet if philosophical reflection leads it toward the Intellect, there will be two avenues of approach to this reality: on the one hand, philosophical discourse, and on the other hand, inner experience. Thus, as Plotinus says, there will be two forms of self-knowledge: on the one hand, knowledge of self as a rational soul which depends on the Intellect but remains on the plane of Reason, and, on the other, self-consciousness as the process of self becoming Intellect. Plotinus describes this in the following way: "Knowing oneself, then, is to know oneself no longer as a human being but as someone who has become wholly other—someone who has torn himself away upward and is carrying along with him only the best part of the soul."[53]

The self then discovers that what is highest within the soul is Intellect and Spirit, and that, unconsciously, it constantly lives from the life of the Intellect. As had been stated by Aristotle and repeated by Porphyry, however, the goal of life is that "life according to the Spirit" or "life according to the Intellect." We must therefore become aware of this unconscious activity, and turn our attention to that transcendence which opens itself to the self: "It is as with a person waiting for a voice which he wishes to hear: he sets aside all other sounds and turns his ear toward the best of sounds, in order to hear it approaching. In the same way, we must leave aside the noises which come from the sensible world, unless they are necessary, in order to keep the soul's conscious power pure and ready to hear the sounds from above."[54]

Here we arrive at the first stage of the mystical experience, for what is involved is the transcendence of the activity proper to the rational soul: it is a "becoming other" and a "being torn upward." The self, having identified itself with the rational soul, is now identified with, and becomes, the Intellect. Yet how are we to imagine what it means to "become Intellect"? Plotinus conceives the Intellect on the model of Aristotelian Thought: as perfectly adequate and transparent self-knowledge. At the same time, he believes that the Intellect contains all the Forms or Ideas within itself—which means, since Intellect is the totality of Forms which thinks itself, that each Form is, in its own way (*qua* Idea of Man or Idea of Horse), the totality of Forms: in the Intellect, everything is interior to everything else. "To become Intellect" is thus to think of ourselves from the viewpoint of totality—not by itemizing this totality, but on the contrary by experiencing its concentration, inwardness, and profound harmony.[55] As Plotinus says, "We must see the Spirit as our own self."[56]

"To become Intellect," then, is ultimately to arrive at a state of the self in which it achieves that inwardness, that meditative retreat toward itself, and that self-transparency which characterize the Intellect. This is symbolized by the idea of a light which sees itself, by means of itself.[57] "To become Intellect" is thus to achieve a state of perfect transparency in our relation to ourselves, precisely by cutting off the individual aspect of the self (which is linked to a soul and a body) in order to leave nothing but the pure inwardness of thought to itself: "One has become Intellect oneself, when, letting other things go from oneself, one looks at the Intellect by means of this Intellect—when one looks at oneself by means of oneself."[58] To become a determinate individual is to separate oneself from the All by adding a difference which, as Plotinus says, is a negation.[59] By cutting off all individual differences, and therefore our own individuality, we can become the All once again. To become Intellect is thus to see ourselves, and all things, within the totalizing perspective of the Divine Spirit.

At this stage, however, the self has not yet reached the end of its ascent. According to Plotinus' image, the Intellect in which we are submerged is like a wave, which, as it swells, raises us up toward a new vision.[60]

Here again, philosophical discourse can demonstrate that beyond the uni-totality represented by the Intellect, which is only a derived unity, we must necessarily admit an absolute and primary unity.[61] Yet here philosophical discourse reaches its limit: it cannot express what absolute Unity is, since to speak is to attach complements or attributes to subjects by means of verbs—but the One, since it is absolutely one, can have no complement or attribute. We can therefore speak of it only by referring to that which it is not. If we appear to attribute positive predicates to it—for example, by saying "the One in the cause of everything"—we are saying not what it is in itself but what we are in relation to it; that is to say, we are its effects. In other words, although we think we are speaking about the One, in fact we are speaking only about ourselves.[62] As relative beings, we are always relative to ourselves, and cannot attain the absolute.

Our only access to this transcendent reality is nondiscursive, unitive experience. Experience of the Intellect corresponds to a state of the self in which it achieves inwardness and perfect transparency with itself. The experience of the One corresponds to a new state of the self, in which it loses and finds itself once again. It loses itself, in that it gets the impression of no longer being itself, or of belonging to itself but being the possession of something else.[63] At the same time, however, this annihilation of personal identity is perceived as "a flourishing of the self" and an "intensification of the self."[64] By "cutting off all things,"[65] we no longer find Totality at this level; we find that Presence which is behind all things, including itself, prior to all determination and individuation.

In fact, such an experience is ineffable, and as he describes it Plotinus can say nothing about the One: he describes only the subjective state of the person who experiences it. Yet this experience is what truly leads to the One. Plotinus here distinguishes very clearly between discursive teaching and nondiscursive experience. Theology, which can only be discursive, provides us with teaching and instruction about the good and the One, but what leads us to the One is virtue, purification of the soul, and the effort to live the life of the Spirit. Teaching is like an inner signpost which tells us in which direction we must go; but in order to reach the One, we must begin actually to walk—on a road which we travel alone, toward the Alone.[66]

Yet philosophical discourse may appear once again, in order to explain how such experience of the One is possible. The self can reach the One precisely because it lives the life of the Spirit. Within the Spirit, or the Intellect, there are two levels: the level of the thinking Intellect, which corresponds to the state of the Intellect when it is completely constituted and thinks itself as the totality of Forms. On the other hand, there is the level of Intellect when it is being born—when it is not yet Intellect and does not yet think, but emanates from the One like a ray of light and is therefore in immediate contact with it. As a result of this being touched by the One, Plotinus tells us, the Spirit is "drunk with love," "drunk on nectar," and "flourishes in enjoyment."[67] To become the Intellect which thinks is already a mystical experience for the self; but to become the Intellect which loves means to rise to a higher mystical experience. It is to situate ourselves at the point of origin where all things emanate from the good—this being none other than the point at which the Intellect is born. We can imagine a point situated on a line and coming to coincide with the point where the line emanates from the center. The birth-point of the line is infinitely close to the center, yet infinitely separated from it, because it is not the center but a point of emanation.[68] Such is the relationship between the relative and the absolute.

The relations which, in Plotinus, exist between philosophical discourse and existential choice are well summed up in the following phrase, which Plotinus directs against the Gnostics: "When one says 'God' without truly practicing virtue, 'God' is nothing but a word."[69] Only moral or mystical experience can give content to philosophical discourse.

POST-PLOTINIAN NEOPLATONISM AND THEURGY

Philosophical Discourse and the Will to Harmonize Traditions

Neoplatonism after Plotinus, as represented above all by Iamblichus, Syrianus, Proclus, and Damascius, might seem at first to be a development of Plotinus' hieratic system. In fact, however, it is characterized by a gigantic attempt at synthesizing the most disparate elements of the philosophical and religious tradition of all antiquity. In conformance with a long tradition, Platonism was identified with Pythagoreanism. At the same time, Aristotelianism was reconciled with Platonism, insofar as Aristotle's writings, interpreted in a Platonic sense, represented the first stage in the overall *cursus* of Neoplatonic teaching. This consisted in the explanation of some of Aristotle's treatises,[70] and then of Plato's dialogues,[71] ordered in accordance with the stages of spiritual progress.

Harmonization did not stop here, however. There was also an attempt to create agreement with the philosophical tradition on the one hand, and on the other with the Orphic writings and the *Chaldean Oracles*, considered to be traditions revealed by the gods. The task was thus to systematize all revealed doctrines—Orphism, Hermeticism, and Chaldeanism—with the philosophical tradition, whether Pythagorean or Platonic.

We thus arrive at what may seem like incredible juggling acts. The Neoplatonists were able to find the various classes of gods of the *Chaldean Oracles* in each of the articulations of the dialectical argument concerning the well-known hypotheses on the One, as developed in Plato's *Parmenides*. Hierarchies of notions taken artificially from Plato's dialogues came to correspond, term for term, with Orphic and Chaldean hierarchies of beings. Thus, the Chaldean and Orphic revelations came to penetrate Neoplatonic discourse. We ought not, however, to imagine therefore that Neoplatonic philosophical discourse is nothing but confusion. In fact, every scholastics is a rational attempt at exegesis and systematization. It obliges the mind to undertake intellectual gymnastics which is, in the last analysis, educational, and which develops our logical rigor and ability to analyze concepts. We cannot help admiring Proclus' attempt in his *Elements of Theology* to explain, *more geometrico*, the stages of the procession of beings, while his commentaries on Plato are veritable monuments of exegesis. To take another example: Damascius' reflections on the problems implied by the notion of "Principle of the All" achieve great profundity. It is not surprising that Proclus' "system" exercised a fundamental influence on the whole history of Western thought, especially during the Renaissance and in the period of German Romanticism.

The activity of the Neoplatonists later than Plotinus was devoted above all to the exegesis of texts by Plato and Aristotle. Some of their commentaries on Aristotle were translated into Latin, and played a considerable role in the interpretations of this philosopher that were proposed in the Middle Ages.

Way of Life

For the later Neoplatonists, as for Plotinus, philosophical discourse was intimately linked to concrete practices and a way of life. For Plotinus, however, life according to the Spirit consisted in a philosophical life—that is, in *askēsis* and moral and mystical experience. The situation was wholly different for the later Neoplatonists. To be sure, they preserved the philosophical practice of *askēsis* and of virtue;[72] but they considered what they called "theurgical" practice equally important, or even, in the case of Iamblichus, apparently even more important. The word "theurgy" does not appear until the second century A.D.; it seems to have been created by the author or authors of the *Chaldean Oracles* to designate rituals capable of purifying the soul and its "immediate vehicle," the astral body, and thus allowing it to contemplate the gods.[73] These rituals included ablutions, sacrifices, and invocations using ritual words that were often incomprehensible. What differentiated theurgy from magic was that it did not claim to force the gods, but aimed at submitting to their will by carrying out the rites which they themselves supposedly ordained. As

Iamblichus says, the only thing that can bring about our union with the gods is not theoretical philosophy, but rites which we do not understand.[74] It is not by intellectual activity that we can carry them out, for in this case their efficacy would depend on us. It is the gods who take the initiative; they have chosen the material signs, or "sacraments," which attract the gods, allow contact with the divine, and enable us to see the divine forms. Thus, we are in the presence of a kind of doctrine of salvific grace. In this conception, the idea of mystical union does not disappear but is included within the overall perspective of theurgy. Like the other gods, the supreme deity can also manifest himself to the soul in the mystical experience by means of what Proclus calls the "one of the soul," or the supreme, transcendent part of the soul.[75] This "one of the soul" thus somehow corresponds to the *sign*, which attracts the gods into the soul in ordinary theurgical practice.

This invasion of Platonism by theurgy is mysterious to us. It is hard to understand why Neoplatonism of the end of antiquity introduced theurgical practice into philosophical practice. As H.-D. Saffrey has pointed out, such an attitude can be explained by the later Neoplatonists' conception of man's place with regard to the divine.[76] Whereas Plotinus believed that the human soul was always in unconscious contact with the Intellect and the spiritual world, the later Neoplatonists believed that because the soul had fallen into the body, it needed to go through material and sensible rites in order to be able to rise toward the divine. This was similar to the move made by Christianity, in which man, once corrupted by original sin, needs the mediation of the incarnate Logos and the sensible signs of the sacraments in order to enter into contact with God. For Neoplatonism and Christianity, the two spiritual movements which dominated the end of antiquity and opposed each other, man cannot save himself by his own strength but must wait for the divine to take the initiative.

Philosophy and Philosophical Discourse

PHILOSOPHY AND THE AMBIGUITY OF PHILOSOPHICAL DISCOURSE

The Stoics made a distinction between philosophy, defined as the lived practice of the virtues of logic, physics, and ethics,[1] and "discourse according to philosophy," which was theoretical instruction in philosophy. The latter was in turn divided into the theory of physics, the theory of logic, and the theory of ethics. This distinction had a quite specific meaning within the Stoic system, and it could be used in a more general way to describe the phenomenon of "philosophy" in antiquity. Throughout this investigation, we have recognized the existence of a philosophical life—more precisely, a way of life—which can be characterized as philosophical and which is radically opposed to the way of life of nonphilosophers. On the other hand, we have identified the existence of a philosophical discourse, which justifies, motivates, and influences this choice of life. Philosophy and philosophical discourse thus appear to be simultaneously incommensurable and inseparable.

Their incommensurability derives first of all from the fact that for the ancients, one was a philosopher not because of the originality or abundance of the philosophical discourse which one conceived or developed, but as a function of the way one lived. Above all, the goal was to become better; and discourse was philosophical only if it was transformed into a way of life. This was true of the Platonic and Aristotelian traditions, which taught that the philosophical life culminated in life according to the spirit. Yet it was equally true for the Cynics, for whom philosophical discourse was reduced to a minimum—sometimes to mere gestures. Yet the Cynics were in no way regarded as being anything less than philosophers, even model philosophers.

Let us consider another example: the Roman statesman Cato of Utica, who opposed the dictatorship of Caesar and ended his life by a famous suicide.[2] Posterity admired him as a philosopher, and even as one of the rare Stoic sages to have ever existed; this was because he practiced the Stoic virtues with exemplary rigor in his political activity. The same holds true of other Roman statesmen, such as Rutilius Rufus and Quintus Mucius Scaevola Pontifex, who practiced Stoicism to the letter. They showed an exemplary disinterestedness in the administration of provinces; and as the only ones who took seriously the prescriptions of the laws against luxury, they defended themselves before the tribunals in Stoic style, without recourse to rhetorical tricks.[3] We might also mention Marcus Aurelius, who was officially called "philosopher" during his lifetime, although no one knew that he had written his *Meditations* and therefore he did not appear to be a theoretician.[4] Another philosopher, although he did not teach, was the senator Rogatianus, Plotinus' disciple mentioned above, who, on the day he was to assume his duties as a praetor, renounced his wealth and his political office.

Philosophical life and philosophical discourse are incommensurable, above all, because they are of completely heterogeneous natures. The essential part of the philosophical life—the existential choice of a certain way of life, the experience of certain inner states and dispositions—wholly escapes expression by philosophical discourse. This appears most clearly in the Platonic experience of love, perhaps even in the Aristotelian intuition of simple substances, and especially in the Plotinian unitive experience. This last is completely ineffable in its specificity, since whoever speaks about it once the experience is over is no longer at the same psychic level as when he was living the experience. It is also true, however, of the Epicurean, Stoic, and Cynic life experiences. The lived experience of pure pleasure, or of coherence with oneself and with nature, is of a wholly different order from the discourse which prescribes or describes it from the outside. Such experiences are not of the order of discourse and propositions.

They are thus incommensurable—but also inseparable. There is no discourse which deserves to be called philosophical if it is separated from the philosophical life, and there is no philosophical life unless it is directly linked to philosophical discourse. This, moreover, is the locus of a danger that is inherent to philosophical life—namely, the ambiguity of philosophical discourse.

All schools denounced the risk taken by philosophers who imagine that their philosophical discourse can be sufficient to itself without being in accord with the philosophical life. They constantly attacked those who, to use the terms of the Platonist Polemo, seek to be admired for their skill at syllogistic arguing but contradict themselves in the conduct of their lives.[5] In the words of an Epicurean saying, they develop empty discourses.[6] According to the Stoic Epictetus, they talk about the art of living like human beings, instead of living like human beings themselves.[7] And as Seneca put it, they turn love of wisdom *(philosophia)* into love of words *(philologia)*.[8] Traditionally, people who developed an apparently philosophical discourse without trying to live their lives in accordance with their discourse, and without their discourse emanating from their life experience, were called "Sophists." This was true from Plato and Aristotle to Plutarch, who declares that once these Sophists have gotten up from their chairs and have put down their books and manuals, they are no better than the rest of mankind "in the real acts of life."[9]

Conversely, the philosophical life cannot do without philosophical discourse, so long as such discourse is inspired and animated by philosophy; for it is an integral part of such a life. We can consider the relationship between philosophical life and philosophical discourse in three different ways, which are closely linked. First, discourse justifies our choice of life and develops all its implications. We could say that through a kind of reciprocal causality, the choice of life determines discourse, and discourse determines our choice of life, as it justifies it theoretically. Second, in order to live philosophically, we must perform actions on ourselves and on others; and if philosophical discourse is truly the expression of an existential option, then from this perspective it is an indispensable means. Finally, philosophical discourse is one of the very forms of the exercise of the philosophical way of life, as dialogue with others or with oneself.

Let us look first at the way in which philosophical discourse theoretically justifies our choice of life. As we have seen throughout the history of ancient philosophy, in order to establish the rationality of their choice of life, philosophers must rely on a discourse which itself aims, insofar as is possible, for rigorous rationality. Whether it is the choice of the good, as in Plato; or the choice of pure pleasure, as for the Epicureans; or the choice of moral intent, as for the Stoics; or the choice of life in accordance with the Intellect, in the case of Aristotle and Plotinus—on each occasion, it will be necessary to disengage the presuppositions, implications, and consequences of each respective attitude with great precision. For instance, as we saw in the case of Stoicism and Epicureanism, it will be necessary, from the perspective of the existential option, to seek man's place within the world and thus elaborate a physics. We will also have to define man's relationship to his fellow men and thus elaborate an "ethics." Finally, we shall define the very rules of reasoning used within physics or ethics, and thereby elaborate a "logic" and a theory of knowledge. We will therefore have to use a technical language, and speak of atoms, incorporeals, Ideas, Being, and the One, as well as of the logical rules of discussion. Even for the Cynic choice of life, in which philosophical discourse is reduced to a minimum, we can glimpse in the background a reflection on the relation between "convention" and "nature." An attempt at conceptualization and systematization, more or less pronounced, is apparent throughout ancient philosophy.

Second, discourse is a privileged means by which the philosopher can act upon himself and others; for if it is the expression of the existential option of the person who utters it, discourse always has, directly or indirectly, a function which is formative, educative, psychagogic, and therapeutic. It is always intended to produce an effect, to create a *habitus* within the soul, or to provoke a transformation of the self. Plutarch alludes to this creative role when he writes: "Philosophical discourse does not sculpt immobile statues, but whatever it touches it wants to render active, efficacious, and alive. It inspires motive impulse, judgments which generate useful acts, and choices in favor of the good."[10] From this perspective, we can define philosophical discourse as a spiritual exercise—in other words, as a practice intended to carry out a radical change in our being.

The various types of philosophical discourse attempt to realize this transformation of the self in a number of ways. Purely "theoretical" and dogmatic discourse, even when reduced to itself, as it were, can already bring this about by sheer force of evidence. For example, when Epicurean and Stoic theories constrain their followers to make the choice of life they imply, they somehow do this by means of their rigorously systematic form, or by the attractive features they sketch of the sage's way of life.

They can further increase their persuasive vigor by concentrating on highly dense summaries, or—even better—on short, striking maxims like the Epicureans' fourfold remedy. This is why Stoics and Epicureans advised their disciples to remember these fundamental dogmas, night and day, and not only mentally but by writing. It is in this perspective that the exercise constituted by Marcus Aurelius' *Meditations* must be understood.

In this work, the emperor-philosopher formulates the dogmas of Stoicism for himself. Yet this was no matter of summaries or reminders which one would only need to read; these were not mathematical formulas, received once and for all and intended to be applied mechanically. The point was not to resolve theoretical or abstract problems, but to place oneself in a frame of mind such that one felt obliged to live like a Stoic. It was thus not enough to reread "words"; one also had to formulate, in a striking manner, maxims which invited the reader or listener to action. What counted was the act of writing and of talking to oneself.[11] In general, one can say that the advantage of the systematic structure of the Stoic and Epicurean theories was that doctrinal refinements could be reserved for specialists, while the essential part of the doctrine remained accessible to a wider public. There was an analogy here with Christianity, where discussions are reserved for theologians while the catechism suffices for average parishioners. Such philosophies could thus become "popular," and "missionary."

There was also a wholly different type of discourse which also seems to be theoretical; it took the form of questions, investigations, and *aporiai*. These proposed neither dogmas nor system, but obliged their disciples to undertake a personal effort and active exercise. Such discourse also tended to produce an aptitude, or *habitus*, in the interlocutor's soul, and to lead him to a determinate choice of life.

The Platonic dialogue—the *Sophist* or *Philebus*, for example— was a more intellectual exercise; yet we must recognize that it still was, above all, an "exercise." As we have seen, its principal and unique goal was not to solve the problem raised, but "to make people better dialecticians." Being a better dialectician meant not only being skillful at invention or at denouncing tricks in reasoning. Before anything else, it meant knowing how to dialogue, together with all the demands that this entails: recognizing the presence and the rights of one's interlocutor, basing one's replies on what the interlocutor admits he knows, and therefore agreeing with him at each stage of the discussion. Above all, it meant submitting oneself to the demands and norms of reason and the search for truth; finally, it meant recognizing the absolute value of the Good. It therefore meant leaving behind one's individual point of view, in order to rise to a universal viewpoint; and it meant trying to see things within the perspective of the All and the deity, thereby transforming one's vision of the world and one's own inner attitude.

The third aspect of the relations between philosophy and philosophical discourse is that philosophical discourse is one of the forms of exercise of the philosophical way of life. We have seen that dialogue is an integral part of the Platonic way of life. Life in the Academy implied constant intellectual and spiritual exchange not only in dialogue, but also in scientific research. This community of philosophers was also a community of scholars, who practiced mathematics, astronomy, and political reflection.

Even more than the Platonic school, the Aristotelian school was a community of scholars. The Aristotelian choice of life was an attempt "to live according to the Intellect"—that is, to find pleasure and the meaning of life in research. It meant leading the life of a scholar and a contemplative, and undertaking research, often collective, on every aspect of human and cosmic reality. For Aristotle, philosophical and scientific discourse could not be merely dialogical; for him, too, it was an essential element of life in accordance with the mind. This scholarly activity could, moreover, transcend itself and become mystical intuition, when the human intellect, by means of nondiscursive contact, enters into a rapport with the divine Intellect.

Such a community of research, discussion, care for oneself and for others, and mutual correction could also be found in other schools; we have seen it in Epicurean friendship, as well as in Stoic and Neoplatonic direction of conscience.

Another exercise of the philosophical way of life is meditative discourse—a kind of dialogue which philosophers carry out with themselves. Dialogue with oneself was a widespread custom throughout antiquity; for instance, we know that Pyrrho used to astonish his fellow citizens because he spoke to himself out loud, and that the Stoic Cleanthes used to admonish himself in the same way.[12] Silent meditation could be practiced while standing motionless—this was Socrates' way—or while walking, as in the following verses by Horace: "Do you go silently, tiptoeing through the healthful woods, harboring in your mind all the thoughts worthy of a sage and a good man?"[13] Likewise the Stoic Epictetus: "Go for a walk alone, and converse with yourself."[14] Meditation is part of an ensemble of practices, not all of which fall within the order of discourse, but all of which testify to the philosopher's personal engagement. They are means by which philosophers can transform and influence themselves. These are the spiritual exercises, which we shall now investigate.

SPIRITUAL EXERCISES

Throughout our investigation, we have encountered "exercises" (askēsis, meletē) in every school, even among the Skeptics; that is to say, we have found voluntary, personal practices intended to cause a transformation of the self. These are inherent to the philosophical life. I would now like to highlight the common tendencies that can be discerned in the practices of the various schools.

Prehistory

There are never any absolute beginnings in the history of thought. We can therefore assume that a prehistory of spiritual exercises existed among the Presocratic thinkers and in Archaic Greece. Unfortunately, all that we know about the Presocratics is extremely lacunary, the testimonies are late, and the fragments which have been preserved for us are very difficult to interpret, because we cannot always grasp with certainty the meaning of the words used. For instance, Empedocles speaks in the following terms of an unusual personage who may perhaps be Pythagoras: "Among them lived a man of extraordinary wisdom who had been able to acquire a great wealth of thoughts [*prapidōn*]; he was powerful in all sorts of works. For when he made a great effort in his thoughts [*prapidessin*], he easily saw all of the things that had happened in the lifetimes of ten or twenty men."[15]

It has been suggested that this is an allusion to the memory exercises practiced by Pythagoras.[16] We shall return to this point, but for the moment let us note that this recollection takes place by means of "a great effort of thought." The word *prapides,* which is used twice in our text, originally meant the diaphragm, the tension of which can stop the breath and therefore, figuratively, reflection and thought. Like the word "heart," it had both a physiological and a psychological meaning. Following Louis Gernet, Vernant therefore believes that our Empedocles text is alluding to a "spiritual exercise" of remembrance, which consisted in "techniques of controlling one's breathing by the diaphragm which were to allow the soul to concentrate itself, in order to free itself from the body and travel in the Beyond."[17]

Yet can we say that the word *prapides* has a physiological meaning in the context of an attempt to remember, when two lines earlier it denoted thoughts and reflections and thus seemed to have a psychological meaning? In another text by Empedocles—"Happy is he who has acquired great wealth of divine thoughts [*prapidōn*]; unhappy is he who maintains a dark opinion of the gods"[18]—we find the same "psychological" meaning of *prapides,* which is moreover confirmed by its opposition to a term meaning "opinion." In this context, the affirmation of the existence of "techniques for controlling the breath" rests only on the ambiguity of the word *prapides;* but nothing proves that this word denotes the diaphragm in this phrase by Empedocles.

I do not wish to say that no techniques for controlling the breath existed in the Greek philosophical tradition; the idea of the soul as breath is enough to allow us to suppose the existence of such techniques.[19] It may be that the Platonic exercise which consisted in concentrating the soul, which is usually dispersed throughout all the parts of the body, ought to be understood from this perspective. It is also striking that in stories which tell of the deaths of philosophers—for instance, those of the Cynics Diogenes and Metrocles—we frequently hear of people who supposedly ended their lives by holding their breath.[20] This allows us to suppose that similar practices were mentioned in the biographical tradition. Here, however, I simply wish to give one example (among many) of the uncertainties and difficulties which lie in wait for all reconstructions and hypotheses dealing with the Presocratics and with Archaic Greece.

Jean-Pierre Vernant adds that these techniques of breath control must be placed within the context of the "shamanic" tradition.[21] Shamanism is a social phenomenon fundamentally linked to hunting cultures.[22] Only in Siberia and in South America has it remained a primary social phenomenon, but there it was adapted to and mixed with other cultures and religions at a fairly ancient date. Its substratum remains most visible in Scandinavia and Indonesia. It revolves around the figure of the shaman, who knows how to use ritual actions to enter into contact with the world of animal or human spirits, whether living or dead, in order to ensure good luck in hunting and pasturing, or else to cure the souls of the living or the dead. Since the work of Karl Meuli[23] and E. R. Dodds,[24] scholars have looked to shamanism for the origins of Greek philosophers' conceptions of the soul and of the body-soul dichotomy. Shamanism has also been considered the origin of techniques of spiritual concentration, of concepts of psychic journeys outside the body, and, since the work of Mircea Eliade,[25] the origin of techniques of ecstasy. I myself am extremely reticent about this kind of explanation, primarily for two reasons.

In the first place, even if we accept this shamanic prehistory, it remains true that the spiritual exercises which interest us no longer have anything in common with shamanic rituals. On the contrary, they respond to a rigorous need for rational control, which, so far as we know, emerges with the first Greek thinkers, with the Sophists, and with Socrates. Overly narrow comparativism thus runs the risk of falsifying our conception of Greek philosophy.

Second, it seems to me that historians of philosophy have a highly idealized and spiritualized idea of shamanism which leads them to see shamanism everywhere they turn. For instance, Henri Joly has written: "That Socrates was the last shaman and the first philosopher is now an anthropologically accepted truth."[26] But can we really talk about Socrates in these terms? What does Joly mean by "anthropologically accepted truth?" Furthermore, can one really say that Socrates was the first philosopher? What does the word "shaman" mean here? Does it mean that, in conformity with the essence of shamanism (that is to say, from the perspective of hunting and fishing, the alliance between human souls and animal spirits, conceived on the model of matrimony), Socrates had a ritual spouse, believed to be "a feminine spirit of the nourishing world—a daughter of the forest spirit who gives mankind game, or of the aquatic spirit who gives fish"? Did he take on the form of an animal for the duration of the ritual, in his dress and his behavior? Did he bellow and leap about, like a male animal fighting his rivals and preparing to couple with his female? I am here alluding to a description of the shaman's activity recently given by my colleague Roberte Hamayon.[27] She has also, it seems to me, shed remarkable light on the ambiguity inherent in the use of the term "trance" (which is close to that of "ecstasy") in order to group together the totality of shamanistic bodily conduct.[28] It might seem to be enough to say that the shaman is "in a trance," without describing the details of his gestures; but what are truly important are precisely the details of these bodily gestures. Trembling or leaping does not express the same kind of relation when it is directed toward different types of spirits:[29]

> The symbolism of the alliance with animal spirits, because it implies the shaman's ritual animalization, is enough to account for the bizarreness of his behavior. It allows us to disregard questions about his normal or pathological nature, or the artificial or spontaneous character of his conduct. There is no need to appeal to any particular psychology or any physical conditioning. By the movements of his body, the shaman communicates with the animal spirits, just as the different species communicate with one another despite their lack of a common language. When he leaps or when he remains motionless, he is not out of his mind, nor has he fainted, nor is he hysterical or catatonic. He is playing his part. For him, the point is not to reach some state, or to live through some experience, as certain Western interpretations would have it; rather, the point is to carry out the action which his people are waiting for. There is thus no need to appeal to the vocabulary of "trance," "ecstasy," or "altered states" of consciousness—a vocabulary which is ambiguous because it implies a link between physical state, psychic state, and symbolic act, a link which has not been proved.

In order to be able to talk about Socrates as if he were a shaman, we must, it seems to me, eliminate from the idea of "shaman" all that gives it specificity. For Joly, the fact that Socrates stood off by himself and remained motionless in order to meditate, as well as the fact that he "applied his spirit to himself,"[30] proves that he had recourse to "well-known techniques of breath control."[31] "Well-known" seems to me quite exaggerated; "alleged" or "possible" would seem more exact, as we have seen. I myself think that if one wants to meditate quietly, it is *necessary* to remain motionless and silent, and that such behavior has nothing to do with the shaman's "retreat." Dodds speaks in this context of a religious "retreat"—a period of rigorous training in solitude and fasting which can include a psychological change of sex. After this period, the shaman's soul can leave his body and travel throughout the world of the spirits. Yet the realities are much more complex, since they are always linked to a specific ritual relationship with animal spirits or the souls of the dead. Eliade and Dodds imagine shamanism to be the power of one individual to modify the relations of his soul and his body at will; but what we really find is the art of practicing a certain symbolic conduct, which is related to certain concrete situations. Insofar as the shaman's "retreat" is concerned, I quote Hamayon once again: "The alliance with an animal spirit is the basis for the wild, spontaneous aspect of the shaman's ritual behavior, and also for the nonritualized behavior which marks the inception of his career: running away, refusing to eat meat, sleepiness, and so on. When these behaviors are manifested at puberty, they are taken as expressing entry into contact with animal spirits and as constituting a test of virility."[32]

It is hard to see how all this relates to Socrates' behavior. Dodds also wanted to see traces of shamanism in the stories told about historical characters such as Abaris, Aristeas of Proconnesus, Hermotimus of Clazomenae, and Epimenides, who supposedly traveled outside their bodies. The description of Aristeas given by a late writer from the second half of the second century A.D. (thus, nine centuries after the fact) seems, moreover, to confirm the idealized representation which scholars usually have of shamanism:

"As he lay on the ground, scarcely breathing, his soul, abandoning his body, wandered like a bird and saw everything beneath it: earth, sea, rivers, towns, the customs and passions of mankind, and natures of every kind. Then, returning to its body and making it rise, using it once again as an instrument, it told what it had seen and heard."[33]

In a meticulous study, James Bolton has shown that it was in fact under the influence of Heraclides of Pontus—one of Plato's pupils, who was interested in this type of phenomena—that the story of Aristeas had been interpreted in this way.[34] According to Bolton, however, we have every reason to believe that Aristeas, who lived in the seventh century B.C., really did make a voyage of exploration in what is now the south of Russia and the steppes of Asia, and that upon his return he wrote a poem entitled *Arimaspeia*, which told of his adventures. It thus seems that, in the case of Aristeas, there was no psychic voyage but an authentic terrestrial voyage. Aristeas had been gone for six years and was thought to be dead. People thus believed that it was his soul which had made the voyage, in a state of apparent death. Here again, we see the uncertainty that weakens this kind of "shamanistic" interpretation.

It is possible that traces of shamanism can be discerned in certain religious aspects and rituals of archaic Greece, but we must surely exercise the greatest prudence when we use shamanism to interpret the figures and practices of those sages who, from Aristeas to Pythagoras, were supposed to have possessed mastery over their souls, thanks to an ascetic life-discipline. It this area, it seems entirely legitimate to hesitate, as does Jean-Pierre Vernant when he writes, with regard to figures like Abaris and Aristeas: "For our part, we would be tempted to establish a comparison with yoga-type techniques rather than with acts of shamanism."[35]

We can now return to the Empedocles text from which we started. It suggests two facts well known from other sources: that

Pythagoras believed in reincarnation, and that he was credited with the power to remember his previous existences. It was said that he remembered having been Euphorbus, son of Panthoos, who was killed by Menelaus during the Trojan War.[36] The ancients also described how, mornings and evenings, the Pythagoreans practiced memory exercises in which they recalled all the events of the current or the previous day.[37] It has been said that these exercises were ultimately intended to help people recall their previous lives.[38] Yet this interpretation can be supported only by one single, very late witness: Hierocles, the fifth-century A.D. commentator on a Neopythagorean apocryphon entitled *The Golden Verses,* where one finds, among other things, advice on the subject of examining one's conscience. After showing the moral importance of this practice, Hierocles adds: "This remembrance of daily life becomes an exercise suitable for reminding us of what we have done in our previous lives, and thus for giving us the feeling of our immortality."[39] Yet we must note that when two earlier witnesses, Diodorus Siculus and Cicero, mention the Pythagorean practice of remembering the events of the preceding days, they speak only of exercises intended to increase memory capacity.[40] For Porphyry, it was more a question of examining one's conscience, since it was necessary to account to oneself for one's past actions, and also foresee how one was going to act in the future.[41]

We have many descriptions of life in the school of Pythagoras. Unfortunately, they are often projections of an ideal of the philosophical life which was proper to schools much later than Pythagoreanism, so they cannot be trusted for the reconstruction of the Pythagorean model of life. We know that Plato praised this way of life in his *Republic,* but he gives us no substantive details about it.[42] All we can say with certainty is, first, that the Pythagoreans, during and after the time of Pythagoras, exerted political influence on several southern Italian cities, thereby furnishing a model for the Platonic ideal of a city organized and governed by philosophers.[43] We can also say that after the defeat of this political activity, there existed, in southern Italy as well as in the rest of Greece, Pythagorean communities which led an ascetic life of the type we have already discussed.

We also know very little about the spiritual practices that may have been followed by other Presocratic philosophers. We can only note that when discussing peace of mind, one of their favorite themes, philosophers like Seneca and Plutarch allude to a work by Democritus devoted to *euthumia*, or the good disposition of the soul, equivalent to joy.[44] According to Seneca, Democritus sought it in a state of balance of the soul, which we can achieve if we adapt our actions to what we are capable of doing. Joy thus corresponds to self-knowledge, and we must "mind our own business." Action on oneself is possible.

It is noteworthy that an abundant collection of moral sayings circulated under the name of Democritus.[45] He had also written a work entitled *Tritogeneia*—one of the epithets of the goddess Athena, whom he identified with wisdom or prudence; and he defined this wisdom as the art of reasoning well, speaking well, and doing what needs to be done.[46]

Among the Sophists, Antiphon is interesting specifically for having proposed a therapeutics which consisted in healing grief and pain by means of the word.[47] We do not know how he practiced it, but we can find valuable indications of his knowledge of human psychology in the fragments of his works which have been preserved. Here, we shall limit ourselves to a few examples.

Antiphon knew that one cannot become wise without having personally experienced what is shameful or bad—in other words, without having won a victory over oneself. He also knew that a person who wants to harm his neighbor but does not do so right away, for fear of failure or of unpleasant consequences, often winds up abandoning his project.[48] This means that prudence consists in reflection and in adopting a critical distance toward ac-

tion; thus, we can glimpse the role played by reflection in the conduct of life. He also was reputed to be an excellent interpreter of
dreams. We may note the following remark on the uniqueness and
seriousness of life: "There are people who do not live their present
life; it is as if they were preparing themselves, with all their zeal, to
live some other life, but not this one. And while they do this, time
goes by and is lost. We cannot put life back in play, as if we were
casting another roll of the dice."[49] It is as though we were already
hearing Epicurus or Seneca telling us that "while we wait to live,
life passes us by."

These few examples allow us to suppose that there was an entire
prehistory of the philosophical life and of the practices associated
with it.[50] Yet given the paucity of surviving fragments and the
difficulty of interpreting them, to describe them with precision
would require a very lengthy study.

Exercises of Body and Soul

Although many texts allude to them, there is no systematic treatise
which exhaustively codifies the theory and technique of philosophical exercises *(askēsis)*. We can assume that such practices
were mainly the subject of oral instruction, and that they were
linked to the custom of spiritual guidance. Treatises entitled *On
Exercise* did exist, but they are now lost. Under this title, we have
only a brief treatise by the Stoic Musonius Rufus.[51] Musonius first
affirms that people who undertake to philosophize need to exercise. He then distinguishes exercises proper to the soul, and those
common to the soul and the body. The former consist in "always
having at one's disposition," and therefore handy for meditation,
the arguments which establish the fundamental dogmas governing our actions. They also include representing things to ourselves
in a new way, and wishing and seeking only for things which are
truly good—that is to say, purity of moral intent. We practice the

exercises common to body and soul "if we accustom ourselves to the cold, to heat, to hunger, to frugal nourishment, to hard beds, to abstinence from pleasant things, and to tolerance of unpleasant things." Thus, our bodies will become insensitive to pain and ready for action; at the same time, the soul will fortify itself thanks to such exercises, becoming courageous and temperate.

These remarks by Musonius are precious because they show that the notion of philosophical exercises has its roots in the ideal of athleticism and in the habitual practice of physical culture typical of the gymnasia. Just as the athlete gave new strength and form to his body by means of repeated bodily exercises, so the philosopher developed his strength of soul by means of philosophical exercises, and transformed himself. This analogy was all the more clear because it was precisely in the gymnasium—the place where physical exercises were practiced—that philosophy lessons were often given as well.[52] Exercises of body and soul thus combined to shape the true person: free, strong, and independent.

We have seen several examples of these practices in the context of the various schools. Let us now look at the profound kinship that existed among all these exercises. We will see that they ultimately can be reduced to two movements, opposed but complementary, in the acquisition of self-consciousness: one of concentration of the self, and the other of expansion of the self. What unified these practices was their striving for a single ideal: the figure of the sage, who, despite apparent differences, was conceived by the various schools as having many common features.

Relation to Self and Concentration of the "I"

ASKĒSIS

Almost all the schools advocated the practice of *askēsis* (a Greek word meaning "exercise") and self-mastery. There was Platonic *askēsis,* which consisted in renouncing the pleasures of the flesh and in adopting a specific dietary regime, which, under the influence of Neopythagoreanism, sometimes went as far as vegetarianism. This *askēsis* was intended to weaken the body by means of fasting and sleeplessness, so that the individual could better live the life of the spirit. Then there was Cynic *askēsis* (also practiced by certain Stoics), which advocated enduring hunger, cold, and insults, as well as eliminating all luxury, comfort, and artifices of civilization, in order to cultivate independence and stamina. There was Pyrrhonian *askēsis,* which trained the individual to view all things as indifferent, since we cannot tell if they are good or bad. There was that of the Epicureans, who limited their desires in order to accede to pure pleasure. And there was that of the Stoics, who corrected their judgments of objects by recognizing that we must not become attached to indifferent things. All these schools called for a kind of self-duplication in which the "I" refuses to be conflated with its desires and appetites, takes up a distance from the objects of its desires, and becomes aware of its power to become detached from them. It thus rises from a partial and particular vision to a universal perspective, be it that of Nature or that of the Spirit.

DEATH, THE "I," AND THE PRESENT

Spiritual exercises almost always correspond to the movement by which the "I" concentrates itself upon itself and discovers that it is not what it had thought. It ceases to be conflated with the objects to which it had become attached.

The thought of death plays a decisive role here. We have seen how Plato defined philosophy as an exercise of death: since death is the separation of the soul and the body, the philosopher separates himself spiritually from the body. From a Platonic point of view, we are thus brought back to that *askēsis* which consists in discovering the pure "I," and in transcending the egoistic self which is withdrawn into its individuality. It does this by separating the self from everything that has become attached to it and to which it has become attached, and that prevents it from becoming aware of itself—like the sea god Glaucus, covered with barnacles, seaweed, and pebbles, mentioned by Plato.[53] Becoming aware is an act of *askēsis* and detachment, as we can also see from Plotinus, who urges the "I" to separate itself from what is foreign to it:

> If you do not see your own beauty yet, do as the sculptor does with a statue which must become beautiful: he pares away this part, scratches that other part, makes one place smooth, and cleans another, until he causes a beautiful face to appear in the statue. In the same way, you too must pare away what is superfluous, straighten what is crooked, purify all that is dark, in order to make it gleam. And never cease sculpting your own statue, until the divine light of virtue shines within you.[54]

The exercise we have just mentioned can be found in the Stoics—for instance, in Marcus Aurelius.[55] Marcus exhorts himself to separate from "himself" (meaning, he says, from "his thought") what others do or say, and what he himself has done or said in the past. He also encourages himself to separate from his "I" everything in the future which may worry him (by this he means his body, and even the soul which animates his body), including events which stem from the mutual linkage of universal causes—in other words, destiny—and things which have become attached to him because he has attached himself to them. He promises himself that if he separates himself from the past and the future, and lives within the present, he will attain a life of peace and serenity.

In this exercise, the "I" is completely circumscribed within the present. It tries to live only that which it lives—that is, the present—and it "separates" itself from what it has done and said in the past, and from what it will experience in the future. "We live only the present, so infinitely small," says Marcus. "The rest either has already been lived, or else it is uncertain."[56] The past no longer concerns us, and the future does not concern us yet.[57] Here, we encounter the Stoic opposition between what depends on us and what does not depend on us. What depends on us is the present—the site of action, decision, and freedom; what does not depend on us comprises the past and the future, about which we can do nothing. For us, the past and the future can mean only imaginary pains and pleasures.[58]

It is important to understand this exercise of concentration on the present. We must not imagine that the Stoic remembers nothing and never thinks about the future. It is not thoughts about the future and the past which he rejects, but the passions, vain hopes, and vain regrets they can entail. The Stoic wants to be active; in order to live and to act, we must make projects, and take the past into consideration in order to foresee our actions. Since all action is inevitably present, however, we must think about the past and the future only as a function of our action and insofar as such thoughts may be useful for our action. It is thus choice, decision, and action which determine the thickness of the present.

The Stoics distinguished two ways of defining the present. The first consisted in understanding it as the limit between the past and the future. From this perspective, there is never any present time, since time is infinitely divisible. This is an abstract, mathematical division, in which the present is reduced to an infinitesimal instant. The second way consisted in defining the present with regard to human consciousness; it then represented a certain thickness and duration, corresponding to the attention of lived consciousness.[59] When we speak of concentration on the present, it is this present to which we refer.

Self-awareness is nothing other than the consciousness of the "I" acting and living within the present moment. As Marcus Aurelius never tires of repeating: I must concentrate my attention on what I am thinking at this moment, what I am doing at this moment, and what is happening to me at this moment, so that I see things as they present themselves to me at this moment, so that I may rectify my intention in the action I am accomplishing. I must want to do only that which serves the human community, so that I may accept, as willed by fate, what is happening at this moment, and which does not depend on me.[60]

This exercise of self-awareness can thus be reduced to an exercise of attention to oneself *(prosokhē)* and vigilance.[61] It supposes that, at each instant, we renew our choice of life—that is to say, the purity of our intentions, the conformity of our individual will with the will of universal Nature—and that we keep constantly present in our minds the rules of life which express that choice. Philosophers must be perfectly aware, at each instant, of what they are and of what they are doing.

Like Platonic self-awareness, such concentration on the present moment also presupposes an "exercise of death." The thought of the possibility of death gives value and seriousness to each of life's moments and actions:

> Act, speak, and always think like one who might depart from life at any moment.

> Accomplish each of life's actions as if it were your last, keeping yourself far from all frivolity.

> Your way of life achieves perfection when you spend each day as if it were your last.

> Let death be before your eyes every day, and you will never have a base thought or an excessive desire.[62]

From this perspective, the person who applies all his attention and all his consciousness to the present will feel that he has everything within the present moment, for within this moment he has both the absolute value of existence and the absolute value of moral intent. There is nothing further left to desire. An entire lifetime and all eternity could not bring him any more happiness: "If one has wisdom for one moment, one will not be any less happy than a person who has it throughout all eternity."[63] Happiness is happiness through and through, just as a circle remains a circle whether it is tiny or immense.[64] Unlike a dance or a theater play, which remain unfinished if they are interrupted, moral actions are wholly perfect at each moment.[65] One such present moment is thus equivalent to an entire life. With regard to such a moment, we can say: "I have realized my life; I have had all that could be expected from life. Now I can die."

> At the moment we go to sleep, let us say, in joy and gaiety: "I have lived. I have traveled the path which Fortune assigned to me." If a god gives us the next day as a bonus, let us receive it with joy. He who awaits tomorrow without worries is fully happy and enjoys tranquil self-possession. Whoever has said to himself "I have lived" can arise each day to an unexpected gift.
>
> Hurry up and live, and consider each day as a completed life. . . . He who believes every day that his life has been complete enjoys peace of mind.[66]

We can see how this exercise leads us to consider time and life in a completely different way, and ultimately engenders a true transfiguration of the present. It is all the more interesting to note that in the course of this spiritual process, Epicureanism and Stoicism coincide at various points.

In Epicureanism, too, concentrating on oneself and becoming aware of oneself were linked to an *askēsis,* which consisted in limiting one's desires to those that are natural and necessary and that ensure stable pleasure for the flesh—in other words, for the individual.[67]

Aristotle had remarked, "It is a pleasure to sense that one is alive."[68] But to be alive means precisely to sense. Thus, what we should say is: "It is a pleasure to sense that one senses." For Epicurus, sentient beings could, as it were, become aware of themselves—and this was precisely philosophical pleasure, the pure pleasure of existence.

In order to achieve this self-awareness, however, it is again necessary to separate the self from what is foreign to it—not only from the passions engendered by the body, but also from the passions engendered by the soul's vain desires. Here we once again see concentration on the present, because the reason we let ourselves be dragged along and worried, waiting and hoping for the future, is that the soul is thinking about the past and the future.[69] This happens when the soul has not yet cut off its desires which are neither natural nor necessary, such as the pursuit of wealth and honors, which can be satisfied only by a lengthy effort, as difficult as it is uncertain:

> The foolish live waiting for good things to happen. Since they know these things are uncertain, they are consumed by fear and anxiety. Later on—and this is the worst of their torments—they find that they have longed in vain for money, power, and glory; for they have not derived any pleasure from these things, which they hoped for so passionately and worked so hard to attain.

> The life of a fool is hard and worrisome. It is wholly devoured by the future.[70]

Concerning the past, the Epicureans admitted that it can provide us stable pleasure, but only insofar as we "reactualize" it.[71] Thus, Epicurus writes that his physical sufferings are assuaged by the memory of the philosophical conversations he had with his disciples.[72] And this may mean not only that the memory of past pleasures provides him with pleasure in the present, but that the philosophical reasoning he recalls likewise helps him to overcome his suffering.

As for the Stoics, the fundamental Epicurean spiritual exercise consists in concentration on the present—that is to say, on the consciousness of the "I" in the present—and in refraining from projecting our desires on the future. The present is enough for happiness, because it allows us to satisfy our simplest and most necessary desires, which provide stable pleasure. This is one of the favorite themes of the poet Horace:

> Let the soul be happy in the present, and refuse to worry about what will come later.

> Think about arranging the present as best you can, with serene mind. All else is carried away as by a river.[73]

For the Stoics, this exercise is closely linked to the thought of death, since this is what gives value to each of life's days and instants. This is why we must live each moment as if it were our last:

> While we are talking, jealous time has fled. So seize the day, and do not trust the morrow!

> Persuade yourself that each new day that dawns will be your last. Then you will receive each unexpected hour with gratitude.[74]

"With gratitude" because, from the perspective of death, each instant appears as a wonderful gift—an act of grace which is unexpected in its uniqueness. "Recognize the value of each additional moment, and receive it as though it happened by wonderful, incredible luck."[75]

We must become aware of the splendor of existence.[76] Most people are unaware of it and consume themselves in vain desires, which conceal life itself from them. In the words of the Stoic Seneca: "While we postpone living, life passes us by."[77] He seems to have been echoing an Epicurean saying: "We are born only once; twice is not permitted. Thus, we must cease to exist for all eternity. Yet you, who are not master of tomorrow—you put off joy until tomorrow. Life is vainly consumed in such delays, and each of us dies without ever having known peace."[78]

Like the Stoic, the Epicurean finds perfection in the present moment. For him, the pleasure of the present moment does not need to last in order to be perfect. A single instant of pleasure is as perfect as an eternity thereof.[79] Here, Epicurus is heir to the Aristotelian theory of pleasure.[80] For Aristotle, just as the act of vision is complete and finished, in its specificity, at each moment of its duration, so pleasure is specifically complete at each moment. Pleasure is not a movement which unfolds within time, nor does it depend on duration. It is a reality in itself which is not situated within the category of time. We can say of Epicurean pleasure, as of Stoic virtue, that their quantity does not change their essence: a circle is a circle, be it immense or minuscule. This is why to hope for an increase in pleasure from the future is to be ignorant of pleasure's very nature; for we can achieve stable, appeasing pleasure only if we know how to limit ourselves to what we can obtain within the present moment, without letting ourselves be swept along by the unreasonable limitlessness of our desires. Stoic virtue and Epicurean pleasure are thus perfect at each moment, and both Stoics and Epicureans can agree with Horace's dictum: "He who is happy and master of himself is the one who can say, every day: 'I have lived.'"

"I have lived," in other words, because I have known the atemporal nature of pleasure, and the perfection and absolute value of stable pleasure; but also because I have become aware of the atemporal nature of being. Nothing can prevent me from having been within being, or from having attained the pleasure of feeling myself exist.[81] The Epicurean meditation on death is intended to make us aware of both the absolute value of existence and the nothingness of death, to give us the love of life and to suppress the fear of death: "The exercise of living well and the exercise of dying well are one and the same thing."[82] To die well means to understand that death, *qua* not-being, is nothing for us; but it also means rejoicing at each instant that we have acceded to being, and knowing that death cannot diminish the plenitude of the pleasure of being. As Carlo Diano has rightly remarked, there is a profound ontological intuition behind the idea that death is nothing for me: being is not not-being, and there is no passage from being to nothingness. Perhaps Wittgenstein was thinking of Epicurus when he wrote: "Death is not an event of life. It is not experienced. If by 'eternity' we mean not an infinite temporal duration but atemporality, then whoever lives in the present lives eternally."[83]

Here we see that Spinoza was wrong, in a sense, to oppose meditation on death to meditation on life. In fact, they are inseparable from each other.[84] They are fundamentally identical, and both are an indispensable condition for becoming self-aware. From this point of view, moreover, we would be wrong to establish a radical opposition between the exercise of death in Plato, on the one hand, and in the Stoics and Epicureans, on the other. In both cases, the goal of this exercise is to become self-aware by means of the thought of death, for the self which thinks of its death always, in one way or another, thinks of itself in the atemporality of the Spirit or of being. We can therefore say that, in this sense, the exercise of death is one of the most fundamental philosophical exercises.

CONCENTRATION ON THE SELF AND EXAMINATION OF THE CONSCIENCE

From the perspective of lived philosophy, which we are here setting forth, becoming self-aware is an essentially ethical act, thanks to which our way of being, living, and seeing is transformed. To be aware of ourselves thus means to be aware of our moral state. This is what the tradition of Christian spirituality calls the examination of the conscience, a practice which was very widespread in the philosophical schools of antiquity.[85] This practice has its roots, first of all, in the simple fact that in all schools, the beginning of philosophy means becoming aware of the state of alienation, dispersion, and unhappiness in which we find ourselves before we convert to philosophy. An Epicurean principle states: "The knowledge of our errors is the beginning of our salvation."[86] To which

corresponds the Stoic principle: "The starting point of philosophy
. . . is our consciousness of our own weakness."[87] Yet the point is
not simply to think about our faults. We must also take stock of
the progress we make.

So far as the Stoics are concerned, we know that Zeno, the
school's founder, recommended that philosophers examine their
dreams in order to become aware of the progress their soul had
made. This implies the existence of the practice of examining the
conscience: "He thought that each person could become aware of
the progress he was making by means of his dreams. Such progress
was real if one no longer dreamed that one was defeated by some
shameful passion, or that one had yielded to or committed something bad or unjust, but if the soul's faculties of representation
and affectivity, relaxed by reason, shone as if in a diaphanous sea
of serenity, untroubled by waves."[88] As we have seen, Plato had already noted that dreams reveal the state of the soul.[89] And the
theme reappears in Christian spirituality.[90]

Although this is not stated explicitly in the texts, we can reasonably assume that the examination of conscience was practiced
within the Epicurean school, for it was virtually inseparable from
the confession and fraternal correction which the school considered so important.

We find traces of this practice in the second-century B.C. *Letter
of Aristeas,* which affirms that the good king has a duty to have all
his actions of the day noted, so that he can correct whatever errors
he may have committed.[91]

Around the beginning of the Christian period, Neopythagoreanism takes up in a moral sense the mnemonic exercises practiced by the ancient Pythagoreans. We can see this in the *Golden
Verses:*

Do not let sleep fall upon your soft eyes
Before you have gone over each act of your day three times:
Where have I failed? What have I done? What duty have I omitted?

Begin here, and continue the examination. After this,
Find fault with what was badly done, and rejoice in what was good.[92]

These lines from the *Golden Verses* were frequently cited or alluded to later on by writers advocating examination of the conscience— by Stoics such as Epictetus, independent philosophers such as Galen, and especially Neoplatonists such as Porphyry and Iamblichus when they describe the life of Pythagorean communities as the ideal model for the philosophical life.

Galen, a physician, was independent of all philosophical schools.[93] Because he wished to care not only for bodies but also for souls, he linked the examination of the conscience to spiritual guidance. He advised people to have their faults pointed out by someone older and more experienced, and then to examine themselves, mornings and evenings.

Seneca stated that he himself practiced this exercise. He claimed to be following the example of a Neopythagorean philosopher named Sextius, who lived in the time of Augustus:

> Every day, we must call upon our soul to give an account of itself. This is what Sextius did. When the day was over and he had withdrawn to his room for his nightly rest, he questioned his soul: "What evils have you cured yourself of today? What vices have you fought? In what sense are you better?" Is there anything better than to examine a whole day's conduct? What a good sleep follows the examination of one's self! How tranquil, deep, and free it is, when the mind has been praised or warned, and has become the observer and secret judge of its own morals! I make use of this power, and every day I plead my cause before myself. When the torch has been taken away and my wife, already used to my habits, has fallen silent, I examine my entire day and measure what I have done and said. I hide nothing from myself, nor am I indulgent with myself.[94]

Elsewhere, Seneca develops this analogy with judicial procedure: "Be your own accuser, then judge, and finally defense attorney."[95] Here we find the notion of the "inner court" of the conscience—an image that can be found in (among other texts) Hierocles' commentary on the Pythagorean *Golden Verses.*[96] This is the "inner court" described by Kant, who observed that when the self is its own judge, it splits into an intelligible self (which imposes its own law on itself, viewing itself from a universal perspective) and a sensible, individual self.[97] We thus encounter once again the split implied in *askēsis* and in becoming aware of one's self. Here, the "I" comes to identify with impartial, objective Reason.

This examination may sometimes have been carried out in writing, as is implied when Epictetus recommends that we observe the precise frequency of our episodes of negligence.[98] We should note, for instance, if we get angry once a day, or every two, three, or four days.[99]

Usually, however, the examination of conscience did not become entangled in such minutiae. On the contrary, it was much less a matter of keeping a score—be it positive or negative —of the soul's states than of having a means to reestablish self-consciousness, self-attention, and the power of reason. We can see this in Marcus Aurelius, for instance, who recalls the fundamental rules of life which govern our relations with others, as he exhorts himself to prepare for the difficulties he will encounter with other people.[100] Similarly, Galen recommends that when we get up in the morning and before we undertake the actions of the day, we ask ourselves if it is better to live in slavery to the passions, or, on the contrary, to make use of rationality in all things.[101] Epictetus likewise advises us to examine ourselves in the morning, so that we may recall not only the progress we must make but also the principles which must guide our actions:

As soon as you rise in the morning, ask yourself, "What must I still do to attain impassibility and absence of worry? Who am I? A body? A possession? A reputation? None of those things. But what, then? I am a rational being." What is required of such a being? Go over your actions in your mind: "Of the things that lead to happiness, which have I neglected? What have I done that is contrary to friendship, to social obligations, or to the qualities of the heart? What duty have I omitted in these matters?"[102]

We glimpse even broader perspectives when Epictetus, exhorting the philosopher to learn how to live alone with himself, gives the example of Zeus, who, when alone after the periodic conflagration of the universe and prior to the beginning of a new cosmic period, "rests within himself, reflects on his divine government, and entertains himself with thoughts that are worthy of him." Epictetus continues: "We, too, should converse with ourselves, should learn how not to need others and not to feel aimless when we are by ourselves. We must pay attention to the divine and to our relation to the rest of the world; must consider what our attitude toward events has been and what it is now—what things cause us grief, and how they might be treated and extirpated."[103] Here, examination of the conscience appears as part of an exercise which is much more vast: that of meditation. The movement of concentration upon and attention to oneself turns out to be closely related to the opposite movement of dilation and expansion by which the "I" finds its place within the perspective of the All, of its relation to the rest of the world, and of destiny as this is manifested in events.

Relation to the Cosmos and Expansion of the "I"

THE SELF'S EXPANSION INTO THE WORLD

We have seen how one of the spiritual exercises which Plato recommended consisted in a kind of dilation of the self into the totality of the real. The soul was to "strive ceaselessly to embrace the whole universality of the divine and the human" and toward "the contemplation of the whole of time and of being."[104] Thus, the soul, as it were, stretches into immensity. "It rises into the heights and governs the whole world,"[105] while the body alone remains to inhabit the city: "Its thought, considering all human affairs as mere petty nothingness of which it takes no account, flies in every direction, . . . sounding what is beneath the earth, measuring the earth's surface, studying the path of the stars across the vault which overlooks the sky, exploring the whole nature of each of these realities in its totality, without ever coming back down to what is immediately close to hand."[106] The Aristotelian contemplation of nature, from the loving gaze directed at the stars to the marvelous pleasure provided by the works of Nature, likewise brings about this elevation of thought.

Among the Epicureans, too, there is an expansion of the self into the cosmos—an expansion that provides us with the pleasure of plunging into the infinite. For the Epicureans, the world we see is only one of the innumerable worlds which extend throughout infinite time and space:

> For the spirit plunges into immeasurable and infinite space, and extends itself so as to traverse it in all directions, never seeing any borders or limits at which it might stop.

> Since space stretches to infinity beyond the walls of this world, the spirit seeks to know what is in this immensity, into which it can plunge its gaze as far as it wishes and where it can soar in free, spontaneous flight.

> The walls of the world fly apart. I see things hurled about within the immense void. . . . The earth does not stop me from distinguishing all that is happening beneath my feet, in the depths of the void. At the sight, I find myself seized by a kind of shudder of divine pleasure.[107]

Let us note in passing that, despite what certain historians may believe, it was not necessary to wait for Copernicus for the "walls of the world to fly apart" or for the transition to be made from the "closed world to the infinite universe."[108]

Like the consciousness of existence, the Epicurean contemplation of nature means being elevated to atemporality, as is stated in an Epicurean saying: "Remember that, although born mortal and having received a limited life, you have nevertheless risen, through the science of nature, up to eternity, and that you have seen the infinity of things: those that shall be and those that have been."[109]

The Stoics likewise advocated an exercise of expansion of the "I," an expansion into the infinite—not into the infinity of countless universes (for the world was finite and unique according to Stoic thought), but into the infinity of time, in which the same unfolding of events which constitutes the world repeats itself eternally. The "I" plunges into the totality of the world and feels with joy that it is an integral part of this world:

> Tell us instead how natural it is for man to unfold his thought into the infinite. The human soul is a grand and noble thing. The only limits it accepts are those it has in common with God himself. . . . Its homeland is that which encloses the sky and the world by its circular movement.
>
> The soul achieves all the fulfillment and completion of happiness that the human condition can attain when it reaches the heights, and enters the heart of nature. . . . It likes to soar amid the stars, . . . When it arrives there, it nourishes itself and grows. Freed from its bonds, it returns to its origin.
>
> The soul travels through the entire world, and the void which surrounds it, and its form. And it extends into the infinity of endless time, and embraces and conceives of the periodic rebirth of the universe.
>
> To embrace the paths of the stars in our gaze, as if they were carrying us along in their revolutions, and constantly to think of the transformations of the elements into one another—such representations purify us of the stains of terrestrial life.

Constantly imagine the totality of the world, and the totality of the real.[110]

In the Platonic tradition, where references to the *Republic,* the *Phaedrus,* and the *Theaetetus* are dominant, the soul's flight through cosmic space is a very frequent theme: "When men aspire to a life of peace and serenity, they contemplate nature and all that is within it. . . . In thought, they accompany the moon, the sun, and the movements of the other stars, fixed or wandering. To be sure, their bodies remain on earth, but they give wings to their souls, so that they can rise into the ether and observe the powers which dwell there, as is fitting for men who have become citizens of the world."[111]

In an epigram that is probably correctly attributed to him, the astronomer Ptolemy, who was influenced by Platonic, Stoic, and Aristotelian doctrines, likewise describes his feelings at being associated with divine life, when he soars in thought through the celestial spheres: "I know I am mortal and last only a day. Yet when I accompany the dense ranks of stars in their circular course, my feet no longer touch the earth. Beside Zeus himself, I drink my fill of ambrosia, like a god."[112]

In all the schools that practiced it, this exercise of thought and imagination consists, in the last analysis, in the philosopher's becoming aware of his being within the All, as a minuscule point of brief duration, but capable of dilating into the immense field of infinite space and of seizing the whole of reality in a single intuition. The "I" thus experiences a twofold feeling: that of its puniness, as it sees its corporeal individuality lost in the infinity of space and time; and that of its greatness, as it experiences its power to embrace the totality of things.[113] We can call this an exercise of detachment and of taking one's distance, intended to teach us to see things with impartiality and objectivity. It is what the moderns would call "the viewpoint of Sirius." As Ernest Renan wrote in 1880, "When we place ourselves in the viewpoint of the solar system, our revolutions are scarcely as big as the movements of an atom. From the viewpoint of Sirius, they are even smaller."[114] Such a rational, universal viewpoint has nothing to do with the alleged trance of the shaman.

THE VIEW FROM ABOVE

From the heights to which he rises in thought, the philosopher looks down at the earth and at mankind, and judges them at their true value. As we read in a Chinese philosophical text, he "sees things in the light of the heavens."[115] The vision of the totality of being and time, mentioned in Plato's *Republic,* inspires us with contempt for death; while in the *Theaetetus,* all human affairs are petty nothingness for the philosopher who wanders over the whole extent of the real. He who is used "to embracing the whole world in his gaze" finds mankind's possessions small indeed.[116]

This theme recurs in the famous *Dream of Scipio,* in which Cicero tells how Scipio Aemilianus dreams he sees his ancestor Scipio Africanus. He is then transported to the Milky Way, where he sees the earth from above. It seems like a mere speck to him, so that he is ashamed of the tiny dimensions of the Roman Empire. His ancestor points out to him the vast spaces of the deserts, in order to make him see the insignificance of the space through which all-important fame can spread.[117]

Influenced by his Neopythagorean source, Ovid places the following words in the mouth of Pythagoras at the end of his *Metamorphoses:* "I yearn to travel amid the lofty stars. Leaving the earth, this inert way-station, I want to be borne by the clouds. . . . From above, I will see men wandering haphazardly, trembling with fear at the thought of death, because they lack reason."[118] Epicureans and Stoics also recommended this attitude. From the heights of the serene regions, Lucretius lowers his gaze to mankind and sees them "wandering everywhere, seeking for the path of life at random."[119] For Seneca, the philosopher's soul, transported amid the stars, casts its gaze down upon the earth, which seems like a speck to it. It then laughs at the luxuries of the wealthy; the wars over the borders which people erect between each other seem ridiculous to it; and armies invading territories are mere ants fighting over a narrow space.[120]

This is also the view of the Cynic Menippus in Lucian's brilliant story *Icaromenippus*. When the hero arrives on the moon, he sees people stupidly quarreling over national boundaries and the rich gloating over their lands, which, notes Menippus, are no larger than the atoms of Epicurus. When he sees mankind from above, Menippus also compares them to ants. In another work, entitled *Charon*, the ferryman of the dead looks at human life on earth from a vertiginous height, and considers how foolish men's actions are when one examines them while bearing in mind that their agents will soon die.

It is significant that Lucian's observer should be the ferryman of the dead. To view things from above is to look at them from the perspective of death. In both cases, it means looking at things with detachment, distance, and objectivity, seeing them as they are in themselves, situating them within the immensity of the universe and the totality of nature, without the false prestige lent to them by our human passions and conventions. The view from above changes our value judgments on things: luxury, power, war, borders, and the worries of everyday life all become ridiculous.

Becoming aware of ourselves, whether in the movement of concentration on the self or in the movement of expansion towards the All, inevitably requires the exercise of death. One might say that this exercise has been, since Plato, the very essence of philosophy.

PHYSICS AS A SPIRITUAL EXERCISE

We have already mentioned the spiritual exercise of physics. This expression sounds strange to our modern ears, yet it corresponds well to the image of physics which has been traditional in ancient philosophy at least since Plato.

In general, ancient physics did not claim to be propounding a system of nature which was totally rigorous in all its details. To be sure, there were indisputably general principles of explanation—for instance, the antithesis between necessity and optimal choice in the *Timaeus,* or between atoms and the void in Epicurus. There was also a global vision of the universe. For explanations of particular phenomena, however, ancient philosophers made no claims to certainty. They were content to propose one or several probable or reasonable explanations which would satisfy the mind and afford it pleasure. As Plato remarks with regard to metals: "Similarly for the other varieties [of metals], it would be by no means complicated to discuss them by pursuing the type of story known as the likely myth. When, for the sake of recreation, a person sets aside the accounts concerning eternal beings, and examines those likely ones concerned with the realm of becoming, he procures a pleasure of which he will not have to repent and acquires a moderate, reasonable amusement in his life."[121]

Here, as always, we must make allowances for Platonic irony, which pretends to treat lightly what matters most. Nevertheless, Plato does believe that natural things, produced by the gods, ultimately escape our knowledge. In general, we can say that ancient writings on physics are not treatises which set forth, once and for all, a definitive, systematic theory of physical phenomena examined for their own sake. Their finality lies elsewhere. Instead, the goal was to learn to deal with problems in a methodical way (as advocated by Aristotle); or else to devote oneself to what Epicurus called the constant exercise *(energēma)* of the science of nature *(physiologia),* which, he says, "brings the highest degree of serenity in this life";[122] or else to elevate the spirit by the contemplation of nature.

Such exercises thus had a moral finality, whose tone differed from school to school but which can always be recognized. This is already the case in the *Timaeus,* when Plato urges the human soul to imitate the world soul in the movement of its thoughts and thereby attain the goal of human life.[123] According to Aristotle, the practice of research brings joy to the soul and thereby enables it to attain life's supreme happiness; often, the philosopher will attain merely what is probable *(eulogon),* which is only satisfying for the mind but in the process affords it joy.[124] For Epicurus, the exercise of the science of nature frees us from the fear of the gods and of death.

In a text by Cicero, inspired by the philosophy of the New Academy,[125] we find perhaps the best description of physics conceived as a spiritual exercise. As a good disciple of Arcesilaus and Carneades, he begins by taking up the Platonic reflections on the uncertainties of our knowledge of nature, particularly on the difficulties of observation and experimentation. Despite these uncertainties, physical research has a moral finality:

> I do not think we need to renounce the questions of the physicists. The observation and contemplation of nature are a kind of natural food for the soul and the mind. We rectify and dilate [I read *latiores*] ourselves; we look down at human things from on high, and as we contemplate the higher, celestial things, we feel contempt for human things, finding them petty and narrow. The search for the largest things, as well as for the most obscure, brings us pleasure. If something probable presents itself to us in the course of this research, our mind is filled with a noble, human pleasure.

At the beginning of his *Natural Questions,* Seneca likewise sees elevation of the soul as the principal justification of physics: "To contemplate these things, study them, devote ourselves to them, be absorbed by them—doesn't this mean transcending the mortal condition and having access to a superior condition? What profit, you ask, could you derive from your studies? Consider this one, if there is no other: when the measure of God has been taken, I will know that everything is small."[126]

The contemplation of nature had an existential meaning, whether or not it was accompanied by an effort at rational explanation. According to the poet Menander, who perhaps was influenced by Epicurus: "In my view, the greatest happiness—. . . before we return whence we came, with the greatest of haste—is to have contemplated, free of worry, these august beings: the sun which shines on all, the stars, the clouds, water, fire. Whether one lives a few years or one hundred, this same spectacle presents itself to our eyes, and we will never see another one so worthy of our praise."[127] This is a constant tradition within ancient philosophy: what gives meaning and value to human life is the contemplation of nature, and it is thanks to this contemplation that every day is a festival for people of good will.[128]

It is in Stoicism that the exercise of physics takes on its full value. More than anyone, the Stoic is conscious of being in contact with the entire universe at every moment, for the entire universe is implied within each present moment:

> Whatever happens to you was prepared in advance for you for all eternity, and the interweaving of causes has always woven together your substance and your encounter with this event.
>
> This event which comes to meet you has happened to you, has been coordinated with you, has been placed in relation to you because it has been spun together with you since the beginning, from the most distant causes.
>
> Each event which comes to meet you has been linked to you by destiny, and has been spun together with you from the All, since the beginning.[129]

Thus, the self's concentration on the present moment and its dilation into the cosmos are realized in one single instant. In the words of Seneca, "He enjoys the present without depending on what does not yet exist. . . . He is without hope and without desire; he does not hurl himself toward an uncertain goal, for he is satisfied with what he has. Nor is he satisfied with little, for what he possesses is the universe. . . . Like God, he says: 'All this belongs to me.'"[130] At each moment, therefore, and with each event that I encounter, I am in relation with the entire past and future development of the universe. The Stoic choice of life consists precisely in being able to say "Yes!" to the universe in its totality, and therefore to want what happens to happen as it happens. As Marcus Aurelius says to the universe: "I love along with you!" It is physics that allows us to understand that all is within all, and that, as Chrysippus said, a single drop of wine can be mixed with the entire sea and diffused throughout the whole world.[131]

Consent to fate and to the universe, renewed on the occasion of each event, is thus lived and practiced physics. This exercise consists in placing our individual reason in accord with Nature, which is universal Reason. This is the same as making ourselves equal to the Whole, plunging into the All,[132] ceasing to be "human beings" and becoming "Nature." This tendency to strip ourselves of "the human" is constant throughout the most diverse schools—from Pyrrho, who remarked on how hard it is to strip ourselves of the human, to Aristotle, for whom life according to the mind is superhuman, and as far as Plotinus, who believed that in mystical experience we cease to be "human."[133]

Relations with Others

Throughout our presentation of the various philosophical schools, we have encountered the problem of the philosopher's relation to others—of his role within the city, for instance, and of his life with other members of his school. Here again, there are remarkable constants in the practice of philosophy. First of all, we must recognize the capital importance of spiritual guidance.[134] It had two aspects: the process of moral education in general, and the relationship which individually linked master to disciple. Ancient philosophy was spiritual guidance according to both these aspects. In the words of Simplicius, who wrote at the very end of the history of ancient thought:

> What place shall the philosopher occupy within the city? It will be that of a sculptor of men, and an artisan who fabricates loyal, worthy citizens. He will thus have no other trade than to purify himself and to purify others, so that everyone may live life in conformity with nature, as is fitting for mankind. He will be the common father and pedagogue of all citizens—their reformer, their counselor, and their protector—offering himself to all in order to cooperate in the accomplishment of every good thing, rejoicing along with those who enjoy good fortune and offering condolences to the afflicted.[135]

So far as general moral education is concerned, we have already seen that the philosopher has taken the place of the city. As Ilsetraut Hadot has shown, the Greek city was particularly concerned about the ethical training of its citizens.[136] This is attested by the custom of setting up stelae in the cities, engraved with maxims of Delphic wisdom. Each philosophical school tried, in its own way, to take over this educative mission. Platonists and Aristotelians tried to influence the legislators and governors, considered the educators of the city; while Stoics, Epicureans, and Cynics tried to convert individuals, by means of missionary propaganda which was directed to all the people, with no distinctions of sex or social condition.

Spiritual guidance thus appears as a method of individual education. It had a twofold purpose. First, the goal was to allow the disciple to become aware of himself—that is to say, of his defects and his progress. According to Marcus Aurelius, this was the role that the Stoic Junius Rusticus had played in his life—"to have had an idea of my need to correct my moral state and to take care of it."[137] Next, the goal was to help the disciple to make the particular reasonable choices demanded by everyday life. By "reasonable" we mean "probably good," for most schools agreed that when it comes to deciding on actions which do not depend entirely on us—navigating, going to war, getting married, having children—we cannot wait until we are certain before we act, and must make our choices according to probability. At this point, a counselor is indispensable.

Paul Rabbow and Ilsetraut Hadot have given excellent analyses of the methods and forms of individual spiritual guidance, the practice of which is attested in almost all the philosophical schools.[138] Socrates, as he appears in Plato's *Dialogues* and Xenophon's *Memorabilia,* can be considered the paradigm of the "spiritual guide" who, through his discourse and his way of being, gnaws at or shocks his interlocutor's soul, thereby obliging him to place his own life in question. We can use the same term to describe the influence wielded by Plato over Dionysius of Syracuse, and the moral and political advice he gave him. According to tradition, Plato paid attention to the particular character of each of his disciples. Of Aristotle, he supposedly said, "I need a brake for him"; whereas he said of Xenocrates, "For him, it is a spur I need." He would often say to Xenocrates, who was always severe and serious, "Make a sacrifice to the Graces."[139]

In his *Seventh Letter,* Plato sets forth the principles which must underlie spiritual guidance as well as political action: "When one advises a sick person who is following a bad diet, the first thing to do to bring him back to health is to change his way of life." The patient must change his life in order to be treated. Whoever accepts such a change of life can be counseled: "Such, then, is my state of mind when someone comes to me and asks for advice on one of the most important things of his life—for instance, on the acquisition of wealth or the care that ought to be given to the body or the soul. If his everyday life seems to me to have taken a specific turn, or if he seems to agree to obey my advice on that for which he is consulting me, I advise him with all enthusiasm, and do not stop until I have fulfilled my sacred duty."[140]

Here we encounter the principle of the ethics of dialogue: we can engage in dialogue only with people who sincerely *want* to engage in dialogue. Thus, we will not try to force a person who refuses to change his way of life. We will not irritate or annoy him, reproach him vainly, or help him to satisfy desires of which we do not approve. The same holds true for the city which refuses to change its way of life: the philosopher may say that he abhors the city's depravity, if that is of any use—but let him refrain from violence! "When it is impossible to bring a better regime to power without banishing and killing people, it is better to keep still and pray for our own personal good, and for that of the city."

With regard to the Cynics, there are anecdotes in which a master tests the mettle of one of his disciples by humiliating him or reprimanding him.[141] From the school of Epicurus, we have precious testimony on the practice of spiritual guidance, particularly in its epistolary form. The practice of spiritual guidance was a topic of study in Epicurus' school, as we learn from Philodemus' treatise *On Free Speech*, which was taken from the lessons given on this theme by Zeno the Epicurean.[142] Here, the master's frankness appears as an art, which is defined as aleatory or "which proceeds by guesswork" *(stokhastikos)*, insofar as it must take moments and circumstances into account. The master must expect defeats, and must try and try again to rectify the disciple's behavior by having compassion for his difficulties. For this to happen, however, the disciple must not hesitate to admit his difficulties and errors, and must speak with absolute freedom (here we see that the Epicurean tradition recognized the therapeutic value of the word). In return, the master must listen with sympathy, without sarcasm or malevolence. In response to the disciple's "confession," the master must also speak openly, remonstrating with the disciple while making him understand the true purpose of his reprimands. As Philodemus remarks, Epicurus had not hesitated to make rather stinging reproaches in a letter to his disciple Apollonides. The chiding had to be serene, without lacking in benevolence. Interestingly, Philodemus adds that the philosopher must not be afraid to address reproaches to politicians.

From Epicurus' school, we have an example of spiritual guidance in a letter sent by Metrodorus, one of Epicurus' disciples, to the young Pythocles:

> You tell me that the spur of the flesh urges you on to abuse the pleasures of love. If you do not break the laws and do not disturb established morality in any way, if you do not disturb any of your neighbors, if you do not exhaust your strength and do not waste your fortune—then give in to your inclinations without any scruples. However, it is impossible not to be stopped by at least one of these barriers. The pleasures of love have never profited anyone. At best, they may fail to do harm.[143]

We know little about the guidance of the conscience in ancient Stoicism; but we can assume that the Stoic treatises on casuistry written by Antipater of Tarsus and Diogenes of Babylon, of which we find traces in Cicero's treatise *On Duties*, summarized lengthy experience of guidance of the conscience. Nevertheless, the history of Stoicism provides us with several figures of soul-directors: Seneca in his *Letters to Lucilius*, Musonius Rufus in his writings, and Epictetus in his *Discourses*, as reported by Arrian. Seneca's spiritual guidance is highly literary; throughout his letters, the striking formulas, images, and even sonorities are chosen intentionally. Yet the psychological observations and the descriptions of Stoic exercises they contain are extremely valuable.

We have every reason to believe that Junius Rusticus, Marcus

Aurelius' Stoic master, served as a director of conscience for him. The future emperor was often angry at him, no doubt because the philosopher was in the habit of speaking quite freely.

In Porphyry's *Life of Plotinus,* as well as in other life-accounts of philosophers from the end of antiquity, many anecdotes reveal practices of spiritual guidance. For instance, there is the well-known story of how Plotinus advised travel to Porphyry, who was haunted by thoughts of suicide.[144] Elsewhere, we learn an interesting detail about Aidesius, a philosopher who taught in Pergamum in the fourth century, and how he corrected his students' arrogance:

> Aidesius' way of being was affable and close to the people. After dialectical jousts, he used to go out for a walk in Pergamum with his most distinguished disciples. He wanted his disciples to have a feeling of harmony in their hearts and of care for the human race, so when he saw that they were insulting and haughty because of the pride they derived from their opinions, and that they had wings even larger than those of Icarus but even more fragile, he made them come down—not into the sea but onto the earth, and into what is human. If he came across a vegetable merchant, he was pleased, and stopped to talk with her about prices, about how much money she earned, and about vegetable farming. He did the same with weavers, blacksmiths, and carpenters.[145]

A text by Plutarch gives a good summary of the foregoing observations on the phenomenon of guidance of the conscience in the philosophical schools, and the freedom of speech which reigned there. If, he writes, a person who has come to listen to a philosopher is troubled by something in particular—if, that is, he is oppressed by a passion which needs to be suppressed, or by suffering which needs to be relieved—then we must bring it out into the open and treat it.

If a fit of anger or superstition, a sharp disagreement with the people around us, or a passionate desire caused by love, "moving the unmoved chords of the heart,"[146] comes to trouble our thoughts, we must not try to talk with the master about other things, in order to avoid being blamed. It is precisely discourses dealing with these passions which we must hear during class; and when the class is over, we must go to the master in private and ask him further questions. We must avoid doing the opposite, which is what most people do. They appreciate and admire philosophers when they talk about other subjects, but if the philosopher leaves other things aside and speaks to them frankly in private of the things which are important to them, and reminds them of them, they find him indiscreet and will not put up with him.[147]

Most people, Plutarch continues, consider philosophers to be nothing but Sophists, who, as soon as they get up from their chairs and have put down their books and their beginner's manuals, are worse than other men "in the real acts of life." Yet the way of life of true philosophers is different from this.

Ancient philosophers thus developed many varieties of therapy of the soul, which were practiced by means of various forms of discourse: exhortation, reprimands, consolation, instruction. The Greeks had known since the time of Homer and Hesiod that it is possible to modify people's decisions and inner dispositions by the careful choice of persuasive words;[148] and in the time of the Sophists, the rules of the art of rhetoric were constituted in accordance with this tradition. Like the spiritual exercises by which an individual tried to influence and modify himself, philosophical spiritual guidance utilized rhetorical techniques in order to provoke conversion and bring about conviction.

Above all, the custom of spiritual guidance and the therapy of souls led ancient philosophers to a profound knowledge of the "human heart"—of its motivations, conscious and unconscious, and its deepest intentions, both pure and impure. Without entering into details, Plato's *Phaedrus* had presented the possibility of a rhetoric which could adapt its genres of discourse to the various kinds of souls; here, an entire program of conscience-guiding was present *in nuce*. Book II of Aristotle's *Rhetoric* partially realizes this project, as it describes all that must be known about the auditor's dispositions—the influence exerted on him by his passions, social status, and age. Also important were the descriptions of virtues and vices in Aristotle's various *Ethics,* where they were intended to enlighten the legislator on the right way to govern. We have seen that the Epicurean treatise *On Free Speech* made precise studies of individual reactions to rebukes, confessions, and guilt. In the Epicurean Lucretius and the Stoic Seneca, we find remarkable descriptions of the tortures which the human soul can inflict on itself ("Each person tries to flee himself. . . . Yet despite ourselves, we remain attached to this self which we hate").[149] And of the sort of boredom which "reaches the point of nausea" and makes us say "How long must we see the same things?"[150] And of the hesitation to convert to philosophy—a hesitancy that Seneca describes in the prologue to his treatise *On Peace of Mind,* where his friend Serenus makes a kind of confession:

> By observing myself attentively, I have discovered in myself certain very obvious defects which I could put my finger on; others which hide in deep regions; and others, finally, which are not continuous but only reappear at intervals. . . . The disposition in which I find myself most often (why should I not confess everything to you, as I would to a doctor?) is to be neither wholly delivered from the things I fear and hate, nor completely under their sway.[151]

Serenus gives a long analysis of every aspect of his indecisiveness—his hesitations between the simple life and a life of luxury, between an active life in the service of mankind and the leisure which brings tranquillity, between the desire to become immortal and the will to write only for moral usefulness.

We also find very interesting observations in the lengthy commentary which the Neoplatonist Simplicius devoted to the *Manual* of Epictetus.

The traditional practice of guidance of the conscience enables us to better understand the demands of the purity of moral action. Let us take, as an example, the *Meditations* of Marcus Aurelius, where we find an ideal description of the way we must practice action upon others. For instance, one cannot help admiring the extreme delicacy with which Marcus defines the attitude we must adopt in order to act upon other people's consciences, the benevolence we must show to a person who has made a mistake, and how we should address him: "not chiding him and making him feel that we are putting up with him, but with frankness and goodness, . . . with gentleness, without irony, not reproachfully but with affection, with a heart exempt from bitterness—not as if we were in school, nor in order to be admired by some bystander, but truly person to person, even if others are standing nearby."[152]

Here Marcus seems to be saying: gentleness is such a delicate thing that merely to want to be gentle means ceasing to be gentle, because any kind of artifice or affectation destroys gentleness. Besides, we can act effectively upon other people only when we do not try to act upon them—when, that is, we avoid all violence, even spiritual, toward ourselves and others. It is this pure gentleness and delicacy which have the power to make people change their minds, even to convert and transform them. Similarly, when we want to do good to others, our intention to do good will be truly pure only if it is spontaneous and unselfconscious. The perfect benefactor is unaware of what he is doing: "We must be one of those who do good unconsciously."[153]

Here we have reached the supreme paradox: a will so strong that it suppresses itself *qua* will, and a habit which becomes nature and spontaneity. At the same time, it appears that the perfection of our relations to others culminates in love and respect for others. For all schools, moreover, what motivates our choice of life and choice of discourse is the love of mankind. It was this love which inspired the Socrates of Plato's *Apology* and *Euthyphro*,[154] Epicurean and Stoic propaganda, and even Skeptic discourse.[155]

THE SAGE

The Figure of the Sage and Choice of Life

Throughout antiquity, wisdom was considered a mode of being: a state in which a person is, in a way which is radically different from that of other people—a state in which he is a kind of super-man. If philosophy is that activity by means of which philosophers train themselves for wisdom, such an exercise must necessarily consist not merely in speaking and discoursing in a certain way, but also in being, acting, and seeing the world in a specific way. If, then, philosophy is not merely discourse but a choice of life, an existential option, and a lived exercise, this is because it is the desire for wisdom. To be sure, the idea of perfect knowledge is contained within the notion of wisdom. Yet as we saw with regard to Plato and Aristotle, such wisdom does not consist in the possession of information about reality. Instead, it too is a way of life, which corresponds to the highest activity which human beings can engage in and which is linked intimately to the excellence and virtue of the soul.

In each school, the figure of the sage was the transcendent norm which determined the philosopher's way of life. In the description of this norm, beyond apparent differences among the various schools, we can discern profound areas of agreement and common tendencies. Here we encounter the same phenomenon we described with regard to spiritual exercises.

First of all, the sage remains identical to himself, in perfect equanimity of soul: he is happy no matter what the circumstances. Thus, in Plato's *Symposium,* Socrates maintains the same attitude whether he is obliged to put up with hunger and cold or has everything he needs. With the same ease, he could abstain from things or else enjoy them. It was said of Aristippus, one of Socrates' disciples, that he adapted himself to every situation; he could enjoy whatever turned up and did not suffer from the things he lacked.[156] Pyrrho always remained in the same inner state, which means that he did not modify his resolutions or his attitude in any way when exterior circumstances changed. Self-coherence and permanence within identity also characterize the Stoic sage, for wisdom consists in always wanting the same thing and in not wanting the same thing.

The sage finds his happiness within himself, and so is independent *(autarkēs)* with regard to external things and events—like Socrates, who, according to Xenophon in his *Memorabilia,* lived by being sufficient unto himself, without concerning himself about superfluous things. This is one of the characteristics of the sage, according to Plato, who makes Socrates say: "If there is anyone who is self-sufficient so far as happiness is concerned, it is the sage; and of all people, he is the one who has the least need of others."[157] According to Aristotle, the sage lives a contemplative life because he does not need external things on which to exercise himself, and he therefore finds happiness and perfect independence in such a life.[158] To depend only on ourselves and to be self-sufficient by reducing our needs to the minimum are the particular ideals of the Cynic philosophers. The Stoics, for their part, preferred to say that virtue, all by itself, is sufficient for happiness.

The sage always remains identical to himself and is self-sufficient (at least for Pyrrho, the Cynics, and the Stoics) because external things cannot disturb him. He considers them to be neither good nor bad; for a variety of reasons, he refuses to apply value judgments to them and therefore declares them to be indifferent. For Pyrrho, everything is indifferent because we cannot know whether things are good or bad; we therefore cannot make any distinctions among them. For the Stoics, all things which do not depend on us are indifferent. The only thing that does depend on us, and is not indifferent, is moral good—that is, the intention to do good because it is the good. All other things are neither good nor bad in themselves; it depends on us to use them in a good or a bad way. This is true of wealth and poverty, health and illness. Their value thus depends on the sovereign usage the sage makes of them. The sage's indifference is not a lack of interest with regard to everything, but a conversion of interest and attention toward something other than that which monopolizes the care and attention of other people. As for the Stoic sage, as soon as he discovers that indifferent things depend not on his will but on the will of universal Nature, they take on infinite interest for him. He accepts them with love, but he accepts them all with *equal* love; he finds them beautiful, but all of them inspire him with the same admiration. He says "Yes!" to the entire universe and to each of its parts and events, even if specific parts and events seem painful or repugnant. Here we rejoin Aristotle's philosophy of nature: we must not have a puerile aversion to any given reality produced by nature, for, as Heraclitus said, there are gods even in the kitchen. The sage's indifference corresponds to a complete transformation of his relation to the world.

Equanimity of soul, absence of need, and indifference to indifferent things: these are the foundations of the sage's peace of mind and lack of worries. The origin of the soul's worries can be highly diverse. For Plato it is the body, which, through its desires and passions, brings disorder and worry to the soul. Yet there are also the cares of private life, and especially of political life. Xenocrates is supposed to have said that "philosophy was invented in order to erase the worries that caused the cares in life."[159] The Aristotelian contemplative life, which remains far from the business of politics and the uncertainties of action, brings serenity. According to Epicurus, people's worries are caused by vain terrors about death and the gods, but also by disorderly desires and participation in the affairs of the city. For the sage who knows how to limit his desires and his actions, and knows how to suppress pain, the psychological serenity he thereby acquires will allow him to live on earth "like a god among men." Pyrrho finds peace by refusing to decide whether things are good or bad; and for the Skeptics, inner peace followed "like a shadow" after the suspension of judgment—that is, the refusal to form value judgments about things. Finally, according to the Stoics, the sage knows how to reconcile efficacious action and inner serenity, for, uncertain of success, he always acts in consent to destiny while striving to keep his intentions pure.

The figure of the sage appears as a kind of unconquerable, unalterable nucleus of freedom, which is perfectly described in a well-known text by Horace: "He who is just and firm in his resolve is shaken neither by the fury of citizens who ordain evil nor by the face of a threatening tyrant. Neither is his spirit shaken, either by the Auster, turbulent leader of the stormy Adriatic, or by the great hand of thunder-bearing Zeus. Let the world break and collapse—he will be unafraid when struck by its debris."[160]

In the figure of the sage, we again find the twofold movement that was apparent in the context of the exercises of wisdom. The sage becomes aware of his "I," which, through its power over his judgments, guiding them or suspending them, can ensure perfect inner freedom, and independence from all things. Yet this inner freedom is not arbitrary freedom; it is unbreachable and unassailable only if it situates itself, and thereby transcends itself, in the perspective of Nature or the Spirit—or, at least in the case of the Skeptics, of critical reason.

Philosophical Discourse on the Sage

The figure of the sage thus plays a decisive role in the philosophical choice of life, yet it is offered to the philosopher as a ideal described by philosophical discourse more than as a model incarnate in a living human being. The Stoics said that the sage is extremely rare. There are very few—perhaps one, perhaps none at all. Almost all the other schools were in agreement on this point, except for the Epicureans, who did not hesitate to venerate Epicurus as the sage *par excellence*. The only universally recognized sage was Socrates—that disconcerting sage who did not know he was a sage. Sometimes, of course, a given philosopher took it upon himself to consider one of his masters, or some famous figure from the past, as a perfect sage. This is what Seneca does when he speaks of Sextius or Cato; likewise the authors of lives of the philosophers—for example, Porphyry when he speaks about Plotinus.

Historians of philosophy have perhaps neglected the fact that in the teaching of ancient philosophy, a major role was played by the discourse which consisted in describing the sage. It was less important to trace the features of concrete figures of particularly noteworthy philosophers or sages (this was the role of the lives of the philosophers) than to define the sage's ideal behavior, and ask: "What would the sage do in such-and-such circumstances?" In the various schools, this was often the means of giving an idealized description of the specifics of the way of life which was characteristic of them.

The Stoics accorded a large place in their teaching to the discussion of "theses" on the paradoxes of the sage. These demonstrated not only that the sage is the only being who is infallible, impeccable, impassive, happy, free, handsome, and wealthy, but also that he is the only one who can truly and excellently be a statesman, legislator, general, poet, and king. This means that the sage, by his perfect use of reason, is the only person capable of carrying out all these functions.[161]

Some scholars have attached great importance to such paradoxes, considering them "typically Stoic"; but in fact they seem to have corresponded to exercise themes which were purely scholastic. They may already have existed at the time of the Sophists, but in any case they do seem to have been practiced in Plato's Academy. Such subjects were discussed in class in the form of "theses," or questions about which people could argue. Thus Xenocrates once taught a class on the thesis that "only the sage is a good general." Eudamidas, king of Sparta, had come that day to the Academy to listen to Xenocrates. After class, the Spartan, showing admirable good sense, said: "The discourse is admirable, but the speaker is not credible, for he has never heard the sound of trumpets."[162] Eudamidas thus put his finger on the danger of such exercises, in which theories about wisdom are discussed in the abstract without actually being put to the test.

Presumably there is an allusion to this kind of exercise in the final prayer of Plato's *Phaedrus,* in which Socrates seeks to be convinced that the sage is rich. We find the same kind of questions about the sage throughout the history of ancient philosophy: Can the sage be loved? Can he become involved in politics? Does he get angry?

There is, however, one Stoic paradox which is much more significant. It affirms that one does not become a sage gradually, but does so through instant mutation.[163] This places us on the trail of another paradox, which this time is found in all the schools: if the sage represents a mode of being which is different from that of common mortals, can we not say that the figure of the sage tends to become very close to that of God or of the gods?[164] We see this movement most clearly in Epicureanism. On the one hand, for Epicurus, the sage lives like "a god among men."[165] On the other hand, the gods of Epicurus—that is to say, the traditional gods of Olympus, as reinterpreted by Epicurus—live like sages. They are anthropomorphic, and live in what the Epicureans called the "interworlds" (empty spaces between worlds), thereby escaping the corruption inherent in the movement of atoms. Like the sage, they are bathed in perfect serenity, and are not involved in any way in the creation and administration of the world: "Divine nature must enjoy eternal duration in the greatest peace, and it is remote and separate from our affairs. Exempt from all pain and all dangers, strong from its own resources, in no need of our assistance, it is not seduced by benefits or touched by anger."[166]

As we have seen, this conception of divinity was intended to suppress human fear of the gods. The need to give a materialist explanation of the genesis of the universe in philosophical discourse, in order to persuade the soul that the gods do not concern themselves with the world, was based on the Epicurean choice of life. It now appears to us, however, that the goal of such a representation was also to propose the divine as an ideal of wisdom, insofar as the Epicureans conceived of the essence of the divine as consisting in serenity, absence of cares, pleasure, and joy. In a way, the gods are immortal sages, and the sages are mortal gods. The gods are friends and equals of the sages, and the sage finds his joy in the presence of the gods: "He admires the nature and condition of the gods; he tries to get close to them; he aspires, so to speak, to touch them and to live with them; and he calls the sages friends of the gods, and the gods friends of the sages."[167] The gods do not concern themselves with human affairs, so the sage will not invoke them in order to obtain some benefit from them. Instead, he will find his happiness in contemplating their serenity and their perfection, and in associating himself with their joy.

According to Aristotle, the sage devotes himself to the exercise of thought and the life of the spirit. Here again, the sage's model is the divine, for, as Aristotle points out, our human condition renders this activity of our spirit fragile and intermittent, dispersed in time, and subject to error and forgetfulness. By extrapolation, however, we can imagine a mind which would exercise thought perfectly and continuously, within an eternal present. Its thought would think itself, in an eternal act. It would know eternally the happiness and pleasure which the human mind knows only at rare moments. This is the description Aristotle gives of the deity—the first mover and ultimate cause of the universe. The sage, then, experiences intermittently what the deity lives continuously. In the process, he lives a life which transcends the human condition, yet which corresponds to what is most essential in mankind: the life of the spirit.

The relations between the idea of the deity and that of the sage are less clear in Plato, probably because the idea of the divine in Plato is extremely complex and hierarchical. The "divine" is a diffuse reality, which includes entities situated at different levels, such as the good, the Ideas, the divine Intellect, the mythical figure of the Demiurge (or Artisan of the world), and finally the World Soul. On the topic which interests us here, however, Plato announced a fundamental principle: to go in the direction opposed to evil, and thus to go in the direction of wisdom, is "assimilation to the deity insofar as is possible; and one assimilates oneself by becoming just and holy, together with intelligence."[168] Here, the deity appears as the model of human moral and intellectual perfection. In general, moreover, Plato presents the deity or the gods as possessing moral qualities which could be those of the sage: he is true, wise, and good; he feels no envy; and he always wishes to do what is best.

For Plotinus, the relation between the sage and the deity is situated at two levels. First of all, the divine Intellect, in its relation to itself in terms of thought, identity, and activity, possesses the four virtues, conflated with its essence: thought (or prudence), justice, strength, and temperance. In this state, they are the transcendent models of wisdom, and the Intellect lives a life which is "supremely wise, exempt from faults and errors."[169] Since Plotinus believes the soul sometimes elevates itself, at rare moments of mystical experience, to a level which is higher than the Intellect, we also find features of the sage in the description of the One or the Good: absolute independence, absence of need, and self-identity. Clearly, then, Plotinus projects the figure of the sage on his conception of the divine.

It is probably because the figure of the sage and the figure of deity are identified in them that the philosophies of Plato, Plotinus, Aristotle, and Epicurus represent the deity more as a force of attraction than as a creative force. The deity is the model which beings seek to imitate, and the supreme value which orients their choices. As Bernard Frischer remarks, the Epicurean sages and gods are immobile movers, like Aristotle's God: they attract the others by transmitting their images to them.[170]

The Stoic sage knows the same happiness as universal Reason, which is allegorically personified by Zeus; for gods and human beings share the same reason, which is perfect in the gods but perfectible in humans.[171] The sage has attained the perfection of reason by making his reason coincide with divine Reason, and merging his will with divine will. The virtues of the deity are not superior to those of the sage.

The theology of the Greek philosophers is, one might say, a theology of the sage. Nietzsche protested this approach: "Let us separate supreme goodness from the concept of the deity: it is not worthy of a god. Likewise, let us separate supreme wisdom, for it is the vanity of philosophers which has conceived this extravagance—a god who is a monster of wisdom; he had to resemble them as much as possible. No. The deity—the supreme power: that's enough! All flows from this, and from here derives the 'world.'"[172]

Omnipotence or goodness? We shall not discuss this problem,

but we must affirm that, contrary to what Nietzsche seems to be saying, the ideal of the sage has nothing to do with a "classical" or "bourgeois" ethics. Instead, to use Nietzsche's expression, it corresponds to a complete reversal of received and conventional values, and presents itself in the most diverse forms, as we have seen in the context of the various philosophical schools.

To give a new example, it will suffice to mention the description of the "natural"—that is, uncorrupted—state of society given by Zeno the Stoic in his *Republic*. It caused something of a scandal precisely because it presented this state as the life of a community of sages. In that long-ago era, he claimed, there was only one nation: the world itself. There were no laws, for the sage's reason was enough to tell him what he should do; no courts, because he committed no crimes; no temples, since the gods have no need of them, and it is nonsense to consider manmade objects as sacred; no money; no laws governing marriage (only the freedom to unite with whomever one wished, even incestuously); and no laws governing the burial of the dead.

The Sage and the Contemplation of the World

Bernhard Groethuysen has rightly insisted on a highly particular aspect of the figure of the ancient sage: his relation to the cosmos. "The consciousness he has of the world is something particular to the sage. Only the sage never ceases to have the whole constantly present to his mind, never forgets the world, thinks and acts in relation to the cosmos. . . . The sage is part of the world; he is cosmic. He does not let himself be distracted from the world, or detached from the cosmic whole. . . . The figure of the sage and the representation of the world form, as it were, an indissoluble unity."[173]

As we have seen, self-consciousness is inseparable from expansion into the whole, and from a movement whereby the self resituates itself within the totality which contains it. Far from imprisoning the self, this totality allows it to expand throughout infinite space and time: "You will open up a vast field for yourself, by embracing the entire universe in your thought."[174] Here again, the figure of the sage invites us to totally transform our perception of the world.

In a remarkable text by Seneca, the contemplation of the world is linked to the contemplation of the sage: "For my part, I usually spend a lot of time contemplating wisdom. I look at it with the same stupefaction with which, at other times, I look at the world—this world which I often look at as if I were seeing it for the first time."[175] Here we find two spiritual exercises, one of which we know well: the contemplation of the world. The other we have just now seen: the contemplation of the figure of the sage. To judge by the context, the figure which Seneca is contemplating is that of Sextius: "As he reveals to you the wonders of the happy life, he will not deprive you of the hope of attaining it." This is a re-mark of fundamental importance: in order to contemplate wisdom, just as to contemplate the world, we must renew our way of seeing. Here a new aspect of the philosopher's relation to time appears. We must not only perceive and live each moment of time as if it were the last; we must also perceive it as if it were the first, in all the stupefying strangeness of its emergence. In the words of the Epicurean Lucretius: "If all these objects suddenly surged forth to the eyes of mortals, what could be found that was more wonderful than this totality, whose existence the human mind could not have dared to imagine?"[176] Here we have every reason to believe that when Seneca contemplated the world, he was practicing the redis-covery of this naive vision—though it may be the fleeting expres-sion of a kind of spontaneous "wild mysticism," to use the words of Michel Hulin.[177]

What explains this intimate connection between the contem-plation of the world and the contemplation of the sage is, once again, the idea of the sacred—that is to say, the superhuman, and almost inhuman, character of wisdom. As Seneca says elsewhere, in the heart of an ancient wood, in the midst of a lonely wilderness, at the source of great rivers, and before the bottomless depths of dark-watered lakes, the soul has the feeling of the presence of the sacred. Yet Seneca gets the same feeling while admiring the sage: "And if you see a man who is not frightened by danger, who is untouched by passion, who is happy in adversity and peaceful in the midst of storms, who sees human beings from on high and sees the gods at his level, will you not be filled with veneration? . . . In every good person, there lives a god. Which god? We cannot be sure—but it is a god."[178]

To contemplate the world, and to contemplate wisdom, means ultimately to practice philosophy. It means carrying out an inner transformation, and a mutation of vision, which permits us to recognize simultaneously two things to which we rarely pay attention: the splendor of the world and the splendor of the norm represented by the sage: "The starry sky above me, and the moral law within."[179]

CONCLUSION

It is easy to be ironic about the ideal of an almost inaccessible sage—an ideal which the philosopher cannot attain. Modern authors have not resisted this temptation, and have not failed to speak of "nostalgic antirealism, aware of its chimerical nature."[180] Among the ancients, the satirist Lucian had great fun with the unfortunate man who, having spent a lifetime in struggles and sleeplessness, still had not attained wisdom.[181] So speaks the voice of robust common sense, which fails to grasp the whole point of the definition of the philosopher as a nonsage in Plato's *Symposium*— although, as we shall see, this definition enabled Kant to understand the philosopher's true status. It is easy to make fun; and this is justified, if philosophers do nothing but talk about the ideal of the sage. If, however, they have made the decision—which is serious and has grave consequences—truly to train themselves for wisdom, then they deserve our respect, even if their progress has been minimal. What matters is (to use Jacques Bouveresse's formula for an idea of Wittgenstein's) "what personal price have they had to pay" in order to have the right to talk about their efforts toward wisdom.[182]

Despite my reservations about the use of comparativism in philosophy, I wanted to end this chapter by emphasizing the extent to which Michel Hulin's description of the existential roots of the mystical experience (a description inspired by Buddhism) seemed to me to be close to the characteristics of the ideal of the ancient sage, for the resemblances between the two spiritual quests seem striking. Upon rereading Émile Bréhier's *Chrysippe,* however, I was astonished to see that Bréhier had already made an analogous discovery. He writes: "This notion of a sage superior to humanity, exempt from faults and misfortunes, is not peculiar to the Stoics in this period. Since the time of the Cynics [here Bréhier might have said 'since the time of Socrates and Plato'], it was a concept common to all the schools." And in a footnote, he adds the following Buddhist description of the sage: "Victorious, knowing all and understanding all, freed from the burden of circumstance and existence, without needs: such is he who can be glorified as a sage. . . . The solitary traveler is not concerned with either praise or blame. . . . Leader of others, not led by others: such is the person we can celebrate as a sage."[183]

It was precisely this idea of "laying aside one's burden" which had attracted my attention in Hulin's description, and had seemed to me to offer a certain analogy with the spiritual experience that inspired the ideal figure of the ancient sage. Hulin shows that in the first of Buddhism's "noble truths"—"All is suffering"—the word "suffering" signifies not so much suffering as "the alternation of pain and joy—their inextricable blending, their contrast and mutual conditioning." The burden is the opposition which the affirmation of individuality-closed-in-upon-itself establishes between what is pleasant and unpleasant, or between the "good for me" and the "bad for me," and which obliges us always to watch out for our interests. Behind this opposition, we perceive the permanence of a "silent, ever-renewed dissatisfaction," which we might call existential anguish. In order to free ourselves from this "dissatisfaction," we must dare to "set aside the burden." "Stretched and stressed in the pursuit of our worldly interests, we have no idea of the immense relief we would feel if we set aside our burden—that is, if we renounced our effort to affirm ourselves at all costs against the order of the world, and at the expense of others."[184]

PART THREE

INTERRUPTION AND CONTINUITY: THE MIDDLE AGES AND MODERN TIMES

■ ■ ■

Christianity as a Revealed Philosophy

CHRISTIANITY DEFINES ITSELF AS PHILOSOPHY

At its origins, Christianity, as presented in the word of Jesus, announced the imminent end of the world and the coming of the Kingdom of God. Such a message was completely foreign to the Greek mentality and to the perspectives of philosophy; rather, it was inscribed within the intellectual universe of Judaism, which Christianity overthrew, but not without preserving some of its fundamental notions. Nothing, it seems, could have predicted that a century after the death of Christ some Christians would present Christianity not only as a philosophy—that is, a Greek cultural phenomenon—but even as the sole and eternal philosophy.

In fact, however, we ought not to forget that there had long been relations between Judaism and Greek philosophy. The most famous example of this was Philo of Alexandria, a Jewish philosopher contemporary with the Christian era. In this tradition, the notion of an intermediary between God and the World—a mediating element called *Sophia* or the *Logos*—played a central role. Here, the *Logos* was the creative Word ("God said, 'Let there be light'"), which also revealed God. It is from this perspective that we must understand the famous prologue of the Gospel according to John: "In the beginning [or 'In the Principle'—that is, in God—as interpreted by some exegetes] was the *Logos*, and the *Logos* was close to God and the *Logos* was God. . . . Everything was made by him, and without him nothing was made. What was made in him was life, and life was the light of men. . . . And the *Logos* become flesh, and it stayed with us, and we contemplated its glory—the glory which he, as only Son, has from his Father."

Christian philosophy was made possible by the ambiguity of the Greek word *Logos*. Since Heraclitus, the notion of the *Logos* had been a central concept of Greek philosophy, since it could signify "word" and "discourse" as well as "reason." In particular, the Stoics believed that the *Logos*, conceived as a rational force, was immanent in the world, in human beings, and in each individual. This is why, when the prologue to the Gospel of John identified Jesus with the Eternal *Logos* and the Son of God, it enabled Christianity to be presented as a philosophy. The substantial Word of God could be conceived as the Reason which created the world and guided human thought. The Neoplatonist Amelius, a disciple of Plotinus, considered this prologue a philosophical text when he wrote:

> This, then, was the *Logos*, thanks to which all engendered things were produced while he himself exists always (as Heraclitus believed)[1] and which the Barbarian [that is, John the Evangelist] believed "was near to God" and "was God," possessing the rank and dignity of a principle. By him absolutely everything was created; in him was the nature of the living being, of life and of being. And it fell into bodies and, donning flesh, took on human appearance; but at the same time it shows the greatness of its nature. When it is freed, it is once again made divine, and is God, as it was before it fell into the world of bodies, and before it descended into flesh and humankind.[2]

For Amelius, John the Evangelist, whom he calls "the Barbarian," has described in his prologue the World Soul, which is divine yet somehow mixed with the body.[3] But Amelius' interpretation does not matter here; what is important for us is the kinship which the Neoplatonist philosopher recognized between the Evangelist's vocabulary and that proper to philosophy.

Beginning in the second century A.D., Christian authors—called "Apologists" because they tried to present Christianity in a form understandable to the Greco-Roman world—used the notion of the *Logos* to define Christianity as *the* philosophy. Greek philosophers, they claimed, had thus far possessed only portions of the *Logos,* mere elements of the True Discourse and of perfect Reason;[4] but Christians were in possession of the *Logos*—that is, the True Discourse and perfect Reason incarnate in Jesus Christ. If doing philosophy meant living in conformity with Reason, then the Christians were philosophers, for they lived in conformity with the divine *Logos.*[5] The transformation of Christianity into philosophy became even more marked with Clement of Alexandria, in third-century Alexandria.[6] For Clement, Christianity, as the complete revelation of the *Logos,* was the true philosophy, which "teaches us to conduct ourselves so as to resemble God, and accept the divine plan as the guiding principle of all our education."

Like Greek philosophy, Christian philosophy presented itself both as a discourse and as a way of life. In the first and second centuries, the time of the birth of Christianity, philosophical discourse in each school consisted mainly of explicating texts by the school's founders, as we have seen. The discourse of Christian philosophy was also, quite naturally, exegetic, and the exegetical schools of the Old and the New Testament, like those opened in Alexandria by Clement of Alexandria's teacher, or by Origen himself, offered a kind of teaching which was completely analogous to that of contemporary philosophical schools. Just as the Platonists proposed a reading order for the Platonic dialogues which corresponded to the stages of spiritual progress, so Christians like Origen had their disciples read first the biblical Book of Proverbs, then Ecclesiastes, then the Song of Songs. For Origen, these corresponded respectively to ethics, which provides initial purification; physics, which teaches us to go beyond sensory things; and epoptics or theology, which leads to union with God.[7] Here, we begin to see that, as was the case for the philosophers of this period, reading texts is a "spiritual" process closely related to the progress of the soul. The philosophical notion of spiritual progress constitutes the very backbone of Christian education and teaching. As ancient philosophical discourse was for the philosophical way of life, so Christian philosophical discourse was a means of realizing the Christian way of life.

It might rightly be said that there is nevertheless a difference, for Christian exegesis is the explanation of sacred texts, and Christian philosophy is based on a revelation: the *Logos* is the revelation and manifestation of God. Christian theology developed gradually through dogmatic controversies, based always on the exegesis of the Old and New Testaments. Yet within Greek philosophy as well, there existed an entire tradition of systematic theology, inaugurated by Plato's *Timaeus* and the tenth book of the *Laws*, and developed in book twelve of Aristotle's *Metaphysics*. This tradition distinguished the various sources of revelation, and the different degrees and modes of action of divine reality; and during the period of late Neoplatonism, it integrated all kinds of revelations from non-Greek sources. From this point of view as well, Greek philosophy served as a model for Christian philosophy.[8]

Yet although some Christian authors might present Christianity as a philosophy, or even as *the* philosophy, this was not so much because Christianity proposed an exegesis and a theology analogous to pagan exegesis and theology, but because it was a style of life and a mode of being, just as ancient philosophy was. As Dom Jean Leclercq has written: "In the monastic Middle Ages, as well as in antiquity, *philosophia* did not designate a theory or a way of knowing; rather, it signified a lived wisdom, and a way of living in accordance with reason"—that is, in accordance with the *Logos*.[9] Christian philosophy consists in living according to the *Logos*— that is to say, according to reason—to the extent that, as Justin puts it, "those who, before Christ, led a life accompanied by reason [*logos*] are Christians, even if they were known as atheists. Such were Socrates, Heraclitus, and those like them."[10]

With this assimilation of Christianity to a philosophy, we see the appearance within Christianity of spiritual exercises—practices that were proper to secular philosophy. Clement of Alexandria, for instance, writes as follows: "The divine law must inspire fear, so that the philosopher may acquire and conserve peace of mind [*amerimnia*], thanks to prudence [*eulabeia*] and attention [*prosokhē*] to himself."[11] This passage implies the whole thought-world of ancient philosophy. The divine law is both the *logos* of the philosophers and the Christian *Logos*. It inspires circumspection in action, prudence, and attention to oneself—that is to say, the fundamental Stoic attitude. These in turn procure peace of mind, an inner disposition sought by all the schools. In Origen,[12] we re-encounter the highly philosophical exercise of the examination of the conscience. Commenting on a verse from the Song of Songs— "If you do not know yourself, O most beautiful of women"—he interprets this verse as an invitation for the soul to examine itself attentively. The soul must examine its feelings and actions. Does it propose to do good? Does it seek the various virtues? Is it making progress? For instance, has it completely repressed the passion of anger, sadness, fear, and the love of glory? What is its manner of giving and receiving, and of discerning truth?

The phenomenon of monasticism, which developed from the beginning of the fourth century in Egypt and Syria, was interpreted in the sense of "Christian philosophy" by fourth-century Church Fathers who stood in the tradition of Clement of Alexandria and of Origen: Basil of Caesarea, Gregory Nazianzen, Gregory of Nyssa, Evagrius of Pontus, to some degree Athanasius of Alexandria, and later monks such as Dorotheus of Gaza, who wrote in the sixth century. This was the time when some Christians began to wish to attain Christian perfection through the heroic practice of Christ's evangelical advice and the imitation of his life: they retired into the desert, and led lives completely devoted to rigorous *askēsis* and to meditation. They were not educated people, and any connection to philosophy was quite remote from their thinking. They found their models in the Old and the New Testament, and perhaps also—at least, the possibility cannot be excluded a priori—in examples of Buddhist or Manichaean asceticism.[13] We must also recall that communities of contemplative ascetics already existed at the time of Philo and Jesus; these included the Therapeutes (whom Philo describes in his treatise *On the Contemplative Life* and whom he calls "philosophers")[14] and the Jewish sect at Qumrân. Some of the believers in "Christian philosophy" were also practitioners of monasticism themselves; this is the movement which Louis Bouyer has called "learned monasticism."[15] For them, "philosophy" would henceforth designate the monastic life as perfection of the Christian life. Nevertheless, this "philosophy" continued to be linked closely to such secular categories as peace of mind, the absence of passions,[16] and "life in conformity with nature and reason."[17] As in secular philosophy, monastic life thereafter presented itself as the practice of spiritual exercises, some of which were specifically Christian, but many of which had been bequeathed by secular philosophy.[18]

Thus, we reencounter attention to one's self, which was the fundamental attitude of the Stoics, and of the Neoplatonists as well. For Athanasius of Alexandria, such was the very definition of the monastic attitude.[19] When, in his *Life of Antony,* he tells how the saint was converted to the monastic life, he simply says that Antony began to pay attention to himself. Athanasius also reports the words Antony addressed to his disciples on the day of his death: "Live as if you were going to die every day, devoting attention to yourselves and remembering my exhortations."

Gregory Nazianzen spoke instead of "concentration in one-self."[20] Attention to the self, concentration on the present, and the thought of death were constantly linked together within the monastic tradition, as they had been in secular philosophy. For instance, Antony advised his disciples to wake up thinking they might not survive as far as the evening, and to go to sleep thinking that they might not wake up. As Dorotheus of Gaza warned his followers: "Let us pay attention to ourselves, my brothers, and let us be vigilant, while we still have time. . . . Since the beginning of our conversation two or three hours have elapsed, and we have come closer to death; yet we see without fear that we are wasting our time."[21]

Obviously, such attention to oneself is in fact a conversion, and an orientation toward the higher part of oneself. This appears very clearly in a sermon by Basil of Caesarea, who takes as his theme the biblical text, "Pay attention, lest a word of injustice be hidden in your heart."[22] In Basil's commentary we encounter all the themes of Stoicism and Platonism. To pay attention to oneself means to awaken the rational principles of thought and action which God has placed in our souls; it means to watch over the beauty of ourselves (that is to say, our spirit and our soul) and not over what is ours (that is, our body and possessions). Finally, it means keeping watch over the beauty of our soul, by examining our conscience and knowing ourselves. In this way, we can correct our judgments of ourselves, by recognizing both our true poverty and our true riches; the splendors offered by the cosmos, our body, the earth, the sky, and stars; and above all, the destiny of the soul.[23]

Attention to the self presupposes the practice of examination of the conscience, which the famous monk Antony advised his disciples to practice in writing: "Let each of us write down the actions and motions of our soul, as if we had to make them known to others."[24] This is an invaluable psychological remark: the therapeutic value of the examination of the conscience will be greater if it is

externalized by means of writing. We would be ashamed to commit misdeeds in public, and writing gives us the impression that
we are in public: "Let writing take the place of the eyes of others." In any case, the examination of the conscience must be very
frequent and regular. Dorotheus of Gaza recommended self-
examination every six hours, but he also advised his readers to
make a more general estimation of the state of their soul every
week, every month, and every year.[25]

As we have seen, attention to the self and vigilance also presuppose exercises of thought: we must meditate, remember, and have
constantly "at hand" our principles of action, which will be summarized, as far as possible, in short sayings. In monastic literature,
this need is satisfied by the *Apophthegmata* and by what are called
Kephalaia. Like the pagan philosophers' dicta which were collected
by Diogenes Laertius, the *Apophthegmata* were famous and striking sayings that spiritual masters had uttered in specific circumstances.[26] The *Kephalaia* ("capital points") were collections of
fairly short sentences, usually arranged in groups of one hundred.
As in secular philosophy, meditation on such examples and sentences had to be constant. Epicurus and Epictetus recommended
that their disciples practice it day and night; and Dorotheus of
Gaza also advised his followers to meditate ceaselessly, so that they
might have their principles of action "at hand" at the appropriate time.[27] Thus, one could "profit from every event"—in other
words, recognize what needed to be done in the face of each event.

Attention to the self translates into self-mastery and self-
control, which can be obtained only by habit and perseverance in
ascetic practices. These, in turn, are intended to bring about the
triumph of reason over the passions, pushed as far as their complete extirpation. An entire therapeutics of the passions was to be
applied. The road which led to such complete liberation from the
passions *(apatheia)* passed by detachment *(aprospatheia)* from
objects—that is to say, the gradual elimination of desires which

have indifferent things as their object. Like the Stoic Epictetus, but also like the Platonist Plutarch, who had written treatises advising exercises designed to master curiosity and idle chatter, Dorotheus of Gaza recommends that we begin by getting used to cutting back on minor things, in order to prepare ourselves, little by little, for making greater sacrifices.[28] For Dorotheus, it is the egoistic will—our own will, which seeks its pleasure in objects—which will be gradually minimized by such practices:

> In this way, he finally arrives at the point where he has no will of his own. Whatever happens, it makes him as happy as if it came from himself.
>
> He who has no will of his own always does what he wants. Everything that happens satisfies him, and he constantly acts in accordance with his will. For he does not want things to be as he wishes; he wishes them to be as they are.[29]

Here we recognize an echo of the well-known eighth sentence of Epictetus' *Manual*: "Do not seek to have that which happens happen as you wish. Wish that what happens may happen as it happens, and you will be happy." Like the Stoic, the monk wants each present moment just the way it is.

According to another piece of traditional philosophical advice,[30] beginners should try to fight a passion (say, the yearning for luxury) by means of the passion opposed to it (for instance, the desire for a good reputation), before they are able to combat the passion directly by practicing the virtue opposed to it.[31]

Evagrius of Pontus, who had been a disciple of Gregory Nazianzen, was more influenced by Platonic and Neoplatonic conceptions. For instance, he uses the Platonic tripartition of the soul to define the state of virtue: "The rational soul acts according to nature when its desiring part [*epithumētikon*] desires virtue, its combative part [*thumikon*] fights for virtue, and its rational part [*logistikon*] attains the contemplation of beings."[32]

Asceticism was often conceived in a Platonic way, as the separation of body and soul, which was a precondition for the vision of God. This theme appears in Clement of Alexandria, for whom "true piety toward God consists in separating ourselves, irrevocably, from the body and its passions; perhaps this is why Socrates rightly calls philosophy a 'training for death'"—for we must renounce the senses in order to know true reality.[33] Gregory Nazianzen reproached a friend for complaining about his illness as if it were something irremediable, and exhorted him as follows:

> On the contrary, you must do philosophy [that is to say, you must train yourself to live as a philosopher] in your suffering. Now more than ever, this is the moment to purify your thoughts, and to reveal yourself as superior to your bonds [which tie you to the body]. You must consider your illness a pedagogue which leads you to what is profitable to you—that is, teaches you to despise the body and corporeal things and all that flows away, is the source of worries, and is perishable, so that you may belong completely to the part which is above, . . . making this life down below—as Plato says—a training for death, and liberating your soul in this way, as far as possible, both from the body [sōma] and from the tomb [sēma], to use Plato's terms. If you philosophize in this way, . . . you will teach many people to philosophize in their suffering.[34]

Gregory's disciple Evagrius of Pontus takes up the same theme in clearly Neoplatonic terms: "To separate the body from the soul belongs only to Him who has united them, but to separate the soul from the body belongs to the person who tends toward virtue. For our Fathers call *anachōrēsis* [the monastic life] a training for death and a flight from the body."[35]

Porphyry had written, "What nature has bound, she releases; but what the soul has bound, the soul releases. Nature has bound the body within the soul, but the soul has bound itself within the body. Thus, nature releases the body from the soul, but the soul releases itself from the body."[36] Porphyry thus opposed the body's natural bond to the soul, which makes it live, to the emotional bond which attaches the soul to the body. This latter bond can be so strong that the soul identifies itself with the body, and cares only about the satisfactions of the body. According to Evagrius, the death for which the philosopher-monk is in training is the complete uprooting of the passions which bind the soul to the body—an uprooting that will enable him to attain perfect detachment from the body through *apatheia*, or the absence of passion.

CHRISTIANITY AND ANCIENT PHILOSOPHY

The Christians adopted the Greek word *philosophia* to designate monasticism as the perfection of the Christian life, and were able to do so because the word *philosophia* designated a way of life. Thus, when they adopted the word, the "Christian philosophers" were led to bring into Christianity practices and attitudes inherited from secular philosophy. This need not surprise us; there were ultimately many analogies between secular philosophical life and monastic life. To be sure, ancient philosophers did not withdraw into the desert or into a cloister; on the contrary, they lived in the world, where they often took part in political activity. If they were genuine philosophers, however, they must have been converted— that is, they had to profess philosophy, and make a choice of life which obliged them to change all aspects of their behavior in the world, and which, in a certain sense, separated them from the world. They entered into a community, under the direction of a spiritual master, in which they venerated the school's founder and often took meals in common with the other members of the school. They examined their conscience and perhaps even confessed their misdeeds, as seems to have been the practice in the Epicurean school. They lived an ascetic life, and, if they were Cynics, renounced all comfort and wealth. If they belonged to a Pythagorean school or if they were Neoplatonists, they followed a vegetarian diet and devoted themselves to contemplation, seeking mystical union.

Christianity was indisputably a way of life, so there is no problem about the fact that it presented itself as a philosophy. As it did so, however, it adopted certain values and practices which were proper to ancient philosophy. Was this process legitimate? Did such an evolution correspond to the original spirit of Christianity? We cannot give a certain and exhaustive reply to this complex question, because we would first have to give a rigorous definition of what ancient Christianity was; and this exceeds both our competence and the scope of this book. Let us simply examine a few points which seem essential.

First, and most important, we must not forget that although Christian spirituality borrowed certain spiritual exercises from ancient philosophy, these formed part of a broader ensemble of practices which were specifically Christian. The entire monastic life always presupposes the help of the grace of God, as well as a fundamental disposition of humility, which was often manifested in bodily attitudes signifying submission and guilt, such as prostration before one's fellow monks. The renunciation of one's own will was realized through absolute obedience to the orders of one's superiors. Often, training for death was linked to the remembrance of the death of Christ, and asceticism was understood as participation in the Passion. Similarly, the monk saw Christ in every human being: "Aren't you ashamed to get angry and speak evil of your brother? Don't you know that he is Christ, and that it is Christ you are harming?"[37] Here, the practice of the virtues takes on a completely different meaning.

The Christian philosophers tried to Christianize their use of secular philosophical themes by giving the impression that the exercises they advised had already been recommended by the Old or the New Testament. For instance, when Deuteronomy uses the expression "pay attention," Basil concludes that the biblical book is advising the philosophical exercise of "attention to oneself." Such attention to oneself was also called "the guard of the heart," because of a text from Proverbs: "Above all, guard your heart."[38] When the Christian philosophers read the exhortation "Put yourself to the test" in Second Corinthians, this was interpreted as an invitation to examine their conscience;[39] and when, in First Corinthians, they read "I die every day," they understood this as the model of the exercise of death. But such allusions to texts from Scripture obviously could not prevent the Christian philosophers from describing their spiritual exercises by means of the vocabulary and concepts of secular philosophy. Often, such allusions to biblical texts were based only on allegorical interpretation, which ultimately consisted in giving the texts whichever meaning one wanted to give them, without taking the author's intention into account. Many modern philosophers, moreover, still use this interpretive method to explain texts from antiquity.

At any rate, it was by means of this process that the Church Fathers were able, for instance, to interpret such Gospel expressions as "the Kingdom of Heaven" and "the Kingdom of God" as designating the parts of philosophy. We find this interpretation in the opening lines of the *Practical Treatise* by Evagrius of Pontus, which begins: "Christianity is the doctrine of Christ our Savior; it is composed of praxis, physics, and theology."[40] Here we recognize, enumerated in order, the three parts of philosophy which had been taught by the Platonic school since at least the time of Plutarch, and which corresponded to three stages of spiritual progress. It is rather surprising to learn that Christ had proposed a praxis, a physics, and a theology—although one might say that these three parts of philosophy can be discerned in his moral advice and in his teachings on God and on the end of the world.

It is even more surprising, however, when Evagrius defines the three parts of philosophy more closely. For him, it seems, physics is the Kingdom of Heaven, and theology the Kingdom of God.[41] We recognize with some surprise the Gospel notion of the reign of God, designated by the synonymous expressions "Kingdom of Heaven" and "Kingdom of God." The notion came from Judaism, where it corresponded to the future perspective of the reign of God and his Law over the peoples of the earth. In the message of Jesus, the Kingdom is simultaneously both present and imminent, because it has begun to be realized—according to the spirit, not according to the letter—through conversion, penitence, love of one's fellow man, and accomplishment of the will of God. To identify the notion of the Kingdom of God or the Kingdom of Heaven with physics and theology, the parts of philosophy, was to give these notions a completely unexpected meaning. Under the influence of Origen, Evagrius distinguishes the Gospel notions of the Kingdom of Heaven and the Kingdom of God. The Kingdom of Heaven and the Kingdom of God become two states of the soul, or two states of spiritual progress. After *praxis,* a preliminary purification that enables the student to begin acquiring impassivity *(apatheia)* with regard to the passions, he can then progress and try his hand at physics, which is the contemplation of the "natures" *(physeis),* or beings, both visible and invisible, which have been created by God. The progressing student contemplates them *qua* created—that is to say, in their relation to God. Impassivity becomes stronger through this contemplation, and this is what Evagrius calls the "Kingdom of Heaven." As he goes farther still, the progressing student reaches the "Kingdom of God," or the contemplation of the mystery of God in his Trinity; this is the stage of *theology.* This interpretation of the terms "Kingdom of Heaven" and "Kingdom of God" is not peculiar to Evagrius. It was already sketched by Clement of Alexandria and Origen, and is abundantly attested in later writers.[42]

In the years following his conversion, Augustine of Hippo confronted Platonism and Christianity in his book *On the True Reli-*

gion. For Augustine, the essential part of Platonic doctrines over-lapped with the essential part of Christian doctrines. Platonic logic teaches us to recognize that sensory images have filled our soul with errors and false opinions, and that we must cure our soul of this illness so that it can discover divine reality. Physics teaches us that all things are born, die, and fade away; they have existence only by means of the genuine being of God, who has fashioned them. If, then, the soul turns away from sensible things, it will be able to fix its gaze on the immutable Form which gives form to all things, and on that Beauty which is "always equal and similar to itself in every way, neither divided by space nor trans-formed by time." Ethics, finally, will enable us to discover that only the rational and intellectual soul is capable of enjoying the con-templation of God's eternity, and of finding eternal life.[43]

Such, for Augustine, is the essence of Platonism, and such is also the essence of Christianity. As proof, he cites a number of passages from the New Testament, which oppose the visible and the invisi-ble world, the flesh and the spirit. What, however, one might ask, is the difference between Christianity and pagan philosophy? For Augustine, it consists in the fact that Platonism was not able to convert the masses and turn them away from earthly things, in or-der to orient them toward spiritual things; whereas, since the com-ing of Christ, people of all conditions have adopted the Christian way of life, so that a true transformation of humanity is under way. If Plato were to come back to earth, he would say, "This is what I did not dare to preach to the crowd." Although "blinded by corporeal stains," souls have been able "without the help of philo-sophical discussions" "to return within themselves and look to-ward their homeland" because God, through the Incarnation, has lowered the authority of divine Reason down to the human body.[44] From this Augustinian point of view, Christianity has the same content as Platonism: the key is to turn away from sensible reality in order to contemplate God and spiritual reality, but only

Christianity has been able to make the masses adopt this way of life. Nietzsche could have used Augustine to confirm his formula "Christianity is Platonism for the people."[45]

We must admit, then, that under the influence of ancient philosophy, certain values which had been only secondary (not to say nonexistent) within Christianity rose to the first rank of importance. The Gospel idea of the coming of the reign of God was replaced by the philosophical idea of union with God, or deification, achieved by asceticism and contemplation. In some cases, Christian life became less the life of a human being than that of a soul. It became a life according to reason, analogous to that preached by secular philosophers. More specifically, it became a life according to the Spirit, analogous to that of the Platonists; here, the goal was to flee the body in order to turn toward a transcendent, intelligible reality and, if possible, to reach this reality in mystical experience. In any case, attention to the self, the search for impassivity, peace of mind, and the absence of worry, and in particular the flight from the body became the primary objectives of spiritual life. Dorotheus of Gaza declared that peace of mind is so important that we must, if necessary, renounce what we have undertaken in order not to lose it.[46] It is this spirituality, strongly marked by the way of life of ancient philosophical schools, that was inherited by the Christian way of life in the Middle Ages and modern times.

CHAPTER ELEVEN

Eclipses and Recurrences of the Ancient Concept of Philosophy

If ancient philosophy established such an intimate link between philosophical discourse and the form of life, why is it that today, given the way the history of philosophy is usually taught, philosophy is presented as above all a discourse, which may be theoretical and systematic, or critical, but in any case lacks a direct relationship to the philosopher's way of life?

CHRISTIANITY AND PHILOSOPHY, ONCE AGAIN

The causes of this transformation are primarily historical: it is due to the flourishing of Christianity. As we have seen, Christianity presented itself very early as a "philosophy" in the ancient sense of the term. In other words, it presented itself as a way and a choice of life—a life according to Christ—which implied a specific discourse. Many elements from traditional Greco-Roman philosophy had been absorbed and integrated into the Christian way of life, as well as into Christian discourse. Gradually, however, and for reasons which we shall explore later, Christianity, particularly in the

Middle Ages, was marked by a divorce between philosophical discourse and way of life. Some philosophical ways of life, peculiar to the various philosophical schools of antiquity, disappeared completely, such as Epicureanism. Others, like Stoicism and Platonism, were absorbed by the Christian way of life. Although it is true, to a certain extent, that the monastic way of life called itself a "philosophy" in the Middle Ages,[1] nevertheless this way of life, although it integrated spiritual exercises proper to the ancient philosophies, found itself separated from the philosophical discourse to which it had previously been linked. All that persisted was the philosophical discourse of certain ancient schools, in particular the discourses of Platonism and Aristotelianism. Yet, separated from the ways of life which inspired them, they were reduced to the status of mere conceptual material which could be used in theological controversies. "Philosophy," when placed in the service of theology, was henceforth no more than a theoretical discourse; and when, in the seventeenth and especially the eighteenth century, modern philosophy conquered its autonomy, it retained the tendency to limit itself to this point of view. I emphasize the word "tendency," for in fact the original and authentic conception of Greco-Roman philosophy was never to be completely forgotten.

Thanks to the work of Juliusz Domański,[2] I have been able to correct the overly brief and inexact presentation of the "theoreticizing" of philosophy I had proposed in previous studies.[3] I still believe that this phenomenon is closely linked to the relations between philosophy and Christianity, especially as these were defined in the medieval universities. Yet I must admit that the rediscovery of philosophy as a way of life was not as late as I had stated, and that it too began to be sketched in the medieval universities. On the other hand, we must add many nuances and qualifications to our description of this rediscovery of philosophy as a way of life.

PHILOSOPHY AS THE SERVANT OF THEOLOGY

In the closing years of the sixteenth century, the Scholastic author Francisco Suárez published his *Disputationes Metaphysicae*, a work which exercised a considerable influence on many philosophers from the seventeenth to the nineteenth century.[4] In it he declares: "In this work, I take on the role of a philosopher, while remaining well aware that our philosophy must be a Christian philosophy and the servant of divine theology." For Suárez, a "Christian" philosophy is one which does not contradict the dogmas of Christianity, and is Christian in the sense that it can be used to elucidate theological problems. This does not mean that such a philosophy must be specifically Christian in the doctrines it professes; on the contrary, the philosophy in question is essentially Aristotelian, as it had been assimilated and adapted to Christianity in thirteenth-century Scholasticism.

This representation of philosophy as the servant or even the slave of a superior theology or wisdom had a long history.[5] As early as the beginning of the Christian era, we find it in Philo of Alexandria, who proposed a general curriculum for spiritual training and progress.[6] In accordance with the program of Plato's *Republic*, the first step in Philo's curriculum was the study of the cycle of sciences: geometry and music, but also grammar and rhetoric. Commenting on the Book of Genesis, Philo identifies these sciences with Hagar, the Egyptian slave with whom Abraham had to unite before he could achieve union with his wife Sara, who personifies philosophy.[7] The cycle of sciences must be conceived as the slave of philosophy; yet philosophy must, in turn, be considered as the slave of wisdom—and for Philo, wisdom, or real philosophy, was the Word of God as revealed by Moses.[8] Church Fathers like Clement of Alexandria, and especially Origen, took up the proportional relation Philo established between the cycle of sciences and Greek philosophy, on the one hand, and Greek philosophy and Mosaic philosophy on the other. Needless to say, they replaced the Mosaic philosophy with the philosophy of Christ.[9]

We must bear in mind, however, that the Greek philosophy at issue here is Greek philosophy reduced to philosophical discourse. We have seen that Christianity had presented itself as a philosophy—that is to say, as a way of life, even the *only* valid way of life. In tension with this Christian way of life, however, which was sometimes tinged by nuances borrowed from secular philosophy, the philosophical discourse of the various schools persisted. More precisely, what remained was the philosophical discourse of Neoplatonism, since from the third century A.D. onward Neoplatonism, the synthesis of Aristotelianism and Platonism, was the only philosophical school left. It was this Neoplatonic philosophical discourse that the Church Fathers would use, following Clement of Alexandria and Origen, to develop their theology. From this point of view, therefore, philosophy was the servant of theology from Christian antiquity onward. It contributed its own know-how, but was forced to adapt itself to the demands of its mistress.

There was also contamination. In the Trinity, God the Father took on many of the features of the Neoplatonic First God, while the Son was conceived of on the model of the second God of Numenius or the Intellect of Plotinus. The evolution of theological controversies finally led to the notion of a consubstantial Trinity. By drawing distinctions among nature, essence, substance, and hypostasis, Aristotelian logic and ontology, which had been integrated into Neoplatonism, furnished concepts that were indispensable for the formulation of the dogmas of the Trinity and the Incarnation. In return, Aristotelian ontology was refined and made more precise as a result of the nuances introduced by theological discussions.

According to Philo and Origen, the liberal arts were a propaedeutic for Greek philosophy, and Greek philosophy was a propae-

deutic for revealed philosophy. Gradually, however, the preparatory steps tended to fuse together. When Augustine of Hippo, in
his *De doctrina christiana,* enumerates the secular knowledge necessary for the Christian exegete, he places such liberal arts as
mathematics and dialectics almost on the same level as philosophy.[10] We find the same process of leveling-off at the beginning of
the Middle Ages—in Alcuin, for instance, during the Carolingian
period.[11]

From the ninth to the twelfth century, Greek philosophy continued to be used in theological debates, as it had been in the times
of the Church Fathers, thanks to a few works of Plato, Aristotle,
and Porphyry which were known through the translations and
commentaries written at the end of antiquity by Boethius, Macro-
bius, and Martianus Capella. Yet they also served to elaborate a
representation of the world. The Platonism of the School of
Chartres is a well-known phenomenon.[12] Throughout this period,
the liberal arts were part of the cycle of studies in the monastic
schools and cathedrals.[13]

From the thirteenth century onward, two new facts had great
influence on the evolution of thought in the Middle Ages. On the
one hand, there was the birth of the universities; on the other, the
widespread diffusion of translations of Aristotle. The rise of the
universities was concurrent with the flourishing of the cities and a
decline in the monastic schools, which, in the words of Maria-
Dominique Chenu, "unambitiously prepared the young monk for
reading the Bible and for divine service."[14] Within the city center,
the university was an intellectual corporation of masters and students, and, within the Church, it was a body dependent on ecclesi-
astical authority. It organized a scholastic *cursus,* a university year,
classes, discussion exercises, and exams. Teaching was distributed
between two faculties: the Faculty of Arts (where, in principle, the
liberal arts were taught) and the Faculty of Theology.

It was also in the thirteenth century that many of the works of

Aristotle, and of his Greek and Arabic commentators, were discovered. Aristotle's philosophy—that is to say, his philosophical discourse—was to play a key role in both faculties. The theologians would use Aristotle's dialectics—as well as his theory of knowledge and his physics, which opposed form to matter—in responding to problems which Christian dogmas posed to reason. In the Faculty of Arts, the teaching of Aristotle's philosophy (that is, commentaries on the dialectical, physical, and ethical works of Aristotle, who was called "the Philosopher") largely supplanted the teaching of the liberal arts.[15] Philosophy thus became identified with Aristotelianism, and the activity and career of "professor of philosophy" eventually consisted of commenting on the works of Aristotle and resolving the interpretative problems to which they gave rise. This philosophy and theology of professors and commentators has been called "Scholastic." In itself, as we have seen, Scholastics was nothing but the heir to the philosophical method most widely practiced at the end of antiquity, just as the scholastic exercises of *lectio* and *disputatio* merely extended the teaching and exercise methods which were in vogue in the schools of antiquity.[16]

THE ARTISTS OF REASON

I borrow the expression "artists of reason" from Kant, who uses the phrase to designate philosophers interested only in pure speculation.[17] The idea of a philosophy reduced to its conceptual content has survived to our own time. We encounter it every day in our university courses and in textbooks at every level; one could say that it is the classical, scholastic, university conception of philosophy. Consciously or unconsciously, our universities are still the heirs of the "School"—in other words, of the Scholastic tradition.

The "School," moreover, remains to this day, insofar as the popes of the nineteenth and twentieth centuries traditionally recommended Thomism to Catholic universities. The partisans of Neoscholastic or Thomist philosophy have continued, as in the Middle Ages, to view philosophy as a purely theoretical activity. This is why, for example, in the debate concerning the possibility and the significance of a Christian philosophy, a debate which arose around 1930, the problem of philosophy as a way of life was never brought up, so far as I know. The Neoscholastic philosopher Étienne Gilson formulated it in purely theoretical terms: Did Christianity introduce new concepts and problematics into the philosophical tradition? With his characteristic clarity of mind, he saw the essence of the problem: "The most favorable philosophical position is not that of the philosopher, but that of the Christian."[18]

Christianity's great superiority consisted in the fact that it was not "the simple abstract knowledge of the truth, but an efficacious method of salvation." To be sure, Gilson admitted, philosophy in antiquity was both a science and a life; but in the eyes of Christianity, ancient philosophy represented nothing but pure speculation, whereas Christianity itself is "a doctrine which brings with it, at the same time, all the means for putting itself into practice."[19] There could be no clearer affirmation that modern philosophy has come to consider itself a theoretical science because the existential dimension of philosophy no longer had any meaning from the perspective of Christianity, which was simultaneously both doctrine and life.

Yet the "School"—that is, the tradition of Scholastic philosophy—is not all there is. There are also the schools—not the philosophical communities of antiquity, but the universities, which, despite the diversity of their foundations and functions, are still the heirs of the medieval university. Just as, in antiquity, there was a close interaction between the social structure of philosophical institutions and their conception of philosophy, so, since the Middle

Ages, there has been a kind of reciprocal causality between the structure of university institutions and the notions they have entertained about the nature of philosophy.

This, at any rate, is what we glean from a text by Hegel, cited by Miguel Abensour and Pierre-Jean Labarrière in their excellent introduction to Schopenhauer's tract entitled *Against University Philosophy*. Hegel reminds us that philosophy is no longer "practiced as a private art, as it was by the Greeks, but now has an official existence, which therefore concerns the public; and it is principally or exclusively in the service of the State."[20]

It must be admitted that there is a radical opposition between the ancient philosophical school, which addressed individuals in order to transform their entire personality, and the university, whose mission is to give out diplomas which correspond to a certain level of objectifiable knowledge. Obviously, the Hegelian view of a university in the service of the State cannot be generalized. Still, universities come about only though the initiative of a higher authority, be it the State or the various religious communities (Catholic, Lutheran, Calvinist, Anglican). University philosophy therefore remains in the same position it occupied in the Middle Ages: it is still a servant, sometimes of theology, sometimes of science. In any case, it always serves the imperatives of the overall organization of education, or, in the contemporary period, of scientific research. The choice of professors, course topics, and exams is always subject to "objective" criteria which are political or financial, and unfortunately all too often foreign to philosophy.

Furthermore, the university tends to make the philosophy professor a civil servant whose job, to a large extent, consists in training other civil servants. The goal is no longer, as it was in antiquity, to train people for careers as human beings, but to train them for careers as clerks or professors—that is to say, as specialists, theoreticians, and retainers of specific items of more or less esoteric knowledge.[21] Such knowledge, however, no longer involves the whole of life, as ancient philosophy demanded.

With regard to Wittgenstein's ideas on the career of philosophy professor, Jacques Bouveresse has given an admirable analysis of the risk of "intellectual and moral perdition" which lies in wait for the professor:

> In a sense, there is no servitude more intolerable than that which constrains a man professionally to have an opinion in cases in which he may not necessarily have the least qualification. What is at issue here, from Wittgenstein's point of view, is not by any means the philosopher's "wisdom"—that is, the stock of theoretical knowledge he has at his disposition—but the personal price he has had to pay for what he believes he is able to think and say. . . . In the last analysis, a philosophy can be nothing other than the expression of an exemplary human experience.[22]

The dominance of Idealism over all university philosophy, from Hegel to the rise of existentialism and subsequently the vogue of structuralism, has done much to foster the idea that the only true philosophy must be theoretical and systematic.

Such, it seems to me, are the historical factors that have led to the conception of philosophy as pure theory.

THE PERMANENCE OF THE CONCEPT OF PHILOSOPHY
AS A WAY OF LIFE

Yet this transformation is not as radical as it may seem. Throughout the history of Western philosophy, we note a certain permanence and survival of the ancient notion. From the Middle Ages to today, some philosophers have remained faithful to the vital, existential dimension of ancient philosophy. At times, they have been active in the very heart of the university, but more often they were reacting against it. Sometimes they acted alone, but generally they did so from bases which were foreign to the university, such as certain religious or secular communities.

We saw above that thanks to translations of Aristotle made from Greek and Arabic, professors in Faculties of Arts had been able to read nearly all the works of a philosopher from antiquity. It is highly significant that, thanks to these texts, they discovered once again that philosophy is not only discourse but a way of life.[23] This fact is all the more interesting in that the philosopher in question is Aristotle, the philosopher usually considered a pure theoretician. With great perspicacity, however, the Aristotelian commentators saw that the essential point of philosophy for the "Philosopher" was precisely to devote oneself to a life of research, a life of contemplation, and above all an effort to assimilate oneself to the divine Intellect. Thus, Boethius of Dacia, taking up Aristotle's famous assertions at the end of Book X of the *Nicomachean Ethics,* states that mankind's end and happiness consist in living according to the highest part of his being: the intelligence, which is intended to contemplate the truth. Such a life is in conformity with the order of nature, which has subordinated the lower faculties to the higher ones. Only the philosopher, who devotes his life to investigating the truth, lives according to nature; and the life he leads is most delightful.[24] This text is echoed by the following declaration by Aubry of Reims:[25] "When we know we have achieved the end, all that is left is to savor and enjoy the pleasure. This is what is called wisdom, and this savoriness we have found can be loved for its own sake. This is philosophy, and it is here that we must stop." We find the same attitude in Dante, and in Meister Eckhart.[26] As Domański has written, this current of thought "accorded complete autonomy to philosophy, and did not consider it a mere propaedeutic to Christian doctrine."[27]

In the fourteenth century, Petrarch rejected the idea of a theoretical and descriptive ethics, noting that reading and commenting upon Aristotle's treatises on the subject had not made him a better person.[28] He therefore refused to apply the term "philosophers" to "professors sitting in a chair," and reserved the word for those who confirmed their teachings by their acts.[29] It is to Petrarch that we owe the following remark, which is essential to the perspective we are investigating: "It is more important to want the good than it is to know the truth."[30] We find the same attitude in Erasmus when he repeatedly affirms that the only philosopher is the person who lives philosophically, as did Socrates, Diogenes the Cynic, and Epictetus, but also like John the Baptist, Christ, and the Apostles.[31] We must note that when Petrarch and Erasmus speak of the philosophical life, they, like some Church Fathers and some of the monks, have in mind a Christian philosophical life. As we have seen, moreover, they admitted that some pagan philosophers also realized the ideal of the philosopher.

During the Renaissance, we see the renewal not only of the doctrinal tendencies of ancient philosophy, but also of its concrete attitudes: Epicureanism, Stoicism, Platonism, Skepticism. Montaigne's *Essays*, for example, show the philosopher trying to practice the various modes of life proposed by ancient philosophy: "My trade and my art is living."[32] His spiritual itinerary led him from the Stoicism of Seneca to the probabilism of Plutarch,[33] through Skepticism, and finally—definitively—to Epicureanism: "'Today I did nothing.' 'What? Have you not lived? Not only is that the fundamental point, but it is the most illustrious of your occupations . . . Our great and glorious masterpiece is to live appropriately. To know how to loyally delight in our being is a perfection which is absolute, and as if divine.'"[34]

Michel Foucault held that the "theoreticizing" of philosophy began with Descartes, not in the Middle Ages.[35] As I have said elsewhere, I agree with him when he says: "Before Descartes, a subject could have access to the truth only by carrying out beforehand a certain work upon himself which made him susceptible of knowing the truth." We need only recall what I said above with regard to Aristotle and Porphyry. I depart from Foucault, however, when he adds that, according to Descartes, "in order to accede to the truth, it is enough that I be any subject capable of seeing what is evident. . . . Evidence has been substituted for *askēsis.*"

I believe that when Descartes chose to give one of his works the title *Meditations,* he knew perfectly well that the word designated an exercise of the soul within the tradition of ancient spirituality. Each *Meditation* is indeed a spiritual exercise—that is, work by oneself and upon oneself which must be finished before one can move to the next stage. As has been shown with great finesse by the novelist and philosopher Michel Butor, these exercises are presented with tremendous literary skill.[36] For although Descartes speaks in the first person (evoking the fire before which he is sitting, the robe he is wearing, and the paper in front of him), and although he describes the feelings he is experiencing, what he really wishes is that his reader should traverse the stages of the inner evolution he describes. In other words, the "I" used in the *Meditations* is in fact a "You" which is addressed to the reader. Here, once again, we encounter that movement—so frequent in antiquity— by which one passes from the individual self to a self elevated to the plane of universality. Each *Meditation* deals with only one subject—for instance, methodical doubt is discussed in the first *Meditation,* and the discovery of the self as a thinking reality in the second. This enables the reader to assimilate the exercise practiced in each *Meditation.* As Aristotle said, "It takes time for what we have learned to become our nature." Descartes, too, knows that it takes lengthy "meditation" to make the new self-consciousness we have gained enter into our memory. With regard to methodical doubt, he writes: "I have not been able to dispense with giving doubt an entire *Meditation;* and I would that my readers take not only the little time necessary to read it, but some months, or at least some weeks, to consider the things with which it deals, before they move on to something else."[37] With regard to the means for becoming aware of the self as a thinking reality, Descartes writes: "The self must be examined often, and considered for a long time, . . . and this has seemed to me a sufficient cause for dealing with no other matter in the second *Meditation.*" The third *Meditation* also presents itself, in its first lines, as a highly Platonic spiritual exercise, since its goal is radically to separate the self from sensory knowledge: "I shall now close my eyes; I shall stop up my ears; and I shall even erase from my thoughts all images of corporeal things. . . . And thus, conversing only with myself and considering my inner parts, I shall try to make myself, bit by bit, better known and more familiar to myself."

More generally, it does not seem to me that Cartesian evidence is accessible to all perceiving minds. Indeed, in the lines from the *Discourse on Method* which mention the precept of evidence, it is impossible not to recognize the Stoic definition of the adequate or comprehensive representation: "The first was never to accept any thing as true which I do not evidently know to be such; that is to say, carefully to avoid precipitation and preconceptions, and to comprehend in my judgments nothing more than what presents itself to my mind so clearly and distinctly that I should have no occasion to place it in doubt."[38] This is precisely the Stoic discipline of assent.[39] As in Stoicism, this discipline is not equally accessible to just any mind, for it too demands an *askēsis* and an effort, which consists in avoiding "precipitation" *(aproptōsia, propeteia).* The extent to which the ancient conception of philosophy is present in Descartes is not always adequately measured. This is true, for instance, of the *Letters to Princess Elisabeth,* which are to some extent letters of spiritual guidance.

For Kant, the ancient definition of philosophy as *philo-sophia*—the desire for, love of, and exercise of wisdom—was still valuable. Philosophy, says Kant, is "the doctrine and exercise of wisdom (not simple science)," and he knows the distance which separates philosophy from wisdom: "Man does not possess wisdom; he only tends toward it and can feel love for it. Yet this is already sufficiently meritorious."[40] Philosophy, for mankind, consists of

efforts toward wisdom which always remain unfulfilled.[41] The entire technical edifice of critical Kantian philosophy has meaning
only from the perspective of wisdom, or rather from that of the
sage. Kant usually imagines wisdom in the figure of the sage—an
ideal norm, never incarnate in a human being, but according to
which the philosopher tries to live. Kant also calls this model of
the sage the "Idea of the philosopher." "There exists no philosopher corresponding to this model, any more than there exists any
true Christian. Both are models. . . . Models must serve as norms.
. . . The 'philosopher' is only an idea. Perhaps we may glance at
him, and imitate him in some ways, but we shall never totally
reach him."[42] Here, Kant situates himself within the tradition of
Socrates, who in the *Symposium* says that the only thing he knows
is that he is not a sage and has not yet reached the ideal model of
the sage. This Socratism, moreover, foreshadows that of
Kierkegaard, who said he was a Christian only insofar as he knew
he was not Christian. Kant writes: "The Idea of wisdom must be
the foundation of philosophy, just as the Idea of sanctity is the
foundation of Christianity."[43] He uses the expression "Idea of wisdom" as well as "Idea of philosophy or of the philosopher," since
the ideal constituted by wisdom is precisely the ideal which the
philosopher pursues:

> Some ancient philosophers have approached the model of the true
> philosopher, as has Rousseau; yet they have not reached it. Many,
> perhaps, will believe that we already possess the doctrine of wis-
> dom and that we should not consider it a simple Idea, since we own
> so many books filled with prescriptions which tell us how we ought
> to act. Yet these, for the most part, are tautological propositions and
> demands which we cannot stand to hear, for they show us no
> means of attaining them.[44]

As he continues, Kant evokes ancient philosophy:

> A hidden Idea of philosophy has long been present among men. Yet
> either they have not understood it, or else they have considered it a

contribution to erudition. If we take the ancient Greek philosophers—such as Epicurus, Zeno, Socrates—we discover that the principal object of their science has been the destination of man, and the means to achieve it. They thus remained much more faithful to the true Idea of the philosopher than has been the case in modern times, when we encounter the philosopher only as an artist of reason.[45]

After describing the teaching and especially the life of Socrates, Epicurus, and Diogenes, Kant says that the ancients required their to philosophers live as they taught: "Plato asked an old man who told him that he was listening to lectures on virtue: 'When are you finally going to start *living* virtuously?' The point is not always to speculate; ultimately, we must think of actual practice. Nowadays, however, he who lives in a way which conforms with what he teaches is taken to be a dreamer."[46] So long as the sage, perfect in way of life and knowledge, is not realized on this earth, there will be no philosophy. "There is a teacher, [conceived] in the ideal. . . . Him alone we must call philosopher; but . . . he nowhere exists."[47] Philosophy, in the proper sense of the term, does not exist and perhaps shall never exist. All we can do is philosophize—that is, carry out an exercise of reason, guided by our Idea of a "teacher in the ideal."[48]

In fact, two ideas or representations of philosophy are possible: one which Kant calls the "scholastic" concept of philosophy, and another which he calls the "worldly" concept of philosophy.[49] As a scholarly or scholastic concept, philosophy is nothing but pure speculation. It aims only at being systematic, and it aspires to the logical perfection of knowledge. He who is content with the scholastic concept of philosophy, says Kant, is an artist of reason; he is what Plato calls a *philodoxos*, or "friend of opinion."[50] He is interested in many beautiful things, but does not see beauty-in-itself; intrigued by many just things, he does not see justice-in-itself. This is equivalent to saying that he is not perfectly systematic, for he does not see the unity of the universally human interest which animates all philosophical effort.[51] In fact, for Kant, the scholarly concept of philosophy remains at the level of pure theory, and only the concept of "philosophy of the world" is situated within the perspective of the ultimate meaning of philosophy and can truly unify the world.

What is this concept of "philosophy of the world"? Kant also speaks of a "cosmic" or "cosmopolitan" concept.[52] This expression is disconcerting to us; but we must place it in the context of the eighteenth century, the era of the Enlightenment. The word "cosmic" here refers not to the physical "world" but to the human world, which is to say the world of the individual, who lives in a world of other human beings. The opposition between scholastic philosophy and philosophy of the world already existed before Kant—for instance, in the work of J. G. Sulzer (1759).[53] For Sulzer, "philosophy of the world" consisted in human experience and the wisdom which results from it. This distinction corresponds to the Enlightenment's general tendency to force philosophy to leave the closed, fixed circle of the school so that it could become accessible to everyone. We must emphasize this characteristic of the philosophy of the eighteenth century, which tends, as in antiquity, to reunite philosophical discourse and way of life.

Yet the Kantian notion of cosmic philosophy is more profound than philosophy of the world, which was popular in the eighteenth century; for "cosmic" philosophy ultimately refers to the wisdom incarnate in the ideal sage. What has always been the basis for the notion of philo-sophy (that is, the search for wisdom) is, says Kant, the idea of a "cosmic" philosophy, a philosophy "of the world," not the idea of a scholastic philosophy, "especially when the notion was personified, so to speak, and imagined as a model of the philosopher, which exists in the ideal." In other words, it was seen in the figure of the sage. "In this sense, one would be arrogant if one called oneself a philosopher and claimed to be able to equal a model which exists only in the ideal."[54]

Such a sage, or ideal philosopher, would be the "legislator of reason": he would govern himself according to his own law, which would be the law of reason. Although the ideal sage is nowhere to be found, at least "the Idea of his legislation is found everywhere, in all human reason." This enables us to understand that our reason formulates the imperatives which direct human action by the light of the Idea of the ideal sage.[55] In the categorical imperative— "Act only on that maxim whereby thou canst at the same time will that it should become a universal law"[56]—the self realizes itself and transcends itself, even as it universalizes itself. This imperative must be unconditional—that is, it must not be based upon any particular interest. On the contrary, it must incline the individual to act only in the perspective of the universal. Here again, we encounter one of the fundamental themes of the way of life proper to ancient philosophy.

No doubt the reader will still wonder why Kant called this philosophical program, dominated by the idea of wisdom, the "concept of cosmic philosophy." Perhaps we can have a better understanding of the term after reading this Kantian definition:[57] "By 'cosmical concept' [*Weltbegriff*] is here meant the concept which relates to that in which everyone necessarily has an interest"—in other words, since the world (cosmos) in question here is the human world, "that notion which interests everyone."

What interests everyone, or rather what *should* interest everyone, is nothing other than wisdom. The normal, natural, everyday state of human beings ought to be wisdom, but they cannot reach it; this was another of the fundamental ideas of ancient philosophy. It amounts to saying that what interests each person is not only the Kantian-critical question "What can I know?" but especially questions like "What should I do?" "What may I hope for?" "What is humankind?"—which are the fundamental questions of philosophy.[58]

This idea of the interest of reason is very important, for it is linked to the idea of the primacy of practical reason with regard to theoretical reason. As Kant says, "all interest is ultimately practical, and even that of speculative reason is conditional, and it is only in the practical employment of reason that it is complete."[59] In fact, Kantian philosophy is addressed only to those who feel this practical interest for the moral good, who are gifted with moral sentiment, and who opt for a supreme end and a sovereign good. It is, moreover, remarkable that in his *Critique of the Faculty of Judgment,* this interest for the moral good and this moral sentiment appear as the precondition for the interest we can feel for the beauty of nature: "This immediate interest in the beauty of nature is not in fact common. It is peculiar to those whose habits of thought are already trained to the good or else are eminently susceptible of such training."[60]

Kant's theoretical discourse, both on his part and on the part of his audience, is linked to a decision—an act of faith leading to the choice of a certain way of life, inspired, in the last analysis, by the model of the sage. We thus see the extent to which Kant was influenced by the ancient concept of philosophy. Moreover, in the "ethical ascetics" which Kant proposes at the end of his *Metaphysics of Morals,* he sets out the rules for the exercise of virtue, trying to reconcile Epicurean serenity with the tension of Stoic duty.[61]

It would take a large volume to tell the entire history of the reception of ancient philosophy by medieval and modern philosophy. I have chosen to concentrate on a few major figures: Montaigne, Descartes, Kant. We might mention many other thinkers— as different as Rousseau, Shaftesbury,[62] Schopenhauer, Emerson, Thoreau, Kierkegaard, Marx, Nietzsche, William James, Bergson, Wittgenstein, Merleau-Ponty, and still others. All, in one way or another, were influenced by the model of ancient philosophy, and conceived of philosophy not only as a concrete, practical activity but also as a transformation of our way of inhabiting and perceiving the world.

CHAPTER TWELVE

Questions and Perspectives

Now that we have reached the end of this work, the author notices everything he has left unsaid, as well as the questions the reader would like to ask him. If, for instance, the "theoreticizing" of philosophy has been presented as the result of the encounter between Christianity and philosophy, wouldn't it have been better to give an overall study of the relations between philosophy and religion, both in antiquity and in the modern world? In antiquity, the philosopher encountered religion in his social life (in the form of the official cult) and in his cultural life (in the form of works of art and of literature), yet he lived religion philosophically, by transforming it into philosophy. If Epicurus recommended participation in civic festivals and even in prayer, this was to allow the Epicurean philosopher to contemplate the gods as conceived by the Epicurean theory of nature. Even the late Neoplatonists, who practiced theurgy, integrated it into a course of spiritual progress which was essentially philosophical, in order to rise ultimately to a transcendent and unknowable God who was completely foreign to traditional religion. Although they constructed a rational theology according to which philosophical entities corresponded to the gods of the official religion, this theology no longer had much in common with the ancient beliefs which they wanted to defend against Christianity. The philosophical way of life never entered into competition with religion in antiquity, because at the time religion was not a way of life which included all of existence and all of inner life, as it was in Christianity. It was, rather, philosophical discourse which could collide with the received ideas on the gods within the city, as it did in the case of Anaxagoras and of Socrates.

As we have seen, the relations between philosophy and Christianity were much more complex, and it would take a lengthy study to define them. It could be said that almost all philosophies since the Middle Ages have felt the influence of Christianity. On the one hand, their philosophical discourse developed within an intimate relation with Christianity, whether in order to justify Christian doctrine—directly or indirectly—or to combat it. On this point, one must commend the work of Étienne Gilson, who shows how the philosophy of Descartes, Malebranche, and Leibniz is, in the last analysis, situated within the Christian problematic.[1] He might also have added Kant's name,[2] but it must be admitted that by assimilating Christian faith to moral faith, Kant essentially transformed Christianity into a philosophy. Moreover, from the Middle Ages, through Petrarch and Erasmus or the Christian Stoics and Epicureans, to the Christian existentialism of Gabriel Marcel, the philosophical way of life was long identified with the Christian way of life—so much so, that we can discern traces of Christianity even in the existential attitudes of modern-day philosophers.[3] Nor is this surprising, given the strength of this tradition, which suffused the entire Western tradition. One would therefore need lengthy reflection in order to give a more adequate definition of the relations between philosophy and religion.

It may also be useful to give a brief overview of my notion of philosophy. I am quite ready to accept that philosophy, both today and in antiquity, is a theoretical and "conceptualizing" activity. I also believe, however, that in antiquity it was the philosopher's choice of a way of life which conditioned and determined the fundamental tendencies of his philosophical discourse. I also think that this is ultimately true of all philosophy. I do not mean, of course, that the philosopher is determined by a blind, arbitrary choice; I mean that practical reason takes primacy over theoretical reason. Philosophical reflection is, in Kant's words, motivated and guided by "that which interests reason"—in other words, by the choice of a way of life. I would agree with Plotinus that "it is desire that engenders thought."[4] Nevertheless, there is a kind of reciprocal interaction or causality between what the philosopher profoundly wants, what interests him in the strongest sense of the term—that is, the answer to the question "How should I live?"—and what he tries to elucidate and illuminate by means of reflection. Reflection is inseparable from the will. On occasion, this interaction also exists in modern or contemporary philosophies, and we can, up to a point, explain philosophical discourses by the existential choices which motivate them. For instance, we know from one of Wittgenstein's letters that his *Tractatus Logico-Philosophicus*, which is apparently, and indeed truly is, a theory of the proposition, is nevertheless fundamentally a book of ethics in which "what pertains to ethics" is not said but shown.[5] Wittgenstein elaborates his theory of the proposition in order to justify this silence concerning ethics, which is foreseen and deliberate from the beginning of the book. What motivates the *Tractatus* is the will to lead the reader to a certain kind of life, and a certain attitude, which, moreover, is fully analogous to the existential options of ancient philosophy: "to live within the present,"[6] without regretting, fearing, or hoping for anything.[7] We have seen that many modern and contemporary philosophers have remained faithful, in Kant's terms, to the Idea of philosophy. In the last analysis, it is the scholastic *teaching* of philosophy, and especially of the history of philosophy, which has always had a tendency to emphasize the theoretical, abstract, and conceptual side of philosophy.

This is why it is necessary to insist on a few methodological imperatives. In order to understand the philosophical works of antiquity, we must take into consideration the particular conditions of philosophical life at that time. We must discern the philosopher's underlying intention, which was not to develop a discourse which had its end in itself but to act upon souls. In fact, each assertion must be understood from the perspective of the effect it was intended to produce in the soul of the auditor or reader. Whether the goal was to convert, to console, to cure, or to exhort the audience, the point was always and above all not to communicate to them some ready-made knowledge but to *form* them. In other words, the goal was to learn a type of know-how; to develop a *habitus*, or new capacity to judge and to criticize; and to *transform*—that is, to change people's way of living and of seeing the world. If, then, we remember that philosophy's assertions are intended not to communicate knowledge but to form and to train, it will come as no surprise if we find *aporiai* in Plato, Aristotle, or Plotinus in which thought seems to be enclosed—points at which there are reformulations, repetitions, and apparent incoherences.

The relation between a work and its addressee is of the utmost importance, for the content of the work is partially determined by the necessity of adapting itself to the addressee's spiritual capacities. We must never forget to situate the works of ancient philosophers within the perspective of the life of the school to which they belonged, for they almost always bear a relation—direct or indirect—to the teaching. For instance, Aristotle's treatises are, to a large extent, preparations for oral teaching, while Plotinus' treatises are echoes of difficulties which were brought up during his classes. Finally, most works of antiquity, whether philosophical or otherwise, were intimately related to orality. They were intended to be read out loud, often at public readings. Such a close link between writing and speech can explain some of the unnerving particularities of ancient philosophical writings.

The reader will also no doubt wish to ask if I think the ancient concept of philosophy might still exist today. I think I have already answered this question, at least in part, by showing how many philosophers of the modern period, from Montaigne to the present, have considered philosophy not as a simple theoretical discourse but as a practice, an *askēsis,* and a transformation of the self. This concept is therefore still "actual" and can always be reactualized.[8] For my part, I would put the question differently: Isn't there an urgent need to rediscover the ancient notion of the "philosopher"— that living, choosing philosopher without whom the notion of philosophy has no meaning? Why not define the philosopher not as a professor or a writer who develops a philosophical discourse, but, in accordance with the concept which was constant in antiquity, as a person who leads a philosophical life? Shouldn't we revise the habitual use of the word "philosopher" (which usually refers only to the theoretician) so that it applies to the person who practices philosophy, just as Christians can practice Christianity without being theorists or theologians? Do we ourselves have to construct a philosophical system before we can live philosophically? This does not mean, of course, that we needn't reflect upon our own experience, as well as that of philosophers of both past and present.

Yet what does it mean to "live like a philosopher"? What is the practice of philosophy? In this book I have tried to show, among other things, that philosophical practice is relatively independent from philosophical discourse. The same spiritual exercise can be justified after the fact by widely different philosophical discourses, in order to describe and justify experiences whose existential density ultimately escapes all attempts at theoreticizing and systematizing. For instance, the Stoics and the Epicureans, for various and almost opposite reasons, advised their disciples to live always aware of the imminence of death, freeing themselves from the worry of the future and the weight of the past. Yet the person who practices this exercise of concentration sees the universe with new eyes, as if he were seeing it for the first and the last time. In his enjoyment of the present, he discovers the splendor and mystery of existence and of the world's emergence; at the same time, he achieves serenity by experiencing how relative are the things which provoke anxiety and worry. Similarly, Stoics, Epicureans, and Platonists, each for their own reasons, exhorted their disciples to raise themselves to a cosmic perspective, plunge into the immensity of space and time, and thereby transform their vision of the world.

Seen in this way, the practice of philosophy transcends the oppositions of particular philosophies. It is essentially an effort to become aware of ourselves, our being-in-the-world, and our being-with-others. It is also, as Maurice Merleau-Ponty used to say, an effort to "relearn how to see the world" and attain a universal vision, thanks to which we can put ourselves in the place of others and transcend our own partiality.[9]

There is a text by Georges Friedmann that I have often cited in other works. It seems to be of capital importance here, insofar as it shows how a contemporary man, engaged in political struggle, realizes that he can and should live as a philosopher:

"To take flight" every day! At least for a moment, which may be brief, so long as it is intense. A "spiritual exercise" every day—alone or in the company of a person who also wants to better himself.

Spiritual exercises. Leave duration behind. Try to strip yourself of your own passions, of the vanities and the rash of noise surrounding your name (which, from time to time, itches like a chronic affliction). Flee backbiting. Strip yourself of pity and of hatred. Love all free human beings. Become eternal by transcending yourself.

This effort upon yourself is necessary; this ambition is just. Many are those who become completely absorbed in militant politics and the preparation of the social revolution. Few, very few, are

those who, to prepare for the revolution, are willing to make themselves worthy of it.[10]

Yet philosophers in antiquity, in order to practice philosophy,
lived in more or less close proximity to a community of other philosophers, or at least they received their rules of life from a philosophical tradition. Their task was thereby made easier, even if actually living according to such rules of life demanded strenuous
effort. Today there are no more schools, and the "philosopher" is
alone. How shall he find his way?

He will find it as many others have found it before him—as
Montaigne, Goethe, or Nietzsche found it. They, too, were alone,
but in accordance with their circumstances and innermost needs,
they chose the ways of life of ancient philosophy as their models.
Nietzsche, for instance, wrote as follows: "So far as praxis is concerned, I view the various moral schools as experimental laborato-
ries in which a considerable number of recipes for the art of living
have been thoroughly practiced and lived to the hilt. The results of
all their experiments belong to us, as our legitimate property.
Thus, we will not hesitate to adopt a Stoic recipe just because we
have profited in the past from Epicurean recipes."[11] It is lengthy
experience acquired over centuries, and lengthy discussions about
such experience, which give the ancient models their value. To
use the Stoic model and the Epicurean model—successively or al-
ternately—was a way of achieving a certain balance in life for
Nietzsche, but also for Montaigne, Goethe, Kant, Wittgenstein,
and Jaspers.[12] And there are other models that could just as effectively inspire and guide philosophical practice.

The reader might also ask how these ancient models could still
be reactualized, despite the intervening centuries of global evolution. First of all, as Nietzsche remarked, this could happen because
the ancient schools were a kind of experimental laboratory, thanks
to which we can compare the consequences of the various types of

spiritual experience they proposed. From this point of view, the plurality of ancient schools is precious. But the models they offer can be actualized only if they are reduced to their essence or their most profound significance. They must be detached from their antiquated cosmological and mythical elements, so that their fundamental positions, which the schools themselves considered essential, can be brought out. We can go further—for as I have said elsewhere, I believe these models correspond to permanent, fundamental attitudes which all human beings find necessary when they set about seeking wisdom.[13] In *The Inner Citadel* I spoke of a kind of universal Stoicism, which we find not only in the West but also, as Jacques Gernet has shown, in China.[14] As I said, I have long been hostile to comparative philosophy because I thought it could cause confusions and arbitrary connections. Now, however, as I read the works of my colleagues Guy Bugault, Roger-Pol Droit, Michel Hulin, and J.-L. Solère, it seems to me that there really are troubling analogies between the philosophical attitudes of antiquity and those of the Orient.[15] These analogies cannot be explained by historical influences; nevertheless, they do perhaps give us a better understanding of all that can be involved in philosophical attitudes which illuminate one another in this way. The means that enable us to achieve inner peace and communion with other human beings, or with the universe, are not unlimited. Perhaps we should say that the choices of life we have described—those of Socrates, Pyrrho, Epicurus, the Stoics, the Cynics, and the Skeptics—correspond to constant, universal models which are found, in various forms, in every civilization, throughout the various cultural zones of humanity. This is why I earlier mentioned a Buddhist text, as well as some considerations by Hulin, who was inspired by Buddhism: because I thought they could give us a better understanding of the essence of the Greek sage. It is most interesting that in Greece, India, and China, one of the paths to wisdom is indifference, or the refusal to accord things differences in value.

Such differences express the egoistic, partial, and limited viewpoint of the individual—the viewpoint of "the frog at the bottom of the well" or of "a vinegar-fly at the bottom of a barrel," as mentioned by Chuang-tzu: "All I knew of the Tao was what a vinegar-fly stuck inside a barrel can know of the universe. If the master had not lifted the lid, I would still be unaware of the universe in its integral grandeur."[16] Such disinterestedness and indifference bring us back to an original state: the quiet and peace which exists deep within us. It preexists the affirmation of our individuality against the world and against other people, and hence preexists the egotism and egocentricity which separate us from the universe, and which sweep us inexorably into the worried pursuit of pleasure and the perpetual fear of pain.

Spiritual exercises such as "living in the present" and "looking at things from above" can be found in Goethe, Nietzsche, and Wittgenstein.[17] They are quite accessible to the "philosopher," in the sense in which we understand him. I hope to return to this theme in future works.

More generally, I hope I have implied that, in Solère's words, "the ancients were perhaps closer to the Orient than we are."[18] The same point is made by a modern Chinese author who writes: "Chinese philosophers were all Socrates, to various degrees. Knowledge and wisdom were inseparable in the person of the philosopher. His philosophy demanded that he live it, and he himself was its vehicle. Living in accordance with his philosophical convictions was a part of his philosophy."[19] The "philosopher," or lover of wisdom, in the sense in which we understand these terms, can therefore seek models of life in the oriental philosophies, and these will not be so very far from the ancient models.

Such a "philosopher" will, moreover, be exposed to many risks. The first of these will be the temptation to be satisfied with philosophical discourse. There is an abyss between fine phrases and becoming genuinely aware of oneself, truly transforming oneself. It certainly seems, moreover, as if the deepest reason for the "theoreticizing" of philosophy is this tendency—innate, as it were, to the philosopher—which leads him to be satisfied with discourse, or the conceptual architecture which he builds, rebuilds, or admires. Throughout the history of ancient philosophy, and in all the schools, we encounter the same warnings against the danger the philosopher incurs, if he thinks his philosophical discourse can be sufficient unto itself without being linked to a philosophical life. Plato already sensed this ever-present danger when, in order to justify his decision to go to Syracuse, he wrote: "I was afraid that I would see myself as a fine talker, incapable of resolutely undertaking an action."[20]

Another danger, the worst of all, is to believe that one can do without philosophical reflection. The philosophical way of life must be justified in rational, motivated discourse, and such discourse is inseparable from the way of life. Nevertheless, we have to reflect critically on the ancient, modern, and oriental discourses which justify a given way of life. We must try to render explicit the reasons we act in such-and-such a way, and reflect on our experience and that of others. Without such reflection, the philosophical life risks sinking into vapid banality, "respectable" feelings, or deviance. To be sure, we cannot wait until we have read Kant's *Critique of Pure Reason* in order to live as philosophers. Nevertheless, living as a philosopher also means to reflect, to reason, to conceptualize in a rigorous, technical way—or, as Kant used to say, "to think for oneself." The philosophical life is a never-ending quest.[21]

Finally, and despite the tenacious clichés which still clog philosophy manuals, we must never forget that ancient philosophical life was always intimately linked to the care for others, and that this demand is inherent in the philosophical life, especially when it is lived in the contemporary world. In the words of Georges Friedmann: "A modern sage—if such existed—would not turn away from the human sewer, as so many disgusted aesthetes have done."[22] That said, however, Friedmann found the problems in the relations between ancient philosophers and the State almost insoluble. We must agree, for the "engaged" philosopher always runs the risk of letting himself be swept along by political passions and hatreds. This is why it was vital, in Friedmann's view, that in order to improve the human situation we concentrate our strength "on limited groups, even on individuals," and "on the spiritual effort (the transformation of a few)," which, he thought, would eventually be communicated and diffused. The philosopher is cruelly aware of his solitude and impotence in a world which is torn between two states of unconsciousness: that which derives from the idolatry of money, and that which results in the face of the misery and suffering of billions of human beings. In such conditions, the philosopher will surely never be able to attain the absolute serenity of the sage. To do philosophy will therefore also mean to suffer from this isolation and this impotence. But ancient philosophy also teaches us not to resign ourselves, but to continue to act reasonably and try to live according to the norm constituted by the Idea of wisdom, whatever happens, and even if our action seems very limited to us. In the words of Marcus Aurelius: "Do not wait for Plato's Republic, but be happy if one little thing leads to progress, and reflect on the fact that what results from such a little thing is not, in fact, so very little."[23]

Notes

INTRODUCTION

1. The work by G. Deleuze and F. Guattari entitled *Qu'est-ce que la philosophie?* (Paris 1991) is quite distant, both in spirit and method, from the present work; whereas the very interesting little book by A. Philonenko entitled *Qu'est-ce que la philosophie? Kant et Fichte* (Paris 1991) poses the problem of the essence of philosophy with regard to the letters of Fichte and of Kant. The *Historisches Wörterbuch der Philosophie*, vol. 7 *(P–Q)*, (Basel, 1989), cols. 572–927, contains a remarkable array of studies on the definition of philosophy from antiquity to our time.
2. Aristotle, *Politics*, I, 2, 1252a24.
3. É. Weil, *Logique de la philosophie* (Paris, 1950), p. 13.
4. On this point, see Gottfried Gabriel, "La logique comme littérature? De la signification de la forme littéraire chez Wittgenstein," *Le Nouveau Commerce*, 82–83 (1992), p. 84.
5. [On "theoretic" and "theoretical," see page 293, n. 13.—*Trans.*]
6. J. Ruffié, *De la biologie à la culture* (Paris, 1976), p. 357.
7. J. P. Vernant also uses this term; see his *Mythe et pensée chez les Grecs*, vol. 1 (Paris, 1971), p. 96. In English, *Myth and Thought among the Greeks* (London and Boston, 1983).

1. PHILOSOPHY BEFORE PHILOSOPHY

1. The fragments of their works can be found in J. P. Dumont, ed., *Les Présocratiques* (Paris: Gallimard, Pléiade, 1988). [For a discussion in

English, see G. S. Kirk, J. E. Raven, and M. Schofield, *The Presocratic Philosophers*, 2nd ed. (Cambridge, 1983).—*Trans.*]

2. G. Naddaf, *L'origine et l'évolution du concept grec de phusis* (Lewiston, N.Y.: Edwin Mellen, 1992).

3. Heraclitus, in Dumont, ed., *Les Présocratiques*, p. 154, fragment 35 [in English in C. H. Kahn, *The Art and Thought of Heraclitus* (Cambridge: Cambridge University Press, 1979), p. 33, fragment IX.— *Trans.*]. Plato, *Phaedo*, 96a7.

4. See P. Hadot, "Physique et poésie dans le *Timée* de Platon," *Revue de Théologie et de Philosophie*, 115 (1983), pp. 113–133; Naddaf, *L'origine et l'évolution*, pp. 341–442.

5. See Naddaf, *L'origine et l'évolution*, pp. 443–535.

6. On the beginnings of moral education among the Greeks, see I. Hadot, *Seneca und die griechisch-römische Tradition der Seelenleitung* (Berlin: De Gruyter, 1969), pp. 10–38; and eadem, "The Spiritual Guide," in A. H. Armstrong, ed., *Classical Mediterranean Spirituality: Egyptian, Greek, Roman* (New York: Crossroad, 1986), pp. 436–459.

7. On *paideia* in archaic Greece and Athens to the end of the fifth century, see W. Jaeger, *Paideia: The Ideals of Greek Culture*, 3 vols. (New York: Oxford University Press, 1969), trans. G. Highet from the 2nd edition (Berlin: De Gruyter, 1936–1947). See also H.-I. Marrou, *Histoire de l'éducation dans l'antiquité* (Paris, 1950) [trans. G. Lamb as *A History of Education in Antiquity* (New York: Sheed and Ward, 1956)—*Trans.*]; and the chapter "The Origins of Higher Education at Athens," in J. P. Lynch, *Aristotle's School: A Study of a Greek Educational Institution* (Berkeley, 1972), pp. 32–68.

8. See Jaeger, *Paideia*, pp. 29ff., which discusses the difference between education (of the aristocrat, in conformity with the ideals of his caste), and culture (of man as he should be, according to philosophy).

9. Ibid., pp. 26–28.

10. On the conflicts between the philosophers and the city-state, see P. Decharme, *La critique des traditions religieuses chez les Grecs* (Paris, 1904), which is old but still useful.

11. On *sunousia*, see Plato, *Apology*, 19e.

12. The fragments of the Sophists can be found in Dumont, ed., *Les Présocratiques*, pp. 981–1178; and in J. P. Dumont, *Les Sophistes:*

Fragments et témoignages (Paris, 1969). On the Sophists, see
G. Romeyer-Dherbey, *Les Sophistes* (Paris, 1985); J. de Romilly, *Les
grands sophistes dans l'Athènes de Périclès* (Paris, 1988) [trans.
J. Lloyd as *The Great Sophists in Periclean Athens* (Oxford: Claren-
don, 1992—*Trans.*]; Naddaf, *L'origine et l'évolution,* pp. 267–338;
Lynch, *Aristotle's School,* pp. 38–46; B. Cassin, *L'effet sophistique*
(Paris, 1995).
13. Plato, *Sophist,* 222a–2224d; Aristotle, *Sophistical Refutations,* 165a22.

2. THE INCEPTION OF THE IDEA OF "DOING PHILOSOPHY"

1. For opposing views on this subject, see R. Joly, *Le thème
philosophique des genres de vie dans l'Antiquité classique* (Brussels,
1956); W. Burkert, "Platon oder Pythagoras? Zum Ursprung des
Wortes 'Philosophie,'" *Hermes,* 88 (1960), pp. 159–177; C. J. de
Vogel, *Pythagoras and Early Pythagoreanism* (Assen, 1966), pp. 15,
96–102. I agree with Burkert that the anecdote told by Heraclides
Ponticus (see Diogenes Laertius, I, 12; Cicero, *Tusculan Disputations,*
V, 8; Iamblichus, *Life of Pythagoras,* 58) is an instance in which the
Platonic notion of *philosophia* was projected upon Pythagoras.
2. Heraclitus B35, in J. P. Dumont, ed., *Les Présocratiques* (Paris:
Gallimard, Pléiade, 1988), p. 74; in English in C. H. Kahn, *The Art
and Thought of Heraclitus* (Cambridge: Cambridge University Press,
1979), p. 32, fragment IX. In his note *ad loc.* p. 780, Dumont expresses doubts about the authenticity of the word "philosophy"; so
too Diels-Kranz, *Die Vorsokratiker,* vol. 1 (Dublin and Zurich, 1969),
p. 159.
3. Herodotus, *Histories,* I, 30.
4. If Heraclitus really did speak of "philosophers" in his fragment 35,
then he established a link between philosophy and inquiry.
5. On the word *philosophia,* see also E. A. Havelock, *Preface to Plato*
(Cambridge, Mass., 1963), pp. 280–283; Burkert, "Platon oder Pythagoras?" p. 172.
6. Isocrates, *Panegyric,* §47.
7. See B. Gladigow, *Sophia und Kosmos* (Hildesheim, 1965); G. B.
Kerferd, "The Image of the Wise Man in Greece in the Period before

Plato," in F. Bossier, ed., *Images of Man in Ancient and Medieval Thought*, Festschrift Verbeke (Louvain, 1976), pp. 18–28.

8. Homer, *Iliad*, 15, 411.
9. *Homeric Hymn to Hermes*, I, 511.
10. J. Bollack, "Une histoire de *sophie*" (review of Gladigow, *Sophia und Kosmos*), *Revue des Études Grecques*, 81 (1968), p. 551.
11. Solon, *Elegies*, I, 52.
12. Hesiod, *Theogony*, 80–103.
13. See Romeyer-Dherbey, *Les Sophistes*, pp. 45–49; P. Laín Entralgo, *The Therapy of the Word in Classical Antiquity* (New Haven, 1970), with the review by F. Kudlien in *Gnomon* (1973), pp. 410–412.
14. Hesiod, *Theogony*, 55.
15. Ibid., 37.
16. See Epicurus, *Lettres, maximes, sentences*, trans. and ed. J.-F. Balaudé (Paris, 1994), p. 210, saying no. 10.
17. Plato, *Republic*, 486a.
18. Theognis, *Elegiac Poems*, 1072, 213.
19. B. Snell, *Leben und Meinungen der Sieben Weisen* (Munich, 1952).
20. Plato, *Protagoras*, 343a–b.
21. L. Robert, "De Delphes à l'Oxus: Inscriptions grecques nouvelles de la Bactriane," *Académie des Inscriptions et Belles-Lettres: Comptes Rendus* (Paris, 1968), pp. 416–457.
22. See I. Hadot, "The Spiritual Guide," in A. H. Armstrong, ed., *Classical Mediterranean Spirituality: Egyptian, Greek, Roman* (New York: Crossroad, 1986), pp. 441–444.
23. Thrasymachus A VIII, in Dumont, ed., *Les Présocratiques*, p. 1072.

3. THE FIGURE OF SOCRATES

1. Th. Deman, *Socrate et Jésus* (Paris, 1944). On Socrates, see F. Wolff, *Socrate* (Paris, 1985); and E. Martens, *Die Sache des Sokrates* (Stuttgart, 1992).
2. See Wolff, *Socrate*, pp. 112–128, for a "family album" which gives an excellent description of the various personalities involved.
3. Aristotle, *Poetics*, 1447b10. See C. W. Müller, *Die Kurzdialogue der Appendix Platonica* (Munich, 1975), pp. 17ff.
4. Plato, *Apology*, 20–23.

5. Ibid., 23b.

6. Plato, *Republic*, I, 337a.

7. Aristotle, *Sophistical Refutations*, 183b8.

8. Cicero, *Lucullus*, 5, 15. On Socratic irony, see R. Schaerer, "Le mécanisme de l'ironie dans ses rapports avec la dialectique," *Revue de Métaphysique et de Morale*, 48 (1941), pp. 181–209; V. Jankélévitch, *L'Ironie* (Paris, 1964); see also G. W. F. Hegel, *Lectures on the History of Philosophy: Greek Philosophy to Hegel*, trans. E. S. Haldane (Lincoln, Nebraska, 1995), vol. 1, pp. 398ff.

9. Plato, *Symposium*, 174d–175d.

10. *Theaetetus*, 150d.

11. Plato, *Laches*, 197e6.

12. *Theaetetus*, 149a.

13. *Symposium*, 215c; 218b.

14. K. Döring, "Der Sokrates des Aischines von Sphettos und die Frage nach dem historischen Sokrates," *Hermes*, 112 (1984), pp. 16–30. See also C. W. Müller, *Die Kurzdialoge der Appendix Platonica* (Munich, 1975), p. 233, note 1.

15. *Theages*, 130d. Müller, *Die Kurzdialoge*, p. 128, note 1.

16. *Symposium*, 215c–e; 216a.

17. Ibid., 221e.

18. Xenophon, *Memorabilia*, IV, 4, 5.

19. *Apology*, 28b.

20. Ibid., 29a–b.

21. Ibid., 29e.

22. Socrates, in Aristotle, *Nicomachean Ethics*, VII, 3, 1145b21–27.

23. Socrates, in Aristotle, *Eudemian Ethics*, I, 5, 1216b6–8; Xenophon, *Memorabilia*, III, 9, 5.

24. In *L'idée de volonté dans le stoïcisme* (Paris, 1973), p. 194, A.-J. Voelke writes with regard to Socrates' alleged intellectualism: "Socratic dialectics indissolubly unites knowledge of the good and choice of the good."

25. *Apology*, 28bff.

26. *Crito*, 50a.

27. *Phaedo*, 98e.

28. *Apology*, 41d.

29. Ibid., 38a.

30. M. Merleau-Ponty, *Éloge de la philosophie et autres essais* (Paris, 1965), p. 38.
31. *Apology,* 38a.
32. Merleau-Ponty, *Éloge de la philosophie,* p. 44.
33. Ibid., p. 48.
34. *Apology,* 33b; 31a-b.
35. See A. Dihle, *Studien zur griechischen Biographie,* 2nd ed. (Göttingen, 1970), pp. 13–20.
36. Plutarch, *Whether a Man should Engage in Politics When He Is Old,* 26, 796d.

4. THE DEFINITION OF "PHILOSOPHER" IN PLATO'S *SYMPOSIUM*

1. On the use of the word *philosophia* and related words in Plato, see Monique Dixsaut, *Le naturel philosophe* (Paris, 1985).
2. Hölderlin, "Der Rhein."
3. Nietzsche, *The Birth of Tragedy,* §13.
4. D. Babut, "Peinture et dépassement de la réalité dans le *Banquet* de Platon," *Revue des Études Anciennes,* 82 (1980), pp. 5–29, reprinted in *Parerga: Choix d'articles de D. Babut* (Lyon, 1994), pp. 171–196.
5. *Symposium,* 202e.
6. Ibid., 203aff.
7. See the examples in Diogenes Laertius, *Lives of the Philosophers,* II, 27–28.
8. *Symposium,* 175e; 221e.
9. Ibid., 215c.
10. Ibid., 220a-d.
11. Ibid., 203eff.
12. See *Phaedrus,* 278d.
13. See Plato, *Lysis,* 218b1.
14. H.-J. Krämer, *Platonismus und hellenistische Philosophie* (Berlin, 1971), pp. 174–175, 229–230.
15. Kierkegaard, *The Instant,* §10.
16. Pascal, *Pensées,* §553.
17. Plotinus, *Enneads,* III, 5 (50), 9, 44, p. 142 Hadot.
18. *Symposium,* 215b-c.

19. L. Robin, "Notice," in Plato, *Le Banquet* (Paris, 1981), 1st ed. (1929), p. cv, note 2.
20. *Symposium*, 211d–212a.
21. Cicero, *On the Ends of Goods and Evils*, III, 14, 48.
22. Xenophon, *Symposium*, II, 17–19.
23. Nietzsche, *Human, All Too Human*, part 3, "The Wanderer and His Shadow," §86.
24. Isocrates, *Panegyric*, §47.
25. Ibid., §271.
26. I. Hadot, *Arts libéraux et philosophie dans la pensée antique* (Paris, 1984), pp. 16–18.

5. PLATO AND THE ACADEMY

1. *Symposium*, 208e.
2. Ibid., 209b–c.
3. *Phaedrus*, 277a.
4. L. Robin, "Notice," in Plato, *Le Banquet* (Paris, 1981), 1st ed. (1929), p. xcii.
5. Seneca, *Moral Epistles*, 6, 6.
6. See the important work by H.-J. Krämer, *Platonismus und hellenistische Philosophie* (Berlin, 1971).
7. See M.-F. Billot, "Académie," in R. Goulet, ed., *Dictionnaire des philosophes antiques*, vol. 1 (Paris, 1989), pp. 693–789.
8. See Dicearchus in Plutarch, *Table-Talk*, VIII, 2, 719a; Cicero, *Republic*, I, 15–16; Cicero, *On the Ends of Goods and Evils*, 86–87; Augustine, *City of God*, VIII, 4; Numenius, fragment 24, ed. and trans. Des Places; Proclus, *Commentary on the Timaeus*, I, p. 7, 24 Diehl.
9. *Republic*, 600b.
10. J. P. Lynch, *Aristotle's School: A Study of a Greek Educational Institution* (Berkeley, 1972), p. 61.
11. Plato, *Seventh Letter*, 328b–329c.
12. Lynch, *Aristotle's School*, p. 59, note 32 (with bibliography); M. Isnardi Parente, *L'eredità di Platone nell'Accademia antica* (Milan, 1989), pp. 63ff.
13. *Republic*, 519d.

14. K. Gaiser, *Philodems Academica* (Stuttgart, 1988), pp. 153ff.

15. Plato, *Laws*, VI, 756e–758a.

16. *Republic*, 592b.

17. See B. Frischer, *The Sculpted Word: Epicureanism and Philosophical Recruitment in Ancient Greece* (Berkeley, 1982), p. 63.

18. Lynch, *Aristotle's School*, p. 63.

19. On this subject, see Lynch, *Aristotle's School*, pp. 54–63, 93.

20. Gaiser, *Philodems Academica*, p. 154.

21. Plutarch, *Table-Talk*, VIII, 1, 717.

22. *Republic*, 522–534.

23. Ibid., 526e; Plutarch, *Table-Talk*, VIII, 718e–f; see I. Hadot, *Arts libéraux et philosophie dans la pensée antique* (Paris, 1984), p. 98.

24. See F. Laserre, *La naissance des mathématiques à l'époque de Platon* (Fribourg and Paris, 1990).

25. *Republic*, 539d–e.

26. Aristotle, *Sophistical Refutations*, 183b7.

27. See P. Hadot, "Philosophie, Dialectique, Rhétorique dans l'Antiquité," *Studia Philosophica*, 39 (1980), pp. 139–166.

28. Plato, *Meno*, 75c–d.

29. See E. Heitsch, *Erkenntnis und Lebensführung*, Akademie der Wissenschaften und der Literatur, Mainz, fasc. 9 (Stuttgart, 1994).

30. I. Düring, *Aristoteles* (Heidelberg, 1966), p. 9.

31. Plato, *Sophist*, 263e4.

32. See H.-J. Krämer, *Platonismus und Hellenistische Philosophie* (Berlin, 1971).

33. J. Mittelstrass, "Versuch über den sokratischen Dialog," in K. Stierle and R. Warning, eds., *Das Gespräch* (Munich, 1984), p. 26.

34. L. Brisson, "Présupposés et conséquences d'une interprétation ésotériste de Platon," *Les Études Philosophiques*, 4 (1993), p. 480.

35. Aristotle, *Metaphysics*, 1004b25.

36. Plato, *Republic*, 518c.

37. Hadot, *Arts libéraux*, p. 15.

38. Brisson, "Présupposés," p. 480.

39. Plato, *Republic*, 618b.

40. Plato, *Seventh Letter*, 340c–d.

41. Ibid., 327b; 331d; 336c.

42. P. Rabbow, *Paidagogia: Die Grundlegung der abendländischen Erziehungskunst in der Sokratik* (Göttingen, 1960), p. 102.

43. Plato, *Timaeus,* 89d–90a.

44. Plato, *Republic,* 571–572.

45. Plato, *Laws,* VII, 808b–c.

46. Plato, *Republic,* 604b–c.

47. On a similar exercise in the *Crito,* see E. Martens, *Die Sache des Sokrates* (Stuttgart, 1992), p. 127.

48. *Phaedo,* 64a. See R. Di Giuseppe, *La teoria della morte nel "Fedone" platonico* (Il Mulino, 1993).

49. R. Schaerer, *La question platonicienne: Études sur les rapports de la pensée et de l'expression dans les Dialogues* (Neuchâtel, 1969), p. 41.

50. B. Parain, "Le langage et l'existence," in the collection entitled *L'Existence* (Paris, 1945), p. 173.

51. Plato, *Phaedo,* 115c–d.

52. Plato, *Republic,* 486a–b.

53. Plato, *Theaetetus,* 173–176.

54. Ibid., 176b–c.

55. Plato, *Phaedrus,* 249bff.

56. Ibid., 253a.

57. Plato, *Symposium,* 209b–c.

58. Goethe, *Conversations with Eckermann,* May 12, 1825.

59. Plato, *Symposium,* 210–212.

60. Cited in A. Parmentier, *La philosophie de Whitehead et le problème de Dieu* (Paris, 1968), p. 222, note 83: "Concepts are always dressed in emotions; that is to say, in hope or in fear, ardent aspiration, or the pleasure of analysis."

61. Ibid., p. 410, note 131.

62. Plato, *Seventh Letter,* 341c.

63. Plato, *Phaedrus,* 275e.

64. See R. Goulet, "Axiothea," in Goulet, ed., *Dictionnaire des philosophes antiques,* vol. 1 (Paris, 1989), p. 691.

65. Quoted in Gaiser, *Philodems Academica,* p. 148.

66. See Schaerer, *La question platonicienne,* p. 171. Mittelstrass, "Versuch über den sokratischen Dialog," p. 26, points out the danger, linked to the fading of the figure of Socrates, of the transition from dialogue

to monologue, and from a philosophical "form of life" to "professional philosophical research."

67. Schaerer, *La question platonicienne*, p. 67.
68. Ibid., p. 174. As Aristotle said (*Poetics*, 1447b), they are mimetic and poetical works.
69. Brisson, "Présuppposés," p. 480.
70. V. Goldschmidt, *Les Dialogues de Platon* (Paris, 1947), p. 3.
71. Plato, *Statesman*, 285c–d.
72. On Plato's dialogues, see the excellent summary by L. Brisson in his article "Platon," in L. Jaffro and M. Labrune, eds., *Gradus philosophique* (Paris, 1994), pp. 610–613. The following pages owe a great deal to this work.
73. *Parmenides*, 135b.
74. [That is, forms which are apprehensible by the intellect alone.—*Trans.*]
75. See L. Brisson, "Platon," in *Gradus philosophique*, p. 611.
76. This triad appears in the *Euthyphro, Crito, Theaetetus, Statesman, Parmenides, Phaedrus, First Alcibiades, Gorgias, Republic, Timaeus, Laws,* and *Seventh Letter.*
77. Schaerer, *La question platonicienne*, p. 247.

6. ARISTOTLE AND HIS SCHOOL

1. Aristotle, *Metaphysics*, I, 982a15.
2. J. P. Lynch, *Aristotle's School: A Study of a Greek Educational Institution* (Berkeley, 1972), pp. 68–105.
3. Diogenes Laertius, *Lives of the Philosophers*, V, 4.
4. R. Bodéüs, *Le philosophe et la cité: Recherches sur les rapports entre morale et politique dans la pensée d'Aristote* (Paris, 1982), p. 171 [in English, *The Political Dimensions of Aristotle's Ethics*, trans. Jan Edward Garrett (Albany: State University of New York Press, 1993)—*Trans.*]; G. Bien, "Das Theorie-Praxis Problem und die politische Philosophie bei Plato und Aristoteles," *Philosophisches Jahrbuch*, 76 (1968–1969), pp. 264–314.
5. Aristotle, *Politics*, VII, 2, 1324a30. M.-Ch. Bataillard, "La structure de la doctrine aristotélicienne des vertus éthiques," Diss., Université de Paris IV–Sorbonne, p. 348, distinguishes three basic ethical degrees

in Aristotle: the "average man," the "good and beautiful man," and the "contemplative." Compare P. Demont, *La cité grecque archaïque et classique et l'idéal de tranquillité* (Paris, 1990), p. 349; and G. Rodier, *Études de philosophie grecque* (Paris, 1926), p. 215.

6. Aristotle, *Nicomachean Ethics*, X, 1178a9.

7. Ibid., X, 1177a12–1178a6.

8. Aristotle, *Nicomachean Ethics*, X, 1177b27; *Generation of animals*, IX, 737a910.

9. Aristotle, *Nicomachean Ethics*, X, 1178a2.

10. Ibid., 1177b33.

11. Aristotle, *Metaphysics*, XII, 7, 1072b14; 25.

12. Aristotle, *Nicomachean Ethics*, X, 1175a4; 26.

13. [The distinction here is between the French words *théorique* (which means "speculative; having no relation to reality or practice" and derives from the Greek *theorikos*) and *théorétique* (which means "relative to pure knowledge or speculation" and derives from the Greek *theoretikos*). I have tried to convey the distinction by translating the former as "theoretic" (compare the second definition given in the *Oxford English Dictionary*: "Contemplative, as opposed to active or practical") and the latter by "theoretical."—*Trans.*]

14. Aristotle, *Politics*, VII, 3, 8, 1325b16–20.

15. I. Düring, *Aristoteles* (Heidelberg, 1966), p. 472.

16. See W. Jaeger, *Aristotle* (Oxford, 1967), 1st ed. (1934), ch. 13, "The Organisation of Research"; Düring, *Aristoteles*, pp. 524ff.

17. L. Bourgey, *Observation et expérience chez Aristote* (Paris, 1955), pp. 69ff.

18. Aristotle, *Generation of Animals*, 760b30.

19. Aristotle, *Parts of Animals*, 644b31ff.

20. Aristotle, *Generation of Animals*, 645a7–23.

21. Aristotle, *Metaphysics*, XII, 1072b4.

22. On Aristotle's relation to Hellenistic art, see J. Onians, *Art and Thought in the Hellenistic Age: The Greek World View, 350–50 B.C.* (London, 1979), p. 29.

23. L. Robert, "Héraclite à son fourneau," in Robert, *Opera minora selecta*, vol. 3 (Amsterdam, 1969), pp. 1538–1550.

24. Aristotle, *Metaphysics*, XII, 1072a26ff.

25. Kant, *Critique of Judgment*, §42.

26. Aristotle, *Metaphysics*, XII, 1075a7–10: "Just as it is in certain moments for the human intellect, at least when it does not take [following the highly probable conjecture by Diano in his edition of the *Metaphysics* (Bari, 1948)] as its object composite things (for it does not possess the good in such-and-such a part, but it has the highest good, which is different from it, in a kind of indivisible totality), it is the same, for all eternity, for that Thought which is the thought of itself." See also Theophrastus, *Metaphysics*, 9b13–16: "What is perhaps more true is that the contemplation of this kind of Realities takes place by means of the intellect itself, which seizes them immediately and as it were enters into contact with them, which explains why there can be no error with regard to them."

27. Aristotle, *Metaphysics*, I, 982b30.

28. Düring, *Aristoteles*, pp. 29–30.

29. Bodéüs, *Le philosophe et la cité*, p. 26.

30. Ibid., p. 162.

31. Ibid. Bodéüs bases his assertion on the first chapter of the *Nicomachean Ethics* (1094b27ff.), where the auditor plays the role of judge.

32. Ibid., pp. 187ff.

33. P. Aubenque, "La pensée du simple dans la *Métaphysique* (Z,17 et Θ,10)," in Aubenque, ed., *Études sur la Métaphysique d'Aristote* (Paris, 1979), pp. 69–80; Th. de Koninck, "La *noêsis* et l'indivisible selon Aristote," in J.-F. Mattéi, ed., *La naissance de la raison en Grèce: Actes du Congrès de Nice, mai 1987* (Paris, 1990), pp. 215–228.

34. Aristotle, *Nicomachean Ethics*, VI, 1142a12ff. Compare Bodéüs, *Le philosophe et la cité*, p. 190.

35. Aristotle, *Nicomachean Ethics*, VI, 1147a21–22.

36. Plato, *Seventh Letter*, 341c.

37. Aristotle, *Nicomachean Ethics*, X, 1179b4–5.

38. See Bataillard, "La structure de la doctrine aristotélicienne des vertus éthiques," pp. 355–356.

39. See Aristotle, *Nicomachean Ethics*, I, 1, 1095a4–6; Bodéüs, *Le philosophe et la cité*, pp. 185–186.

40. *Nicomachean Ethics*, X, 10, 1179b24.

41. See Bodéüs, *Le philosophe et la cité*, p. 225; Düring, *Aristoteles*, p. 435.

42. Bodéüs, *Le philosophe et la cité*, p. 16.

7. THE HELLENISTIC SCHOOLS

1. See especially G. Murray, "The Failure of Nerve," in Murray, *Four Stages of Greek Religion* (New York, 1912; 3rd ed., 1955), pp. 119ff. Almost all the works by historians of philosophy later than Murray (Festugière and Bréhier, for instance) are affected by this prejudice.
2. See the excellent work by B. Gille, *Les mécaniciens grecs* (Paris, 1980), particularly the chapter on the Alexandrian school, pp. 54ff.
3. Plato, *Republic*, 496c5–e2.
4. See I. Hadot, "Tradition stoïcienne et idées politiques au temps des Gracques," *Revue des Études Latines*, 48 (1970), pp. 146–147; eadem, *Le problème du néoplatonisme alexandrin: Hiéroclès et Simplicius* (Paris, 1978), p. 37.
5. P. Hadot, *The Inner Citadel: Introduction to the Meditations of Marcus Aurelius* (Cambridge, Mass., 1998), pp. 293ff.
6. For example, Amynias of Samos and Apollophanes of Pergamum. See the articles on these philosophers by B. Puech in R. Goulet, ed., *Dictionnaire des philosophes antiques*, vol. 1 (Paris, 1989).
7. I. Hadot, "Tradition stoïcienne et idées politiques au temps des Gracques," pp. 133–161.
8. Diogenes Laertius, *Lives of the Philosophers*, IX, 61–63.
9. Cf. C. Muckensturm, "Les gymnosophistes étaient-ils des cyniques modèles?" in M. O. Goulet-Cazé and R. Goulet, eds., *Le cynisme ancien et ses prolongements* (Paris, 1993), pp. 225–239.
10. Clement of Alexandria, *Stromata*, II, 20, 125, 1.
11. Sextus Empiricus, *Against the Logicians*, I, 87–88; cf. R. Goulet, "Anaxarque d'Abdère," *Dictionnaire des philosophes antiques*, vol. 1, pp. 188–191.
12. Democritus, fragment 9.
13. Cf. H. C. Baldry, "The Idea of the Unity of Mankind," in H. Schwabl and H. Diller, eds., *Grecs et barbares*, Entretiens sur l'Antiquité Classique, vol. 8 (Geneva: Fondation Hardt, 1962), pp. 169–204; J. Moles, "Le cosmopolitisme cynique," in *Le cynisme ancien et ses prolongements*, pp. 259–280.
14. On the Greek vocabulary designating the school as an institution and a doctrinal tendency, see J. Glucker, *Antiochus and the Late Academy* (Göttingen, 1978), pp. 159–225.

15. Diogenes Laertius, *Lives of the Philosophers*, IV, 16.
16. See J. P. Lynch, *Aristotle's School: A Study of a Greek Educational Institution* (Berkeley, 1972), pp. 106–134.
17. Diogenes Laertius, *Lives of the Philosophers*, III, 41; V, 11, 51, 61, 69; X, 16.
18. C. Diano, "La philosophie du plaisir et la société des amis," in Diano, *Studi e saggi di filosofia antica* (Padua, 1973), pp. 368–369. Compare G. Arrighetti, ed., *Epicuro: Opere* (Turin, 1973), pp. 443, 471. On the organization of the Epicurean school, see N. W. De Witt, *Epicurus and His Philosophy* (Minneapolis: University of Minnesota Press, 1954; 2nd ed. Westport, Conn., 1973); idem, "Organization and Procedure in Epicurean Groups," *Classical Philology*, 31 (1936), pp. 205–211; I. Hadot, *Seneca und die griechisch-römische Tradition der Seelenleitung* (Berlin: De Gruyter, 1969), pp. 48–53.
19. Diogenes Laertius, *Lives of the Philosophers*, IV, 19.
20. Ibid., V, 4; Lynch, *Aristotle's School*, p. 82.
21. Diogenes Laertius, *Lives of the Philosophers*, VII, 5–6; 36.
22. Ibid., 10.
23. Ibid., 27.
24. Sextus Empiricus, *Outlines of Pyrrhonism*, I, 16–17. Compare the translation by M.-O. Goulet-Cazé, in "Le cynisme est-il une philosophie?" in M. Dixsaut, ed., *Contre Platon, I: Le Platonisme dévoilé* (Paris, 1993), p. 279.
25. A.-J. Voelke, *La philosophie comme thérapie de l'âme: Études de philosophie hellénistique* (Fribourg and Paris, 1993).
26. Alexander of Aphrodisias, *In Aristotelis Topica comment.*, in the series *Commentaria in Aristotelem Graeca*, 2.2 (Berlin, 1891), p. 27, 13–16 Wallies.
27. See P. Hadot, "Philosophie, dialectique, rhétorique dans l'Antiquité," *Studia Philosophica*, 39 (1980), pp. 147ff.
28. Cicero, *On the Ends of Goods and Evils*, IV, 3, 7.
29. I. Hadot, "Épicure et l'enseignement philosophique hellénistique et romain," *Actes du VIIIe Congrès de l'Association Guillaume Budé* (Paris, 1969), pp. 347–354.
30. Ibid., pp. 351–352.
31. See P. Hadot, "Les modèles de bonheur proposés par les philosophies antiques," *La Vie Spirituelle*, 147, no. 698 (1992), pp. 40–41.

32. Evidence has been collected in L. Paquet, *Les Cyniques grecs: Fragments et témoignages*, preface by M.-O. Goulet-Cazé (Paris, 1992). See also M.-O. Goulet-Cazé, *L'ascèse cynique* (Paris, 1986); and Goulet-Cazé and R. Goulet, eds., *Le cynisme ancien et ses prolongements*.

33. Diogenes Laertius, *Lives of the Philosophers*, VI, 46; 49; 97.

34. Ibid., 38.

35. Ibid., 69.

36. Ibid., 103. See also Goulet-Cazé, "Le cynisme est-il une philosophie?"

37. Diogenes Laertius, *Lives of the Philosophers*, VI, 36, 75–76, 82–84.

38. Ibid., 38–39.

39. Ibid., 22.

40. Ibid., 54.

41. Ibid., IX, 61–70. The *testimonia* on Pyrrho have been collected in *Pirrone: Testimonianze*, ed. F. Decleva Caizzi (Naples, 1981). See also M. Conche, *Pyrrhon ou l'apparence* (Villers-sur-Mer, 1973).

42. Diogenes Laertius, *Lives of the Philosophers*, IX, 66.

43. Chuang-tzu, in *Philosophes taoïstes*, trans. Liou Kia Hway and B. Grynpas (Paris, 1980), p. 141. See also Shitao, *Les propos sur la peinture du moine Citrouille-amère*, trans. and ed. P. Ryckmans (Paris, 1984), p. 12. Ryckmans uses this example to define supreme Taoist simplicity, which is pure virtuality and the absence of desire. [Lao-tzu, reputed to have lived in the sixth century B.C., was the semilegendary founder of Taoism and traditionally the author of the *Tao-te ching*. Chuang-tzu lived ca. 369–ca. 286 B.C.—*Trans.*]

44. Diogenes Laertius, *Lives of the Philosophers*, IX, 63.

45. Compare the remarks by his disciple Timon, in Sextus Empiricus, *Against the Moralists*, 20: "The nature of the divine and of the good always remains, and from it man derives a life always equal to itself." Here, Pyrrho appears as a dogmatic, as has rightly been pointed out by F. Decleva Caizzi (*Pirrone*, pp. 256–258), and W. Goerler (review of Decleva Caizzi, *Archiv für Geschichte der Philosophie*, 67 [1985], pp. 329ff).

46. Cicero, *On the Ends of Goods and Evils*, II, 13, 43; IV, 16, 43.

47. Diogenes Laertius, *Lives of the Philosophers*, IX, 66.

48. Ibid., 63–64.

49. Ibid., 69.

50. *Epicure: Lettres, maximes, sentences,* trans. and ed. J.-F. Balaudé (Paris, 1994), cited in what follows as Balaudé. This work is an excellent introduction to the knowledge of Epicurus. For a Greek text with Italian translation, see *Epicuro: Opere,* ed. G. Arrighetti (Turin, 1973), cited in what follows as Arrighetti.

51. *Vatican Sentences,* §33, p. 213 Balaudé. I adopt the translation of J. F. Balaudé while adding the mention of Zeus, which no doubt is an addition to the text of the manuscripts but which seems to me justified by the *kan* that precedes it in the Greek text.

52. Diano, "La philosophy du plaisir et la société des amis," p. 360.

53. Cicero, *On the Ends of Goods and Evils,* I, 18, 57–19, 63. See also A.-J. Voelke, "Opinions vides et troubles de l'âme," in Voelke, *La philosophie comme thérapie de l'âme,* pp. 59–72.

54. H.-J. Krämer, *Platonismus und hellenistische Philosophie* (Berlin, 1971), pp. 164–170, 188–211, 216–220.

55. Epicurus, *Letter to Menoecus,* § 128, p. 194 Balaudé.

56. Seneca, *Letters to Lucilius,* 66, 45. See also C. Diano, "La philosophie du plaisir et la société des amis," p. 364.

57. Krämer, *Platonismus,* p. 218.

58. Diano, "La philosophie du plaisir et la société des amis," p. 364.

59. Cicero, *On the Ends of Goods and Evils,* I, 18, 59.

60. Epicurus, *Letter to Menoecus,* §§127–128 (pp. 116, 194 Balaudé).

61. Plato, *Republic,* 558d.

62. Epicurus, *Capital Maxims,* §30, p. 204 Balaudé; Porphyry, *On Abstinence,* I, 49.

63. Lucretius, *On Nature,* III, 31ff.

64. See A.-J. Festugière, *Épicure et ses dieux* (Paris, 1946), pp. 51–52.

65. Epicurus, *Capital Maxims,* §11, 12; *Letter to Pythocles,* §85.

66. Epicurus, *Letter to Pythocles,* §§86–87. See also Balaudé, pp. 106–111, 176.

67. Cicero, *On the Ends of Goods and Evils,* I, 6, 18–20.

68. Cicero, *On Fate,* 9, 18; 10, 22; 20, 46; *On the Nature of the Gods,* I, 25, 69. See Arrighetti, ed., *Epicuro,* pp. 512–513.

69. Lucretius, *On Nature,* II, 289–293.

70. Cicero, *On the Ends of Goods and Evils,* I, 6, 19: "Nothing is more shameful for a physicist than to say that a fact occurs without any

cause." See also D. Sedley, "Epicurus' Refutation of Determinism," in *Syzetesis: Studi sull' epicureismo greco e romano offerti a Marcello Gigante* (Naples, 1983), pp. 11–51.

71. Epicurus, *Letter to Menoecus*, §124–125, p. 192 Balaudé. See also Diano, "La philosophie du plaisir et la société des amis," p. 362.

72. Balaudé, *Épicure*, p. 32.

73. Epicurus, *Letter to Menoecus*, §123; p. 192 Balaudé.

74. *Capital Maxims*, I, p. 199 Balaudé.

75. Festugière, *Épicure et ses dieux*, p. 95.

76. Ibid., p. 98.

77. P. Decharme, *La critique des traditions religieuses chez les Grecs* (Paris, 1904), p. 257.

78. Epicurus, *Letter to Menoecus*, §§124, 135; pp. 192, 198 Balaudé.

79. Philodemus, in *Papyrus Herculan.*, 1005, col. IV, 10–14. Text improved by M. Gigante, *Ricerche Filodemee*, 2nd ed. (Naples, 1983), p. 260, note 35a; in Arrighetti, ed., *Epicuro*, p. 548.

80. Festugière, *Épicure et ses dieux*, pp. 36–70; Diano, "La philosophie du plaisir et la société des amis," pp. 365–371.

81. Seneca, *Letters to Lucilius*, 7, 11; Diano, "La philosophie du plaisir et la société des amis," p. 370.

82. See S. Sudhaus, "Epikur als Beichvater," *Archiv für Religionswissenschaft*, 14 (1911), pp. 647–648; W. Schmid, "Contritio und 'Ultima linea rerum' in neuen epikureischen Texten," *Rheinisches Museum*, 100 (1957), pp. 301–327; I. Hadot, *Seneca*, p. 67.

83. Seneca, *Letters to Lucilius*, 25, 5.

84. *Philodemi Peri Parrhesias*, ed. A. Olivieri (Leipzig, 1914), p. 22; M. Gigante, "Philodème: Sur la liberté de parole," in *Actes du VIIIe Congrès de l'Association Guillaume Budé*, pp. 196–217.

85. This is the subject of B. Frischer's book *The Sculpted Word* (Berkeley, 1982).

86. Epicurus, *Letter to Menoecus*, §135, p. 198 Balaudé.

87. *Vatican Sentences*, §27, p. 212 Balaudé.

88. In Arrighetti, ed., *Epicuro*, p. 427 [52]. Cf. Marcus Aurelius, *Meditations*, IX, 41.

89. Cicero, *On the Ends of Goods and Evils*, I, 20, 65.

90. Pliny the Elder, *Natural History*, XXXV, 144 (and 99); De Witt, *Epicurus and His Philosophy*, pp. 95–96.

91. Horace, *Epistles,* I, 4, 13; Philodemus, *On Death,* Book IV, cols. 38, 24, cited in Gigante, *Ricerche Filodemee,* pp. 181, 215–216.

92. E. Hoffmann, "Epikur," in M. Dessoir, ed., *Die Geschichte der Philosophie,* vol. 1 (Wiesbaden, 1925), p. 223.

93. The fragments of the Stoics have been collected in H. von Arnim, *Stoicorum Veterum Fragmenta,* 4 vols. (Leipzig, 1905–1924; rpt. Stuttgart: Teubner, 1964). J. Mansfeld is preparing a new edition of the fragments.

94. Lynch, *Aristotle's School,* p. 143. See also I. Hadot, "Tradition stoïcienne et idées politiques au temps des Gracques," pp. 161–178.

95. Plato, *Apology,* 41d. See also 30b, 28e.

96. Epictetus, *Manual,* §1; *Discourses,* I, 1, 7; I, 4, 27; I, 22, 9; II, 5, 4.

97. Seneca, *Letters to Lucilius,* 20, 5.

98. *Stoicorum Veterum Fragmenta,* I, 179. Hereafter cited as *SVF.*

99. *SVF* III, 68; *Les Stoïciens,* p. 97.

100. Cicero, *On the Ends of Goods and Evils,* III, 4, 16–22, 75. See the remarkable commentary on this text by V. Goldschmidt, *Le système stoïcien et l'idée du temps* (Paris, 1977), pp. 125–131. See also I. Hadot, *Seneca,* pp. 73–75.

101. Marcus Aurelius, *Meditations,* IV, 27. Hereafter cited as Marcus Aurelius.

102. G. Rodier, *Études de philosophie grecque* (Paris, 1926), pp. 254–255; V. Goldschmidt, *Le système stoïcien,* p. 59, note 7.

103. *SVF* II, 952; *Les Stoïciens,* p. 481.

104. Marcus Aurelius, VIII, 34.

105. Seneca, *Lettres to Lucilius,* 107, 11.

106. Marcus Aurelius, VIII, 35.

107. Epictetus, *Manual,* §5.

108. *SVF* II, 91; Sextus Empiricus, *Against the Logicians,* II, 397. Translated in P. Hadot, *The Inner Citadel* (Cambridge, Mass., 1998), p. 106.

109. Cicero, *On Fate,* 19, 43. See also P. Hadot, *The Inner Citadel,* p. 106.

110. Aulus Gellius, *Attic Nights,* XIX, 1, 15–20; translated in P. Hadot, *The Inner Citadel,* p. 116.

111. Epictetus, *Manual,* §8.

112. See P. Hadot, *The Inner Citadel,* pp. 162–163, 179ff.

113. I have borrowed this translation from I. A. Kidd, "Posidonius on

Emotions," in A. A. Long, ed., *Problems in Stoicism* (London, 1971), p. 201. On appropriate actions, see I. Hadot, *Seneca*, pp. 72–78; Goldschmidt, *Le système stoïcien*, p. 145–168; P. Hadot, *The Inner Citadel*, pp. 198–190.

114. See P. Hadot, *The Inner Citadel*, pp. 193ff.

115. Seneca, *On Clemency*, II, 3, 3.

116. Marcus Aurelius, III, 11.

117. Ibid., VI, 13.

118. See Chapter 9, below (section entitled "The View from Above").

119. Ibid., X, 11; 18.

120. Chrysippus (*SVF* II, 912) speaks of the consent the wise give to Fate. Compare Marcus Aurelius III, 16, 3; VIII, 7.

121. On this exercise, see I. Hadot, *Seneca*, pp. 60–61; P. Hadot, *The Inner Citadel*, pp. 205–209.

122. Philo, *On the Special Laws*, II, 46.

123. Marcus Aurelius, II, 5, 2.

124. See P. Hadot, *The Inner Citadel*, pp. 200–204.

125. *SVF* I, Aristo, 351–352; Diogenes Laertius, *Lives of the Philosophers*, VI, 103.

126. Diogenes Laertius, *Lives of the Philosophers*, VII, 39; 41. See also P. Hadot, "Les divisions des parties de la philosophie dans l'Antiquité," *Museum Helveticum*, 36 (1979), pp. 201–233; idem, "Philosophie, discours philosophique et divisions de la philosophie chez les stoïciens," *Revue International de Philosophie*, 45 (1991), pp. 205–219; idem, "La philosophie éthique: Une éthique ou une pratique?" in P. Demont, ed., *Problèmes de la morale antique* (Université de Picardie, Faculté de Lettres, 1993), pp. 7–37. Compare K. Ierodiakonou, "The Stoic Division of Philosophy," *Phronesis*, 38 (1993), pp. 59–61; in the last analysis, it seems to me that this article confirms my interpretation.

127. The fragments have been collected in F. Wehrli, *Die Schule des Aristoteles*, ten fascicles and two supplements (Basel, 1944–1959; 1974–1978). See also Lynch, *Aristotle's School;* J. Moreau, *Aristote et son école* (Paris, 1962).

128. See R. Goulet, "Aristarque de Samos," *Dictionnaire des philosophes antiques*, vol. 1, p. 356.

129. On this question, see I. Hadot, *Seneca*, pp. 40–45.

130. A.-M. Ioppolo, *Opinione e scienza*, (Naples, 1986), pp. 44–50, 53–54.

131. Cicero, *On the Ends of Goods and Evils*, II, 1, 1–4.

132. Plato, *Apology*, 23b; 38a; 41b–c.

133. See C. Lévy, "La nouvelle Académie a-t-elle été anti-platonicienne?" in *Contre Platon, I: Le platonisme dévoilé*, pp. 144–149; and Ioppolo, *Opinione e scienza*, p. 49.

134. Ioppolo, *Opinione e scienza*, pp. 162–165.

135. Ibid., p. 139, citing Plutarch, *Against Colotes*, 1122c–e.

136. Ioppolo, *Opinione e scienza*, pp. 135–146.

137. Seneca, *On Benefits*, II, 10, 1.

138. Ioppolo, *Opinione e scienza*, pp. 203–209.

139. Cicero, *Tusculan Disputations*, V, 11, 33; *Lucullus*, 3, 7–8.

140. On eclecticism, see I. Hadot, "Du bon et du mauvais usage du terme 'éclectisme' dans l'histoire de la philosophie antique," in R. Brague and J.-F. Courtine, eds., *Herméneutique et ontologie: Hommage à Pierre Aubenque* (Paris, 1990), pp. 147–162. On eclecticism in the Enlightenment, conceived as the attitude which consisted in thinking for oneself, without obeying "authorities," see H. Holzhey, "Der Philosoph für die Welt: Eine Chimäre der deutschen Aufklärung?" in H. Holzhey and W. C. Zimmerli, eds., *Esoterik und Exoterik der Philosophie* (Basel, 1977), p. 132.

141. Cicero, *On Fate*, 11, 24–25.

142. See D. Babut, "Du scepticisme au dépassement de la raison: Philosophie et foi religieuse chez Plutarque," in *Parerga: Choix d'articles de D. Babut* (Lyon, 1994), pp. 549–581.

143. Plutarch, *Table-Talk*, I, 2, 613b.

144. The principal source is the work of Sextus Empiricus. The main texts have been collected in *Oeuvres choisies de Sextus Empiricus*, trans. J. Grenier and G. Goron (Paris, 1948); and in J.-P. Dumont, *Les Sceptiques grecs: Textes choisis* (Paris, 1966).

145. Voelke, *La philosophie comme thérapie de l'âme*, pp. 107–126.

146. Sextus Empiricus, *Outlines*, III, 280, in J. P. Dumont, ed., *Les Présocratiques* (Paris: Gallimard, Pléiade, 1988), p. 212. Voelke compares this "philanthropy" to that of doctors in the classical period (*La philosophie comme thérapie de l'âme*, p. 109).

147. Sextus Empiricus, *Outlines*, I, 27–30, pp. 13–14 Dumont.

148. *Outlines*, I, 36–39, p. 49 Dumont; Diogenes Laertius, *Lives of the Philosophers*, IX, 79–88.

149. Diogenes Laertius, *Lives of the Philosophers*, IX, 88.

150. Sextus Empiricus, *Outlines*, I, 206; II, 188; Voelke, *La philosophie comme thérapie de l'âme*, pp. 123ff.

151. Voelke, *La philosophie comme thérapie de l'âme*, p. 116.

152. Sextus Empiricus, *Against the Moralists*, 141–166, in Dumont, ed., *Les Présocratiques*, pp. 206–212.

153. *Outlines*, I, 15 and 197, pp. 12 and 43 Dumont.

8. PHILOSOPHICAL SCHOOLS IN THE IMPERIAL WORLD

1. See J. P. Lynch, *Aristotle's School: A Study of a Greek Educational Institutions* (Berkeley, 1972), pp. 154–207; J. Glucker, *Antiochus and the Late Academy* (Göttingen, 1978), pp. 373–379.

2. Cicero, *Academics*, 4, 15–12, 43.

3. See I. Hadot, *Le problème du néoplatonisme alexandrin: Hiéroclès et Simplicius* (Paris, 1978), pp. 73–76.

4. See I. Hadot, *Arts libéraux et philosophie dans la pensée antique* (Paris, 1984), pp. 215–261.

5. Ibid., pp. 217–218.

6. R. Goulet and M. Aouad, "Alexandros d'Aphrodisias," in Goulet, ed., *Dictionnaire des philosophes antiques*, vol. 1 (Paris, 1989), pp. 125–126; P. Thillet, Introduction to *Alexandre d'Aphrodise: Traité du Destin* (Paris, 1984), pp. xlix–l.

7. Lynch, *Aristotle's School*, p. 177–189; I. Hadot, *Le problème du néoplatonisme*, pp. 9–10.

8. Cicero, *On the Orator*, I, 11, 47.

9. Proclus, *Commentary on the Timaeus*, vol. 1, p. 76, I Diehl.

10. Aulus Gellius, *Attic Nights*, I, 9, 8.

11. Epictetus, *Manual*, §49. For allusions to commenting on texts during class, see *Discourses*, I, 10, 8; I, 26, 13.

12. Porphyry, *Life of Plotinus*, 14, 10, in *Porphyre: Vie de Plotin*, vol. 2, French translation with commentary by L. Brisson et al. (Paris, 1992), p. 155. See also the study by M.-O. Goulet-Cazé, vol. 1, pp. 262–264.

13. M.-D. Chenu, *Introduction à l'étude de saint Thomas* (Paris: Vrin, 1954), p. 55.

14. Diogenes Laertius, *Lives of the Philosophers*, VII, 53–54.

15. Plato, *Timaeus*, 24c.

16. See L. Robert, "Trois oracles de la Théosophie et un prophète d'Apollon," *Académie des Inscriptions et Belles-Lettres: Comptes Rendus* (Paris, 1968), pp. 568–599; idem, "Un oracle grec à Oinoanda," ibid. (Paris, 1971), pp. 597–619.

17. See P. Hadot, "Théologie, exégèse, révélation, écriture dans la philosophie grecque," in M. Tardieu, ed., *Les règles de l'interprétation* (Paris, 1987), pp. 13–34.

18. Epictetus, *Discourses*, III, 21–23; idem, *Manual*, §49.

19. Plutarch, *On Isis and Osiris*, 382d. See also P. Hadot, "La division des parties de la philosophie dans l'Antiquité," *Museum Helveticum*, 36 (1979), pp. 218–221.

20. I. Hadot, *Le problème du néoplatonisme*, pp. 160–164; eadem, Introduction (ch. 3) to *Simplicius: Commentaire sur le Manuel d'Épictète* (Leiden, 1996).

21. Aulus Gellius, *Attic Nights*, I, 26, 1–111. On Epictetus, see J. Souilhé, Introduction to *Épictète: Entretiens*, vol. 1 (Paris, 1948), p. xxix.

22. Porphyry, *Life of Plotinus*, 3, 35.

23. Aulus Gellius, *Attic Nights*, XVII, 8; VII, 13.

24. W. Burkert, *Lore and Science in Ancient Pythagoreanism* (Cambridge, Mass., 1972).

25. Aristophon, *The Pythagorist*, quoted in J. P. Dumont, ed., *Les Présocratiques* (Paris: Gallimard, Pléiade, 1988), p. 612.

26. Burkert, *Lore and Science*, pp. 150–175.

27. P. C. Van der Horst, ed., *Les Vers d'or pythagoriciens* (Leiden, 1932); M. Meunier, ed., *Pythagore: Les Vers d'or; Hiéroclès: Commentaire sur les Vers d'or* (Paris, 1979).

28. *Porphyre, Vie de Pythagore*, ed. and trans. É. Des Places (Paris, 1982); Iamblichus, *Pythagoras*, ed. and German trans. M. von Albrecht (Darmstadt, 1985).

29. Taurus, in Aulus Gellius, *Attic Nights*, I, 9. See also A.-J. Festugière, "Sur le *De vita pythagorica* de Jamblique," in *Études de philosophie grecque* (Paris, 1971), pp. 437–462.

30. Porphyry, *On Abstinence*, I, 2, 3; 3, 3.

31. Ibid., I, 27, 1.
32. Ibid., I, 29, 1–6.
33. Plato, *Timaeus*, 90a.
34. Porphyry, On *Abstinence*, I, 29, 5–6.
35. [*Nous;* often rendered as "intellect."—*Trans.*]
36. Ibid., I, 29, 4.
37. Plotinus, *Enneads*, II 9 (33), 14, 11.
38. Porphyry, *Life of Plotinus*, 8, 20.
39. Porphyry, On *Abstinence*, I, 41, 5.
40. Porphyry, *Life of Plotinus*, 8, 20.
41. Ibid., 9, 18; 8, 19.
42. Ibid., 23, 7–18.
43. Plotinus, *Enneads*, VI 7 (38), 34, 9–37. See the French translation in P. Hadot, trans., *Plotin: Traité 38* (Paris, 1988).
44. Plato, *Symposium*, 210e4.
45. Ibid., 211d–e.
46. Philo, On *Dreams*, II, 232.
47. Philip Merlan, *Monopsychism, Mysticism, Metaconsciousness: Problems of the Soul in the Neoaristotelian and Neoplatonic Tradition* (The Hague, 1963), pp. 35ff.
48. Porphyry, *Life of Plotinus*, 4, 11; 5, 5.
49. Empedocles, fragment B109; Democritus, fragment B 164. Both in Dumont, ed., *Les Présocratiques*, pp. 417, 887.
50. *Enneads*, IV 7 (2), 27ff.
51. Ibid., IV, 7(2), 10, 30; I, 6 (1), 9, 7.
52. Ibid., V, 3 (49), 4, 14ff.
53. Ibid., V, 3(49), 4, 10.
54. Ibid., V, 1 (10), 12, 14.
55. See P. Hadot, Introduction to *Plotin: Traité 38* pp. 31–43.
56. *Enneads*, V, 8 (31), 10, 40.
57. Ibid., V, 3 (49), 8, 22. See also É. Bréhier, *La Philosophie de Plotin* (Paris, 1982), p. 98.
58. *Enneads*, V, 3 (49), 4, 29.
59. Ibid., VI, 5 (23), 12, 20.
60. Ibid., VI, 7 (38), 36, 19.
61. Ibid., VI, 9 (9), 1–4. See the French translation by P. Hadot, *Plotin: Traité 9* (Paris, 1994).

62. *Enneads*, VI, 9 (9), 3, 37–54.
63. Ibid., VI, 9 (9), 10; 15; 11, 11.
64. Ibid., VI, 9 (9), 11, 12.
65. Ibid., V, 3 (49), 17, 37.
66. Ibid., VI, 7 (38), 36, 6–10; VI, 9, (9), 4, 11–16.
67. Ibid., VI, 7 (38), 35, 19–33. See the commentary in P. Hadot, *Plotin: Traité 38*, pp. 37–43, 343–345.
68. See P. Hadot, *Plotin: Traité 9*, pp. 37–44.
69. *Enneads*, II, 9 (34), 15, 39–40.
70. On harmonization between Plato and Aristotle, see I. Hadot, "Aristote dans l'enseignement philosophique néoplatonicien," *Revue de Théologie et de Philosophie*, 124 (1992), pp. 407–425. On the Neoplatonic commentators' conception of Aristotle's work, see I. Hadot, *Simplicius: Commentaire sur les Catégories*, fasc. 1 (Leiden, 1990), pp. 63–107.
71. See A.-J. Festugière, "L'ordre de lecture des dialogues de Platon aux Ve–VIe siècles," in Festugière, *Études de philosophie grecque*, pp. 535–550.
72. See, for instance, R. Masullo, "Il tema degli 'Esercizi Spirituali' nella vita Isidori di Damascio," in *Talariskos: Studia Graeca Antonio Garzya sexagenario a discipulis oblata* (Naples, 1987), pp. 225–242.
73. See H. Lewy, *Chaldaean Oracles and Theurgy*, 2nd ed. (Paris, 1978; a third edition is in preparation); H.-D. Saffrey, *Recherches sur le néoplatonisme après Plotin* (Paris, 1990), pp. 33–94; P. Hadot, "Théologie, exégèse," pp. 26–29.
74. Iamblichus, *The Mysteries of Egypt*, ed. É. des Places (Paris, 1966), II, 11, p. 96.
75. Cf. A. Sheppard, "Proclus' Attitude to Theurgy," *Classical Quarterly*, 32 (1982), pp. 212–224; H.-D. Saffrey, "From Iamblichus to Proclus and Damascius," in A. H. Armstrong, ed., *Classical Mediterranean Spirituality* (New York, 1986), pp. 250–265.
76. Saffrey, *Recherches sur le néoplatonisme après Plotin*, pp. 54–56.

9. PHILOSOPHY AND PHILOSOPHICAL DISCOURSE

1. Cicero, *On the Ends of Goods and Evils*, III, 72; Diogenes Laertius, *Lives of the Philosophers*, VII, 39; 41.

2. Seneca, *On the Constancy of the Sage*, VII, 1; idem, *On Providence*, II, 9.

3. See I. Hadot, "Tradition stoïcienne et idées politiques au temps des Gracques," *Revue des études latines*, 48 (1970), pp. 174–178.

4. See P. Hadot, *The Inner Citadel* (Cambridge, Mass., 1998), pp. 4, 17–18.

5. Diogenes Laertius, *Lives of the Philosophers*, IV, 18.

6. In Porphyry, *Letter to Marcella*, § 31.

7. Epictetus, *Discourses*, III, 21, 4–6.

8. Seneca, *Letters to Lucilius*, 128, 23. See also J. Pépin, "Philologos/ Philosophos," in *Porphyre: La vie de Plotin*, vol. 2, French translation with commentary by L. Brisson et al. (Paris, 1992), pp. 477–501.

9. Plutarch, *How to Listen*, 43f.

10. Plutarch, *That the Philosopher Should Converse Primarily with the Great*, 776c–d.

11. P. Hadot, *The Inner Citadel*, pp. 48–51.

12. Diogenes Laertius, *Lives of the Philosophers*, IX, 64: VII, 171.

13. Horace, *Epistles*, I, 4, 4–5.

14. Epictetus, *Discourses*, III, 14, 1.

15. Empedocles, B CXXIX, in J. P. Dumont, ed., *Les Présocratiques* (Paris: Gallimard, Pléiade, 1988), p. 428.

16. J.-P. Vernant, *Mythe et pensée chez les Grecs* (Paris, 1971), vol. 1, p. 114. [In English, *Myth and Thought among the Greeks* (London: Routledge and Kegan Paul, 1983).—*Trans.*]

17. L. Gernet, *Anthropologie de la Grèce antique* (Paris, 1982), p. 252. [In English, *The Anthropology of Ancient Greece*, trans. John D. B. Hamilton and Blaise Nagy (Baltimore, Md.: Johns Hopkins University Press, 1981).—*Trans.*]

18. Empedocles, B CXXXII, p. 429 Dumont.

19. On the idea of the soul as breath, see Vernant, *Mythe et pensée chez les Grecs*, vol. 2, p. 111.

20. Diogenes Laertius, *Lives of the Philosophers*, VI, 76; 95.

21. Vernant, *Mythe et pensée chez les Grecs*, vol. 1, p. 96; vol. 2, p. 111.

22. R. N. Hamayon, *La chasse à l'âme: Esquisse d'une théorie du chamanisme sibérien* (Paris: Société d'Ethnologie, 1990). In what follows, I shall draw on Hamayon's exposition of shamanism entitled "Le chamanisme sibérien: Réflexion sur un médium," *La Recherche*, 275 (April 1995), pp. 416–422.

23. K. Meuli, "Scythica," *Hermes*, 70 (1935), pp. 137ff.

24. E. R. Dodds, *The Greeks and the Irrational*, Sather Classical Lectures 25 (Berkeley, 1963; 1st ed., 1951).

25. M. Eliade, *Le chamanisme et les techniques archaïques de l'extase* (Paris, 1968; 1st ed., 1951). [In English, *Shamanism: archaic techniques of ecstasy*, trans. from the French by Willard R. Trask (London: Arkana, 1989).—*Trans.*].

26. H. Joly, *Le renversement platonicien* (Paris: Vrin, 1974), pp. 67–69.

27. Hamayon, "Le chamanisme sibérien," pp. 418–419.

28. R. N. Hamayon, "Pour en finir avec la 'transe,' et l'extase' dans l'étude du chamanisme," *Études Mongoles et Sibériennes*, 26 (1995; Variations Chamaniques, II), pp. 155–190.

29. Hamayon, "Le chamanisme sibérien," p. 419.

30. *Symposium*, 174d.

31. Joly, *Le renversement platonicien*, p. 69.

32. Hamayon, "Le chamanisme sibérien," p. 419.

33. Maximus of Tyre, *Discourse*, XVI, 2, p. 60 Dübner, in F. Dübner, ed., *Theophrasti Characteres* (Paris: Didot, 1877).

34. J. D. P. Bolton, *Aristeas of Proconnesus* (Oxford, 1962).

35. Vernant, *Mythe et pensée chez les Grecs*, vol. 1, p. 114; vol. 2, p. 110, note 4.

36. Porphyry, *Life of Pythagoras*, §45. See also W. Burkert, *Lore and Science in Ancient Pythagoreanism* (Cambridge, Mass., 1972), pp. 139–141.

37. Iamblichus, *Life of Pythagoras*, §§164–165.

38. Vernant, *Mythe et pensée chez les Grecs*, vol. 1, p. 111.

39. M. Meunier, *Pythagore: Les Vers d'or; Hiéroclès: Commentaire sur les Vers d'or* (Paris, 1979), verses XL–XLIV, p. 226.

40. Diodorus Siculus, *Historical Library*, X, 5, 1; Cicero, *On Old Age*, 11, 38.

41. Porphyry, *Life of Pythagoras*, §40.

42. Plato, *Republic*, 600a–b.

43. See Burkert, *Lore and Science*, pp. 109–120, 192–208.

44. Seneca, *On Peace of Mind*, 2, 3; Plutarch, *On Peace of Mind*, 465c; Diogenes Laertius, *Lives of the Philosophers*, IX, 45. See also I. Hadot, *Seneca und die griechisch-römische Tradition der Seelenleitung* (Berlin: De Gruyter, 1969), pp. 135ff.; and P. Demont, *La cité grecque archaïque et classique et l'idéal de tranquillité* (Paris, 1990), p. 271.

45. Democritus, B XXXV ff.; *Les Présocratiques,* pp. 862–873 Dumont.
46. Democritus, B II; *Les Présocratiques,* p. 36 Dumont.
47. Antiphon the Sophist, A VI–VII, in *Les Présocratiques,* pp. 1094–1095 Dumont. See also G. Romeyer-Dherbey, *Les Sophistes* (Paris, 1985), pp. 110–115; M. Narcy, "Antiphon le Sophiste," *Dictionnaire des philosophes antiques,* vol. 1, p. 225–244; W. D. Furley, "Antiphon der Sophist: Ein Sophist als Psychotherapeut?" *Rheinisches Museum,* 135 (1992), pp. 198–216; and P. Demont, *La cité grecque archaïque,* pp. 253–255.
48. Antiphon B LVIII–LIX; *Les Présocratiques,* p. 1114 Dumont.
49. Antiphon, B LIIIa, LII; *Les Présocratiques,* p. 1112 Dumont.
50. On this prehistory, see I. Hadot, "The Spiritual Guide," in A. H. Armstrong, ed., *Classical Mediterranean Spirituality: Egyptian, Greek, Roman* (New York, 1986), pp. 436–444; and I. Hadot, *Seneca,* pp. 10ff.
51. French translation in A.-J. Festugière, *Deux prédicateurs de l'Antiquité: Télès et Musonius* (Paris: Vrin, 1978), pp. 69–71.
52. J. Delorme, *Gymnasion* (Paris, 1960), pp. 316–317, 466.
53. *Republic,* 611d.
54. Plotinus, *Enneads,* I 6 (1), 9, 7ff.
55. Marcus Aurelius, *Meditations,* XII, 3, 1 ff. See also P. Hadot, *The Inner Citadel,* pp. 112ff., 131–137.
56. *Meditations,* III, 10, 1.
57. Seneca, *Letters to Lucilius,* 78, 14.
58. Marcus Aurelius, *Meditations,* VIII, 36; XII, 1.
59. See P. Hadot, *The Inner Citadel,* p. 134–135.
60. Marcus Aurelius, *Meditations,* VII, 54.
61. See Epictetus, *Discourses,* IV, 12.
62. Marcus Aurelius, *Meditations,* II, 11; II, 5, 2; VII, 69; Epictetus, *Manual,* §21; Seneca, *Letters,* 93, 6; 101, 7.
63. Chrysippus, in Plutarch, *On Common Notions against the Stoics,* 1062a.
64. Seneca, *Letters,* 74, 27. Compare J. Kristeva, *Les Samouraïs* (Paris, 1990), p. 380: "The perfect circle, whether it is large or small, is happy because it is just."
65. Marcus Aurelius, *Meditations,* XI, 1, 1.
66. Seneca, *Letters,* 12, 9; 101, 10.
67. On the present in Stoicism and Epicureanism, see P. Hadot, "Le

présent seul est notre bonheur," *Diogène*, 1333 (January–March 1986), pp. 58–81.

68. *Nicomachean Ethics*, IX, 1170b1.
69. Diogenes Laertius, *Lives of the Philosophers*, X, 137. See also *Épicure: Lettres, maximes, sentences*, trans. and ed. J.-F. Balaudé (Paris, 1994), p. 135.
70. Cicero, *On the Ends of Goods and Evils*, I, 18, 60; Seneca, *Letters*, 15, 9.
71. Balaudé, ed., *Épicure*, p. 135.
72. Diogenes Laertius, *Lives of the Philosophers*, X, 22. See also Balaudé, ed., *Épicure*, p. 128.
73. Horace, *Odes*, II, 16, 35; III, 29, 33.
74. Ibid., I, 11, 7; idem, *Epistles*, I, 4, 13.
75. Philodemus, *On Death*, 37, 20, in M. Gigante, *Ricerche Filodemee* (Naples, 1983), pp. 181, 215–216.
76. On inner peace as based on the identity of being, being-oneself, ipseity, and feeling-oneself-exist, see the fine discussion in M. Hulin, *La mystique sauvage: Aux antipodes de l'esprit* (Paris, 1993), p. 237.
77. Seneca, *Letters*, I, 3, 1.
78. *Vatican Sayings*, §14, in Balaudé, ed., *Épicure*, p. 210.
79. *Capital Maxims*, XIX, p. 202 Balaudé; Cicero, *On the Ends of Goods and Evils*, I, 19, 63; II, 27, 87.
80. Aristotle, *Nicomachean Ethics*, X, 3, 1174a17ff. See also H.-J. Krämer, *Platonismus und hellenistische Philosophie* (Berlin, 1971), pp. 188ff.
81. C. Diano, "La philosophie du plaisir et la société des amis," in Diano, *Studi e saggi di filosofia antica* (Padua, 1973), p. 364.
82. Epicurus, *Letter to Menoecus*, §126, p. 193 Balaudé.
83. Wittgenstein, *Tractatus Logico-Philosophicus*, 6.4311.
84. Spinoza, *Ethics*, IV, proposition 67.
85. See H. Jaeger, "L'examen de la conscience dans les religions non chrétiennes et avant le christianisme," *Numen*, 6 (1959), pp. 175–233; idem, in *Dictionnaire de spiritualité*, IV, 2 (1961), cols. 1792–1794; I. Hadot, *Seneca*, pp. 66–71.
86. Quoted in Seneca, *Letters*, 28, 9.
87. Epictetus, *Discourses*, II, 11, 1.
88. Plutarch, *How One Can Become Aware of One's Progress in Virtue*, 82–83.
89. *Republic*, 571d.
90. Evagrius of Pontus, *Practical Monk's Treatise*, §§54–56. See also

F. Refoulé, "Rêves et vie spirituelle d'après Évagre le Pontique," *Supplément de la Vie Spirituelle*, 59 (1961), pp. 470–516.

91. *Letter of Aristeas*, §298. See also I. Hadot, *Seneca*, pp. 68–69. The *Letter* is a text of Jewish origin which dates from the second century B.C. but which was influenced by Greek philosophy.

92. Porphyry, *Life of Pythagoras*, §40; Epictetus, *Discourses*, III, 10, 3.

93. Galen, *On the Diagnosis and Treatment of the Passions Proper to Each Person's Soul*, French translation in V. Barras, T. Birchler, and A. F. Morand, eds. and trans., *Galien: L'âme et ses passions* (Paris, 1995), p. 23.

94. Seneca, *On Anger*, III, 36, 1–3; P. Rabbow, *Seelenführung: Methodik der Exerzitien in der Antike* (Munich, 1954), pp. 180–181.

95. Seneca, *Letters*, 28, 10.

96. *Hierocles, In Aureum . . . Carmen Commentarius*, XIX (40–44), ed. F. Köhler (Stuttgart, 1974), p. 80, 20; trans. Meunier, *Commentaire sur les Vers d'or*, p. 222.

97. Kant, *Metaphysics of Morals*, II: *First Metaphysical Principles of the Doctrine of Virtue*, I, 1, §113.

98. Epictetus, *Discourses*, II, 18, 12.

99. I. Hadot, *Seneca*, p. 70; Rabbow, *Seelenführung*, p. 182.

100. Marcus Aurelius, *Meditations*, II, 1.

101. Galen, *On Diagnosis*, 5, 6, p. 19.

102. Epictetus, *Discourses*, IV, 6, 34.

103. Ibid., III, 13, 6.

104. *Republic*, 486a.

105. *Phaedrus*, 246b–c.

106. *Theaetetus*, 173e.

107. Cicero, *On the Nature of the Gods*, I, 21, 54; Lucretius, *On Nature*, II, 1044–1047; ibid., III, 16 and 30.

108. A reference to the title of A. Koyré, *Du monde clos à l'univers infini* (Paris, 1973).

109. *Vatican Sayings*, 10, p. 210 Balaudé.

110. Seneca, *Letters*, 102, 21; idem, *Natural Questions*, I; idem, *Prologue*, 12. Marcus Aurelius, *Meditations*, XI, 1, 3; VII, 47, 1; X, 17.

111. Philo of Alexandria, *De specialibus legibus*, II, §45.

112. *Palatine Anthology*, IX, 577. French translation by A.-J. Festugière in *La révélation d'Hermès Trismégiste*, vol. 1 (Paris, 1944), p. 317.

113. See P. Hadot, *The Inner Citadel*, pp. 179–182.

114. E. Renan, *Oeuvres complètes*, vol. 2 (Paris, 1948), p. 1037.
115. Fong Yeou-Lan, *Précis de philosophie chinoise* (Paris, 1952), p. 128.
116. *Theaetetus*, 174e.
117. Cicero, *Republic*, VI, 9, 9. See also A.-J. Festugière, *La révélation d'Hermès Trismégiste*, vol. 2 (Paris, 1944), pp. 441–459.
118. Ovid, *Metamorphoses*, XV, 147ff.
119. Lucretius, *On Nature*, II, 8.
120. Seneca, *Natural Questions*, I, Prologue, 7–10.
121. *Timaeus*, 59c–d. See also J. Mittelstrass, *Die Rettung der Phänomene* (Berlin, 1962), p. 110.
122. Epicurus, *Letter to Herodotus*, 37, p. 152 Balaudé.
123. *Timaeus*, 90a.
124. J.-M. le Blond, *Aristote, philosophe de la vie* (Paris, 1944), p. 71.
125. [On the New Academy, see the section entitled "The Platonic Academy" in Chapter 7.—*Trans.*]
126. Seneca, *Natural Questions*, I, Prol. 17.
127. See the translation by Festugière, *La révélation d'Hermès Trismégiste*, vol. 2, pp. 165, 169.
128. Plutarch, *On Peace of Mind*, 477c–e.
129. Marcus Aurelius, *Meditations*, X, 5; V, 8, 12; IV, 26.
130. Seneca, *On Benefits*, VII, 2, 5; 3, 3.
131. Chrysippus, in Plutarch, *On Common Notions*, 37, 1078e.
132. Seneca, *Letters*, 66, 6.
133. Plotinus, *Enneads*, V, 3 (49), 4; 10; VI 7 (38), 34, 16–17.
134. I. Hadot, "The Spiritual Guide," pp. 436–459.
135. Simplicius, *Commentary on the Manual of Epictetus*, XXXII, line 154 in the edition by I. Hadot (Leiden: Brill, 1995).
136. I. Hadot, "The Spiritual Guide," pp. 441–444.
137. Marcus Aurelius, *Meditations*, I, 7, 1.
138. P. Rabbow, *Seelenführung*, pp. 260–279; I. Hadot, "The Spiritual Guide," pp. 444–459.
139. Diogenes Laertius, *Lives of the Philosophers*, IV, 6.
140. Plato, *Seventh Letter*, 330c–331a. Translation based on that of Luc Brisson: Plato, *Lettres* (Paris, 1986), pp. 176–177.
141. See Crates' attitude toward his disciple Zeno, in L. Paquet, *Les Cyniques grecs* (Paris, 1992), p. 166.
142. On this treatise, see M. Gigante, "Philodème: Sur la liberté de parole," *Actes du VIIIe Congrès de l'Association Guillaume Budé, 1968*

(Paris, 1970), pp. 196–200; idem, *Ricerche Filodemee*, 2nd ed. (Naples, 1983), pp. 55–113.

143. Translation based on that of A.-J. Festugière, in *Épicure et ses dieux*, p. 40; *Vatican Sayings*, LI, p. 216 Balaudé.

144. Porphyry, *Life of Plotinus*, 11, 13.

145. Eunapius, *Life of the Philosophers and the Sophists*, p. 57, 10–18 Giangrande. See also R. Goulet, "Aidésius de Cappadoce," in R. Goulet, ed., *Dictionnaire des philosophes anciens*, vol. I, p. 74.

146. [A line from an unknown tragedy.—Trans.]

147. Plutarch, *How to Listen*, 43d.

148. See J. de Romilly, "*Patience mon coeur!*" *L'essor de la psychologie dans la tragédie grecque classique* (Paris, 1984).

149. Lucretius, *On Nature*, III, 1068.

150. Seneca, *Letters*, 24, 26.

151. Seneca, *On Peace of Mind*, I, 1.

152. Marcus Aurelius, *Meditations*, XI, 13, 2; XI, 18, 18. See also P. Hadot, *The Inner Citadel*, pp. 225–226.

153. Marcus Aurelius, *Meditations*, V,6, 3.

154. Plato, *Euthyphro*, 3d6.

155. Sextus Empiricus, *Pyrrhonian Outlines*, III, 280 (Dumont, *Les Sceptiques*, p. 212).

156. Diogenes Laertius, *Lives of the Philosophers*, II, 66.

157. Plato, *Republic*, 387d12.

158. Aristotle, *Nicomachean Ethics*, X, 1177a27ff.

159. Xenocrates, fragment 4 , in R. Heinze, *Xenocrates: Darstellung der Lehre und Sammlung der Fragmente* (Leipzig, 1892).

160. Horace, *Odes*, III, 3, 1–8.

161. É. Bréhier, *Chrysippe*, pp. 216–218.

162. Xenocrates, in Plutarch, *Sayings of Spartans*, 220d.

163. *Stoicorum Veterum Fragmenta*, III, 221, 539–542; Plutarch, *How To Tell If One Is Making Progress*, 75c.

164. See P. Hadot, "La figure du sage dans l'Antiquité gréco-latine," in G. Gadoffre, ed., *Les Sagesses du monde* (Paris, 1991), pp. 9–26.

165. Epicurus, *Letter to Menoecus*, §135, p. 198 Balaudé.

166. Lucretius, *On Nature*, II, 646. See also Balaudé, p. 114.

167. Philodemus, *On the Gods*, III, pp. 16, 14 Diels. Compare the translation by Festugière, in *Épicure et ses dieux* (Paris, 1946), p. 98.

168. Plato, *Theaetetus*, 176b.

169. Plotinus, *Enneads,* V, 3 (49), 17, 1.

170. B. Frischer, *The Sculpted Word: Epicureanism and Philosophical Recruitment in Ancient Greece* (Berkeley, 1982), p. 83.

171. Seneca, *Letters,* 92, 27; *Stoicorum Veterum Fragmenta,* III, §§245–252.

172. Nietzsche, *Posthumous Fragments,* Fall 1887, 10 [90], in Nietzsche, *Werke,* ed. Giorgio Colli and Mazzino Montinari (Berlin, 1973), vol. 8, part 2, pp. 173–174.

173. B. Groethuysen, *Anthropologie philosophique* (Paris, 1952), p. 80 (originally published as *Philosophische Anthropologie* [Munich, 1931]).

174. Marcus Aurelius, *Meditations,* IX, 32.

175. Seneca, *Letters,* 64, 6. See also P. Hadot, "Le sage et le monde," *Le Temps de la Réflexion,* 10 (1989), pp. 175–188.

176. Lucretius, *On Nature,* II, 1023ff.

177. M. Hulin, *La mystique sauvage* (Paris, 1993).

178. Seneca, *Letters,* 41, 3–4. See also I. Hadot, *Seneca,* p. 94.

179. Kant, *Critique of Practical Reason,* Conclusion, vol. 5, p. 161.

180. P. Veyne, ed., *Sénèque: Entretiens, Lettres à Lucilius* (Paris, 1993), p. cx.

181. Lucian, *Hermotimus,* ch. 77.

182. J. Bouveresse, *Wittgenstein, la rime et la raison* (Paris, 1973), p. 74.

183. *Chrysippe,* p. 219, note 1. Bréhier quotes Sutta Nipata, trans. Oldenberg, *Deutsche Rundschau* (January 1910), p. 25.

184. Hulin, *La mystique sauvage,* pp. 243, 238–242.

10. CHRISTIANITY AS A REVEALED PHILOSOPHY

1. Heraclitus, fragment B 1, in J. P. Dumont, ed., *Les Présocratiques* (Paris: Gallimard, Pléiade, 1988), p. 145 Dumont.

2. Amelius, in Eusebius, *Evangelical Preparation,* XI, 19.

3. See L. Brisson, "Amélius: Sa vie, son oeuvre, sa doctrine, son style," in W. Haase and H. Temporini, eds., *Aufstieg und Niedergang der römischen Welt,* II, vol. 36, part 2 (1987), pp. 840–843.

4. Justin, *Apology II,* 8, 1; 13, 3. Translated in A. Wartelle, ed., *Saint Justin: Apologies—introduction, texte, traduction et commentaire* (Paris, 1987).

5. Justin, *Apology I*, 46, 3–4.

6. Clement, *Stromata*, I, 11, 52, 3 (translation based on that by Marcel Caster in the Sources Chrétiennes series, no. 30 [Paris: Éditions du Cerf, 1951]. Compare the interesting text by Gregory the Wonder-Worker, entitled *Thanksgiving to Origen*. It describes Origen's school as a traditional philosophical school, which featured love between master and disciple, and dialectical exercises; but philosophy was subordinated to Christian theology.

7. Origen, *Commentary on the Song of Songs*, Prologue, 3, 1–23, ed. L. Brézard, H. Crouzel, and M. Borret, Sources Chrétiennes, nos. 375–376 (Paris, 1991), I, pp. 128–143. See also I. Hadot, Introduction to *Simplicius: Commentaire sur les Catégories*, fasc. I (Leiden, 1990), pp. 36–44.

8. See P. Hadot, "Théologie, exégèse, révélation, écriture dans la philosophie grecque," in M. Tardieu, ed., *Les règles de l'interprétation* (Paris, 1987), pp. 13–34.

9. J. Leclercq, "Pour l'histoire de l'expression 'philosophie chrétienne,'" *Mélanges de Science Religieuse*, 9 (1952), pp. 221–226.

10. Justin, *Apology I*, 46, 3 Wartelle.

11. Clement of Alexandria, *Stromata*, II, 20, 120, 1 Mondésert (Sources Chrétiennes).

12. Origen, *Commentary on the Song of Songs*, II, 5, 7, vol. 1, p. 359, Brézard/Crouzel/Borret.

13. J. Gribomont, "Monasticism and Asceticism," in M. McGinn, J. Meyendorff, and J. Leclercq, eds., *Christian Spirituality* (New York: Crossroad, 1986), p. 91.

14. See the introduction by F. Daumas to Philo of Alexandria, *De vita contemplativa*, in the Sources Chrétiennes series (Paris, 1963), especially p. 31.

15. L. Bouyer, *La Spiritualité du Nouveau Testament et des Pères* (Paris, 1960), pp. 400–472.

16. There are many examples in Gregory Nazianzen, *Letters*, vols. 1–2, ed. P. Gallay (Paris: Les Belles Lettres, 1964–1967), vol. 1, pp. 39, 60, 71, 74, 114; vol. 2, pp. 14, 85. See also H. Hunger, *Die Hochsprächliche profane Literatur der Byzantiner*, vol. 1 (Munich, 1978), pp. 4–10 (with abundant bibliography); and A.-M. Malingrey, *Philosophia* (Paris, 1961).

17. Athanasius, *Life of Antony*, 14, 4, ed. G. J. M. Bartelink, Sources Chrétiennes, no. 400 (Paris, 1994), p. 175; and 20, 56, pp. 189–191; Evagrius, *Monk's Practical Treatise*, ed. A. and C. Guillaumont, Sources Chrétiennes, nos. 170–171 (Paris, 1971), §86, p. 677.

18. Rufinus, *Historia Monachorum*, 7, 29; in *Patrologia latina*, vol. 21, col. 410d, 453. See also J. Leclercq, "Exercices spirituels," in *Dictionnaire de spiritualité* (Paris, 1961), vol. 4, part 2, cols. 1902–1908.

19. Athanasius, *Life of Antony*, 3, 1, p. 137; 91, 3, p. 369.

20. Gregory Nazianzen, *Letters*, vol. 2, p. 45 (Letter 153).

21. Athanasius, *Life of Antony*, 19, 3, p. 187; Dorotheus of Gaza, *Spiritual Works*, ed. L. Regnault and J. de Préville, Sources Chrétiennes, no. 92 (Paris, 1963), §114, 1–15.

22. Deuteronomy, 15:9.

23. Basil of Caesarea, *In illud attende tibi ipsi*, in *Patrologia Graeca*, 31, cols. 197–217; critical edition by S. Y. Rudberg, in *Acta Universitatis Stockholmensis: Studia Graeca Stockholmensia*, vol. 2 (Stockholm, 1962).

24. Athanasius, *Life of Antony*, 55, 9, p. 285. See also M. Foucault, "L'écriture de soi," *Corps Écrit*, 5 (1983), pp. 3–23, along with my remarks on Foucault's text: P. Hadot, "Réflexions sur la notion de 'culture de soi,'" in *Michel Foucault philosophe* (Paris, 1989), pp. 264–266.

25. Dorotheus of Gaza, *Spiritual Works*, §§111, 13 and 117, 7 (pp. 353, 365).

26. See *Les apophthegmes des Pères: Collection systématique*, chs. 1–9, ed. and trans. J.-G. Guy, in the Sources Chrétiennes series (Paris, 1993).

27. Dorotheus of Gaza, *Spiritual Works*, §60, 27–30.

28. Ibid., §20, 1–33. See also Epictetus, *Discourses*, I, 18, 18; *Manual*, 12, 2.

29. Dorotheus of Gaza, *Spiritual Works*, §20, 28; §187, 14–16.

30. Cicero, *Tusculans*, IV, 75.

31. Evagrius, *Practical Treatise*, §58

32. Ibid., §86.

33. Clement of Alexandria, *Stromata*, V, 11, 67, 1, ed. A. le Boulluec, Sources Chrétiennes, nos. 278–279 (Paris, 1981), p. 137.

34. Gregory Nazianzen, *Letters*, XXXI, vol. 1, p. 39.

35. Evagrius, *Practical Treatise*, §52. Cf. the commentary by A. and C. Guillaumont in their Sources Chrétiennes edition.
36. Porphyry, Sentence 8.
37. Dorotheus of Gaza, *Life of Dositheus*, §6.
38. Proverbs, 4:23; Athanasius, *Life of Antony*, 21, 2, p. 193.
39. Paul's Second Epistle to the Corinthians, 13:5; Athanasius, *Life of Antony*, 55, 6, p. 283.
40. Evagrius, *Practical Treatise*, §1.
41. Ibid., §§2–3.
42. Origen, *De oratione*, 25. See the note by A. and C. Guillaumont in *Evagrius: Traité pratique*, vol. 2, pp. 499–503, Sources Chrétiennes, no. 171.
43. Augustine, *De vera religione*, III, 3, in Bibliothèque Augustinienne, Oeuvres de Saint Augustin, no. 8, 1st series: *Opuscules*, VIII: *La foi chrétienne*, ed. and trans. Pegon (Paris, 1951).
44. Augustine, *De vera religione*, IV, 7.
45. Nietzsche, *Beyond Good and Evil*, Preface.
46. Dorotheus of Gaza, "Instructions," in *Spiritual Works*, §§58–60.

11. ECLIPSES AND RECURRENCES OF THE ANCIENT CONCEPT OF PHILOSOPHY

1. See Chapter 10, above (section entitled "Christianity Defines Itself as Philosophy").
2. J. Domański, *La Philosophie: Théorie ou manière de vivre? Les controverses de l'Antiquité à la Renaissance*, preface by Pierre Hadot (Paris: Éditions du Cerf, 1996).
3. P. Hadot, *Exercices spirituels et philosophie antique*, 3rd ed. (Paris, 1993), pp. 56–57, 222–225.
4. F. Suárez, *Disputationes metaphysicae*, in *Opera omnia*, ed. Vivès (1861), vol. 25, *Ratio et discursus totius operis*, cited in É. Gilson, *L'esprit de la philosophie médiévale* (Paris, 1944), p. 414, where Gilson gives a series of texts on the notion of Christian philosophy.
5. For a history of the notion, see B. Baudoux, "Philosophia *ancilla theologiae*," *Antonianum*, 12 (1937), pp. 293–326; É. Gilson, "La servante de la théologie," in *Études de philosophie médiévale*, Publica-

tions de la Faculté des Lettres de l'Université de Strasbourg, fasc. 3 (Strasbourg, 1921), pp. 30–50. See also the remarks by A. Cantin in his introduction to Peter Damian, *Lettre sur la Toute-Puissance divine*, in the series Sources Chrétiennes, no. 191 (Paris, 1972), p. 251, note 3.

6. See I. Hadot, *Arts libéraux et philosophie dans la pensée antique* (Paris, 1984), pp. 282–287; M. Alexandre, "Introduction," in Philo of Alexandria, *De congressu eruditionis gratia*, in *Oeuvres de Philon d'Alexandrie*, vol. 16 (Paris, 1967), pp. 27–96. See also H. A. Wolfson, *Philo: Foundations of Religious Philosophy in Judaism, Christianity, and Islam* (Cambridge, Mass., 1947), pp. 156–157.

7. Philo of Alexandria, *De congressu*, §11. See also I. Hadot, *Arts libéraux et philosophie*, p. 282.

8. Philo of Alexandria, *De congressu*, 79–80. See also I. Hadot, *Arts libéraux et philosophie*, p. 284; Alexandre, "Introduction," pp. 71–72.

9. See the texts by Clement and Origen cited in Alexandre, "Introduction," pp. 83–97; and in I. Hadot, *Arts libéraux et philosophie*, pp. 287–289.

10. Augustine, *De doctrina christiana*, 40, 60, in Bibliothèque Augustinienne, *Oeuvres de Saint Augustin*, vol. 11, 1st series, *Opuscules*, XI: *Le Magistère chrétien* (Paris, 1997), p. 331 Combès/Farges.

11. Alcuin, *Epistulae*, 280, in *Monumenta Germaniae Historica: Epistulae*, vol. 4, p. 437, 27–31 Dümmler. See also J. Domański, *La Philosophie*, ch. 2.

12. See É. Jeauneau, *Lectio philosophorum*, in *Recherches sur l'École de Chartres* (Amsterdam, 1972).

13. See Ph. Delehaye, *Enseignement morale au XIIe siècle* (Fribourg and Paris, 1988), pp. 1–58.

14. M.-D. Chenu, *Introduction à l'étude de saint Thomas d'Aquin* (Paris, 1954), p. 16.

15. See J. Domański, *La Philosophie*, ch. 2, pp. 43–44, note 18.

16. See P. Hadot, "La préhistoire des genres littéraires philosophiques médiévaux dans l'Antiquité," in *Les Genres littéraires dans les sources théologiques et philosophiques médiévales*, Actes du Colloque International de Louvain-la-Neuve, 1981 (Louvain-la-Neuve, 1982), pp. 1–9.

17. Kant, *Critique of Pure Reason,* trans. Norman Kemp Smith (London, 1933); idem, *Logik,* vol. 9 (Berlin, 1923), p. 25.
18. See É. Gilson, *L'esprit de la philosophie médiévale,* pp. 1–38.
19. Ibid., p. 25.
20. M. Abensour and P.-J. Labarrière, "Preface," in Schopenhauer, *Contre la philosophie universitaire* (Paris, 1994), p. 9. This entire preface is important from the perspective of the ideas we are developing here.
21. See the pages that J. Bouveresse devotes to the career of philosophy professor in his book *Wittgenstein: La rime et la raison* (Paris, 1973), pp. 73–75.
22. Ibid., p. 74.
23. Cf. Domański, *La Philosophie,* chs. 2–3.
24. Boethius of Dacia, *De summo bono,* translated in R. Imbach and M.-H. Méléard, *Philosophes médiévaux: Anthologie de textes philosophiques, XIIIe–XIVe siècle* (Paris, 1986), pp. 158–166.
25. Aubry of Reims, cited in A. de Libera, *Penser au Moyen Âge* (Paris, 1991), p. 147.
26. See Libera, *Penser au Moyen Âge,* pp. 317–347, esp. pp. 344–347.
27. See Domański, *La Philosophie,* ch. 2.
28. Petrarch, *De sui ipsius et multorum ignorantia,* in G. Martelotti, ed., *Petrarca: Prose* (Milan, 1955), p. 744. On the following points, see Domański, *La Philosophie,* pp. 91ff.
29. Petrarch, *De vita solitaria,* II, 7, in Martelotti, ed., *Petrarca: Prose,* pp. 524–526. As Domański remarks (*La Philosophie,* p. 94, note 5), the expression "professors sitting in a chair" comes from Seneca, *On the Brevity of Life,* X, 1.
30. Petrarch, *De sui ipsius et multorum ignorantia,* pp. 746–748: "Satius est autem bonum velle quam verum nosse."
31. Erasmus, *Adagia,* 2201 (3, 3, 1) in *Opera omnia* (Amsterdam, 1969), II, 5, p. 162, 25–166, 18. See also Domański, *La Philosophie,* pp. 114ff. and 115, note 44.
32. Montaigne, *Essais,* II, 6, ed. Thibaudet (Paris: Gallimard, Pléiade, 1962), p. 359.
33. See D. Babut, "Du scepticisme au dépassement de la raison: Philosophie et foi religieuse chez Plutarque," in *Parerga: Choix d'articles de D. Babut* (Lyon, 1994), p. 549–581.

34. Montaigne, *Essais*, III, 13, pp. 1088, 1096. See also H. Friedrich, *Montaigne* (Paris, 1949), p. 337.

35. H. Dreyfus and P. Rabinow, *Michel Foucault: Un parcours philosophique* (Paris, 1984), pp. 345–346.

36. M. Butor, "L'usage des pronoms personnels dans le roman," in I. Meyerson, ed., *Problèmes de la personne* (Paris and The Hague, 1973), pp. 288–290.

37. Descartes, "Réponses aux Secondes Objections contre les . . . *Méditations*," in Ch. Adam and P. Tannery, *Descartes: Oeuvres*, vol. 9 (Paris, 1964), pp. 103–104.

38. Descartes, *Discours de la méthode*, part 2, text with commentary by Étienne Gilson (Paris, 1939), p. 18, 15.

39. See *Stoicorum Veterum Fragmenta*, II, §§130–131; Diogenes Laertius, *Lives of the Philosophers*, VII, 46–48. Avoiding hasty judgment is a Stoic virtue; Descartes probably found it not in Saint Thomas, as Gilson believes (*Discours de la méthode*, p. 198) but rather in the Stoics, either modern (Gilson himself cites Guillaume du Vair, *La philosophie morale des Stoïques*, 1603 edition, p. 55) or ancient, for instance in Diogenes Laertius.

40. Kant, *Opus postumum*, French translation by F. Marty (Paris, 1986), pp. 245–246.

41. Ibid., p. 262.

42. Kant, *Vorlesungen über die philosophische Encyclopädie*, in *Kants gesammelte Schriften*, vol. 29 (Berlin: Akademie, 1980), p. 8.

43. Ibid.

44. Ibid.

45. Ibid., p. 9.

46. Ibid., p. 12.

47. Kant, *Critique of Pure Reason*, trans. Norman Kemp Smith, p. 658.

48. Ibid., pp. 658–659. Cf. Kant, *Critique of Practical Reason*, II, 1.

49. Kant, *Critique of Pure Reason*, trans. Norman Kemp Smith, p. 657.

50. Plato, *Republic*, 480a6.

51. É. Weil, *Problèmes kantiens* (Paris, 1990), p. 37, note 17.

52. Kant, *Logik*, vol. 9, p. 25. On the cosmic conception of philosophy, see J. Ralph Lindgren, "Kant's *Conceptus Cosmicus*," *Dialogue*, 1 (1963–1964), pp. 280–300.

53. See H. Holzhey, "Der Philosoph für die Welt—eine Chimäre der

deutschen Aufklärung," in H. Holzhey and W. C. Zimmerli, eds., *Esoterik und Exoterik der Philosophie* (Basel, 1977), pp. 117–138, esp. p. 133.

54. Kant, *Critique of Pure Reason*, trans. Norman Kemp Smith, p. 562.
55. Weil, *Problèmes kantiens*, p. 34.
56. Kant, *Fundamental Principles of the Metaphysics of Morals*, trans. Thomas Kingsmill Abbott.
57. Kant, *Critique of Pure Reason*, trans. Norman Kemp Smith, p. 657.
58. Kant, *Logik*, vol. 9, p. 25; idem, *Critique of Pure Reason*, trans. Norman Kemp Smith, p. 635.
59. Kant, *Critique of Practical Reason*, end of section III, "Of the Primacy of Pure Practical Reason in Its Union with the Speculative Reason."
60. Kant, *Critique of the Faculty of Judgment*, trans. James Creed Meredith, §42.
61. Kant, *Introduction to the Metaphysics of Morals*, Part II: *Metaphysical Principles of Virtue*, II, §53.
62. See Anthony Ashley Cooper, Third Earl of Shaftesbury, *Characteristicks of Men, Manners, Opinions, Times*. Shaftesbury speaks of spiritual exercises according to Epictetus and Marcus Aurelius.

12. QUESTIONS AND PERSPECTIVES

1. É. Gilson, *L'esprit de la philosophie médiévale* (Paris, 1944), pp. 11–16.
2. S. Zac, "Kant, les stoïciens et le christianisme," *Revue de métaphysique et de morale* (1972), pp. 137–165.
3. R. Rochlitz, "Esthétique de l'existence," in *Michel Foucault philosophe* (Paris, 1989), p. 290, speaks of a "secularized Christian and humanist inheritance."
4. Plotinus, *Enneads*, V, 6 [24], 5, 9.
5. G. Gabriel, "La logique comme littérature? De la signification de la forme littéraire chez Wittgenstein," *Le Nouveau Commerce*, 82–83 (Spring 1992), p. 77.
6. Wittgenstein, *Tractatus Logico-Philosophicus*, 6.4311.
7. See the excellent explanations in J. Bouveresse, *Wittgenstein: La rime et la raison* (Paris, 1973), pp. 89, 21–81.
8. See, for example, the numerous works by Arnold I. Davidson, in par-

ticular "Ethics as Ascetics: Foucault, the History of Ethics, and Ancient Thought," in J. Goldstein, ed., *Foucault and the Writing of History* (Oxford, 1994), pp. 63–80. See also H. Hutter, "Philosophy as Self-Transformation," *Historical Reflections*, 16, nos. 2–3 (1989), pp. 171–198; R. Imbach, "La philosophie comme exercice spirituel," *Critique*, 41, no. 454 (March 1985), pp. 275–283; J.-L. Solère, "Philosophie et amour de la sagesse: Entre les Anciens et nous, l'Inde," in J. Poulain, ed., *Inde, Europe, Postmodernité*, originally Colloque de Céret, 1991 (Paris, 1993), pp. 149–198; and J. Schlanger, *Gestes de philosophes* (Paris, 1994).

9. M. Merleau-Ponty, *Phénoménologie de la perception* (Paris, 1945), p. xvi.

10. G. Friedmann, *La puissance et la sagesse* (Paris, 1970), p. 359.

11. Nietzsche, *Posthumous fragments* (Fall 1881), 15 [59], in Nietzsche, *Werke*, ed. Giorgio Colli and Mazzino Montinari (Berlin, 1973), vol. 5, part 2, pp. 552–553.

12. See Goethe's conversation with Falk, in F. von Biedermann, ed., *Goethes Gespräche* (Leipzig, 1910), vol. 4, p. 469; Wittgenstein, *Tractatus*, 6.4311, where he alludes to the Epicurean conception of death and to the Stoic conception of the future; and K. Jaspers, "Epikur," in Benno Reifenberg and Emil Staiger, eds., *Weltbewohner und Weimaraner: Festschrift E. Beutler* (Zurich, 1960), pp. 132–133.

13. P. Hadot, *The Inner Citadel* (Cambridge, Mass., 1998), pp. 310–313.

14. J. Gernet, *Chine et christianisme*, 2nd ed. (Paris, 1991), p. 191; idem, "La sagesse chez Wang-Fou-tche, philosophe chinois du XVIIe siècle," in G. Gadoffre, ed., *Les Sagesses du monde* (Paris, 1991), pp. 103–104.

15. See G. Bugault, *L'Inde pense-t-elle?* (Paris, 1994); R.-P. Droit, *L'oubli de l'Inde* (Paris, 1989); M. Hulin, *La mystique sauvage* (Paris, 1993); Solère, "Philosophie et amour de la sagesse"; and idem, "L'Orient de la pensée," *Les Cahiers de philosophie*, 14 (1992), pp. 4–42.

16. Chuang-tzu, "Autumn Floods" and "T'ien Tseu-Fang," trans. Liou Kia-Hway, in *Philosophes taoïstes* (Paris: Gallimard, Pléiade, 1980), pp. 202, 244.

17. On Goethe, see P. Hadot, "'Le présent seul est notre bonheur': La valeur de l'instant présent chez Goethe dans la philosophie antique," *Diogène*, 133 (1986), pp. 58–81; and idem, "La terre vue d'en haut et

le voyage cosmique: Le point de vue du poète, du philosophe et de l'historien," in *Frontières et conquête spatiales* (Dordrecht and London, 1988), pp. 31–39. For Nietzsche, see *Nietzsche contra Wagner,* Epilogue, I, in Nietzsche, *Werke,* vol. 6, part 3, pp. 434–435: "All that is necessary, when seen from above and in the optics of the economy of the whole, is also useful in itself. We must not only put up with it; we must love it." And for Wittgenstein, see the *Tractatus,* 6.4311 and 6.45.

18. Solère, "Philosophie et amour de la sagesse," p. 198.

19. Yu-Lin Kin, cited in Yu-lan Feng, *Précis d'histoire de la philosophie chinoise* (Paris, 1952), pp. 31–32.

20. Plato, Seventh Letter, 328c, translation based on that of Luc Brisson, *Platon: Lettres* (Paris, 1986), p. 173.

21. See R.-P. Droit, "Philosophie de printemps," *Le Monde des livres* (April 21, 1995), p. ix. Droit cites Kant, *Reflexionen zur Metaphysik,* no. 6204, in *Kant's Gesammelte Schriften,* Akademie edition (Berlin and Leipzig, 1928), vol. 18, p. 488 (*Kants Handschriftlicher Nachlass,* vol. 5: *Die Metaphysik,* part 2, I): "being enlightened means thinking for oneself."

22. G. Friedmann, *La puissance et la sagesse* (Paris, 1970), p. 360.

23. Marcus Aurelius, *Meditations,* IX, 29, 5. See also P. Hadot, *The Inner Citadel,* pp. 303–306.

Quotations of Ancient Texts

Exact references to citations of ancient texts are usually given in the notes. However, for truly "classical" authors like Aristotle or Plato, I have not given references to any particular translations or editions. Instead, I have simply reproduced the usual references which figure in the margins of all editions—for instance, in the case of Plato: *Symposium*, 208e. Alternatively, I have given the divisions by books, chapters and paragraphs which are habitually used in quoting the works of authors like Cicero or Epictetus. In order to complete the succinct information given in the notes, the following specifications are intended to help the reader who would like to consult the texts, by furnishing information on the collections of ancient texts which I have used.

ARISTAEUS. See *Letter of Aristaeus.*

ARISTOPHANES. *The Clouds,* edited with introduction and commentary by K. J. Dover (Oxford: Clarendon Press, 1968). In English in *Lysistrata; The Acharnians; The Clouds,* translated with introduction by Alan H. Sommerstein (Harmondsworth: Penguin Books, 1973).

ARISTOTLE. *The Complete Works,* revised Oxford translation, edited by Jonathan Barnes, 2 vols., Bollingen series, no. LXXI.2 (Princeton: Princeton University Press, 1984).

AUGUSTINE. *Concerning the City of God against the Pagans,* translated by Henry Bettenson, with introduction by John O'Meara (Harmondsworth: Penguin Books, 1984).

AULUS GELLIUS. *The Attic Nights*, with English translation by John C. Rolfe, 3 vols., Loeb Classical Library (Cambridge, Mass.: Harvard University Press, 1967–1984; orig. pub. 1927–1928).

CICERO. Works, in 28 vols., Loeb Classical Library (Cambridge, Mass.: Harvard University Press).

CLEMENT OF ALEXANDRIA. *Ante-Nicene Fathers: Translations of the Writings of the Fathers Down to* A.D. *325*, vol. 2: *Fathers of the Second Century—Hermas, Tatian, Athenagoras, Theophilus, and Clement of Alexandria* (Grand Rapids, Mich.: Eerdmans, 1983; rpt. of Edinburgh edition).

——— *The Pedagogue*, I–III.

——— *Stromata*, I–II.

DIODORUS SICULUS. *Historical Library*, Greek text and English translation by various authors, under the title *Diodorus Siculus*, vols. I–XII, Loeb Classical Library (Cambridge, Mass.: Harvard University Press, 1933–1967).

DIOGENES LAERTIUS. English translation with Greek text by R. D. Hicks, Loeb Classical Library, nos. 184–185 (Cambridge, Mass.: Harvard University Press, 1925 and various reprints).

EPICTETUS. *The Discourses as Reported by Arrian, the Manual, and Fragments*, with English translation by W. A. Oldfather, 2 vols., Loeb Classical Library (Cambridge, Mass.: Harvard University Press, 1925).

EUSEBIUS OF CAESAREA. *Preparation for the Gospel*, translated by Edwin Hamilton Gifford, 2 vols. Twin book series (Grand Rapids, Mich.: Baker Book House, 1981; orig. pub. 1903), cited as *Evangelical Preparation*.

EVAGRIUS PONTICUS. *The Praktikos and Chapters on Prayer*, translated, with introduction and notes, by John Eudes Bamberger, Cistercian Studies series, no. 4 (Kalamazoo, Mich.: Cistercian Publications, 1978).

HERODOTUS. *The Histories*, with English translation by A. D. Godley, 4 vols., Loeb Classical Library (Cambridge, Mass.: Harvard University Press, 1920).

HESIOD. *The Homeric Hymns and Homerica*, with an English translation by Hugh G. Evelyn-White, Loeb Classical Library (Cambridge, Mass.: Harvard University Press, 1925).

HOMER. *The Iliad,* translated with introduction by Richmond Lattimore (Chicago: University of Chicago Press, 1951).

———— *The Odyssey,* translated by Richmond Lattimore (New York: Harper and Row, 1965).

HORACE. *The Complete Odes and Epodes, with the Centennial Hymn,* translated and edited by W. G. Shepherd, with an introduction by Betty Radice (Harmondsworth: Penguin Books, 1983).

ISOCRATES. Works, with an English translation by George Norlin, 3 vols., Loeb Classical Library (Cambridge, Mass.: Harvard University Press, 1954–1956).

IAMBLICHUS. *On the Pythagorean Life,* text, translation, and notes by John Dillon and Jackson Hershbell, Texts and Translations, no. 29, Graeco-Roman Religion series, no. 11 (Atlanta: Scholars Press, 1991), cited as *Life of Pythagoras.*

LETTER OF ARISTEAS. Translated, with an appendix of ancient evidence on the origin of the Septuagint, by H. St. J. Thackeray, Translations of Ancient Documents series II, Hellenistic-Jewish Texts, no. 3 (London: S.P.C.K., 1917).

LUCRETIUS. *Titi Lucreti Cari De rerum natura libri sex,* edited with prolegomena, critical apparatus, translation, and commentary by Cyril Bailey, 3 vols. (Oxford: Clarendon Press, 1986; orig. pub. 1947), cited as *On Nature.*

MARCUS AURELIUS. *The Meditations of the Emperor Marcus Antoninus,* edited with translation and commentary by A. S. L. Farquharson, 2 vols. (Oxford: Clarendon Press, 1944).

NUMENIUS. *The Neoplatonic Writings,* collected and translated by Kenneth Guthrie, with a foreword by Michael Wagner (Lawrence, Kansas: Selene Books, 1987).

OVID. *The Metamorphoses,* translated by A. D. Melville, with introduction and notes by E. J. Kenney (Oxford: Oxford University Press, 1986).

PHILO OF ALEXANDRIA. Works, with English translation by F. H. Colson and G. H. Whitaker, 12 vols., Loeb Classical Library (Cambridge, Mass.: Harvard University Press, 1929–1962).

PLATO. *The complete Works,* edited, with introduction and notes, by John M. Cooper, associate editor D. S. Hutchinson (Indianapolis: Hackett, 1997).

PLINY THE ELDER. *The Natural History,* with English translation by H. Rackham , 10 vols., Loeb Classical Library (Cambridge, Mass.: Harvard University Press, 1967–1975).

PLOTINUS. *Enneads,* in the edition of his works edited, with English translation, by A. H. Armstrong, 7 vols., Loeb Classical Library (Cambridge, Mass.: Harvard University Press, 1966–1988).

PLUTARCH. *Moralia,* 16 vols., Loeb Classical Library (Cambridge, Mass.: Harvard University Press).

PORPHYRY. *Life of Pythagoras, Letter to Marcella,* edited, with French translation, by Édouard des Places (Paris: Les Belles Lettres, 1982).

——— *On Abstinence from Killing Animals,* translated by Gillian Clark, Ancient Commentators on Aristotle (Ithaca, N.Y.: Cornell University Press, 2000).

——— *Porphyry, the Philosopher, to Marcella,* text and translation with introduction and notes by Kathleen O'Brien Wicker, Index verborum by Lee E. Klosinski, Texts and Translations, no. 28; Graeco-Roman Religion series, no. 10 (Atlanta: Scholars Press, 1987).

——— *Sententiae,* Greek text edited by E. Lamberz (Leipzig: Teubner, 1975).

PROCLUS. *Commentaries on the Timaeus of Plato, in Five Books, Containing a Treasury of Pythagoric and Platonic Physiology,* translated from the Greek by Thomas Taylor, 2 vols. (London: Privately printed, 1820).

SENECA. *Ad Lucilium epistulae morales,* with English translation by Richard M. Gummere, 3 vols., Loeb Classical Library (Cambridge, Mass.: Harvard University Press, 1979; orig. pub. 1917).

SEXTUS EMPIRICUS. *Works,* in 4 vols., English translation by R. G. Bury, Loeb Classical Library, nos. 273, 291, and 311 (Cambridge, Mass.: Harvard University Press, 1935–1936 and various reprints).

SOLON. *Elegy to the Muses,* Greek text in E. Diehl, *Anthologia Lyrica Graeca* (Leipzig: Teubner, 1953), p. 20.

THUCYDIDES. *History of the Peloponnesian War,* 4 vols., with English translation by Charles Forster Smith, Loeb Classical Library (Cambridge, Mass.: Harvard University Press, 1965–1969).

XENOPHON. *Conversations of Socrates,* translated by Hugh Tredennick and Robin Waterfield, edited with new material by Robin Waterfield (London: Penguin Books, 1990).

Selected Bibliography

In addition to the works cited in the notes, readers may consult the following se-
lection—intentionally limited—of works which may contribute information on
the themes dealt with in this book.

Archiv für Begriffsgeschichte, vol. 2 (1982), pp. 166–230 (homage to Jacob
   Lanz). Articles in German on the notion of "philosopher."
Babut, D. *La religion des philosophes grecs, de Thalès aux Stoïciens.* Paris,
   1974.
Boyancé, P. *Lucrèce et l'épicurisme.* Paris, 1963.
Brochard, V. *Les sceptiques grecs.* 2nd ed. Paris, 1932. Reprint, 1959.
Davidson, A. "Introduction" to Pierre Hadot, *Philosophy as a Way of Life.*
   Trans. Michael Chase. Oxford, 1995. Pp. 1–45.
Detienne, M. *Les maîtres de vérité dans la Grèce archaïque.* Paris, 1967. On
   religious and intellectual aspects of Presocratic thought.
Dumont, J.-P. *Éléments d'histoire de la philosophie antique.* Paris, 1993.
Friedländer, P. *Plato, I: An Introduction.* Princeton, 1973.
Hadot, P. *Exercices spirituels et philosophie antique.* 3rd ed. Paris, 1993.
———— *Philosophy as a Way of Life.* Trans. Michael Chase. Oxford, 1995.
———— "La philosophie hellénistique." In J. Russ, ed., *Histoire de la
   philosophie: Les pensées formatrices.* Paris, 1993.
———— "Il y a de nos jours des professeurs de philosophie, mais pas de
   philosophes." In *L'Herne: Henry D. Thoreau.* Paris, 1994. Pp. 188–
   193.

——— "Émerveillements." In *La bibliothèque imaginaire du Collège de France*, ed. F. Gaussen. Paris, 1990. Pp. 121–128.

Hersch, J. *L'Étonnement philosophique: Une histoire de la philosophie.* Paris, 1981. 2nd ed., 1993.

Hijmans, B.-L., Jr. *Askēsis: Notes on Epictetus' Educational System.* Assen, 1959.

Ingenkamp, H.-G. *Plutarch's Schriften über die Heilung der Seele.* Göttingen, 1971.

Jordan, W. *Ancient Concepts of Philosophy.* London and New York, 1990.

Kimmich, D. *Epikureische Aufklärungen: Philosophische und poetische Konzepte der Selbstsorge.* Darmstadt, 1993.

Lakmann, M.-L. *Der Platoniker Tauros in der Darstellung des Aulus Gellius.* Leiden, 1995.

Nussbaum, M. C. *The Therapy of Desire: Theory and Practice in Hellenistic Ethics.* Princeton, 1994.

Perret, J. "Le bonheur du sage." In *Hommage à Henry Bardon.* Collection Latomus, vol. 187. Brussels, 1985. Pp. 291–298.

Philip, J. A. *Pythagoras and Early Pythagoreanism. Phoenix* (Toronto), supplementary volume 7. University of Toronto Press, 1966. pp. 159–162. A critique of the shamanistic interpretation.

Pigeaud, J. *La maladie de l'âme: Étude sur la relation de l'âme et du corps dans la tradition médico-philosophique antique.* Paris, 1981.

Plato's Apology of Socrates: A Literary and Philosophical Study, with a Running Commentary. Edited and completed from the papers of the Late E. de Strycker. Leiden, 1994.

Richard, M.-D. *L'enseignement oral de Platon: Une nouvelle interprétation du platonisme.* Preface by P. Hadot. Paris, 1986. Contains translations of texts and a bibliography on the theories concerning Plato's oral teaching.

Thom, J. C. *The Pythagorean Golden Verses, with Introduction and Commentary.* Leiden, 1995.

Van Geytenbeek, A. C. *Musonius Rufus and Greek Diatribe.* Assen, 1963.

W. Wieland, *Platon und die Formen des Wissens.* Göttingen, 1982. Plato teaches not knowledge but know-how.

Chronology

The sign ± indicates that the date is approximate. This is very often the case for the period in which the philosophers were active. In general, I have chosen dates which correspond to what the ancients called the *akmé:* the point at which the person in question reached his maturity, or the height of his activity and renown. The reader will find valuable bio-bibliographic details on the various philosophers in R. Goulet, *Dictionnaire des philosophes antiques,* volume 1: *Abammon à Axiothea,* volume 2: *Babélyca à Dyscolius* (Paris, 1994).

BEFORE CHRIST

850–750   Composition of the Homeric poems.

700?   HESIOD, Greek poet, author of *Works and Days.*

650±?   ARISTEAS OF PROCONNESUS travels to Central Asia and composes his poem *Arimaspeia.*

640±   EPIMENIDES carries out an expiatory sacrifice in Athens.

600–550   The first thinkers appear in the Greek colonies of Asia Minor: THALES OF MILETUS (who predicts the solar eclipse of May 28, 585), ANAXIMANDER, ANAXIMENES.

600±   The SEVEN SAGES (historical and legendary figures): SOLON, PITTACUS OF MYTILENE, CHILON OF SPARTA, BIAS OF PRIENE,

PERIANDER OF CORINTH, CLEOBULUS OF LINDOS, THALES OF MILETUS.

594± SOLON, Athenian statesman and poet, later considered one of the SEVEN SAGES.

560±? ABARIS, linked to Pythagoras in the Pythagorean and Platonic traditions.

540±? XENOPHANES OF COLOPHON emigrates from Colophon, a Greek colony in Asia Minor, and arrives at Elea, a Greek colony in southern Italy.

540±? THEOGNIS, elegiac poet of aristocratic ethics.

532± PYTHAGORAS. Originally from the island of Samos, he emigrates to the Greek colonies of southern Italy: Crotona, and then Metapontum. He is said to be a reincarnation of the (legendary) philosopher HERMOTIMUS OF CLAZOMENAE.

504± HERACLITUS OF EPHESUS (Ephesus is a Greek colony in Asia Minor).

500± BUDDHA and CONFUCIUS teach their doctrines.

490–429 Life span of the Athenian statesman PERICLES.

470± ANAXAGORAS OF CLAZOMENAE.

460± EMPEDOCLES OF AGRIGENTUM.

450±ff. PARMENIDES OF ELEA, ZENO OF ELEA, MELISSUS OF SAMOS.

450±ff. Heyday of the Sophistic movement, whose adherents include PROTAGORAS, GORGIAS, PRODICOS, HIPPIAS, THRASYMACHUS, ANTIPHON, CRITIAS.

450± HERODOTUS, historian.

440± DEMOCRITUS OF ABDERA.

435± SOCRATES teaches in Athens.

432 ANAXAGORAS is tried for impiety in Athens and is forced to flee the country.

432–431	SOCRATES takes part in the battle of Potidaea.
431–416	ALCIBIADES, Athenian statesman and disciple of SOCRATES.
430±	THUCYDIDES writes his *History of the Peloponnesian War.*
423±	Production of ARISTOPHANES' play *The Clouds,* which ridicules SOCRATES' teachings.
399	SOCRATES is tried for impiety and condemned to death.
399±?	ANTISTHENES, ARISTIPPUS OF CYRENE, and EUCLIDES OF MEGARA, disciples of SOCRATES, found their own schools.
390±	ISOCRATES opens a school in Athens, where he teaches "philosophy" as overall culture.
389–388	PLATO makes his first trip to southern Italy and to Sicily. Meets DIO OF SYRACUSE.
388–387	PLATO founds his school in Athens, in the gymnasium called the Academy *(Academia).* The main members of the Academy are EUDOXUS, HERACLIDES, XENOCRATES, SPEUSIPPUS, ARISTOTLE, and THEAETETUS. There are also two women, AXIOTHEA and LASTHENEIA.
370–301	Chinese philosopher CHUANG-TZU, who portrays LAO-TZU as his master.
367–365	EUDOXUS OF CNIDUS replaces PLATO as head of the Academy during the latter's second trip to Sicily to visit Dionysius II of Syracuse.
361–360	HERACLIDES OF PONTUS replaces Plato as head of the Academy during the latter's third trip to Sicily.
360±ff.	DIOGENES THE CYNIC, disciple of ANTISTHENES.
360±?	AESCHINES OF SPHETTOS, disciple of SOCRATES, teaches in Athens and composes dialogues in which SOCRATES is a character.
350±?	XENOPHON, disciple of SOCRATES, writes his memoirs *(Memorabilia)* of SOCRATES.

349–348   Death of PLATO. SPEUSIPPUS succeeds him as head of the
            school.

339–338   XENOCRATES is elected scholarch of the Academy, succeed-
            ing SPEUSIPPUS.

The Hellenistic Period

336   Alexander the Great assumes the throne of Macedonia.

335   ARISTOTLE founds his own school in Athens. Important
            members of the school include THEOPHRASTUS,
            ARISTOXENUS, DICEARCHUS, CLEARCHUS. According to
            epigraphic documents, CLEARCHUS travels to a Greek city
            which eventually becomes Ai Khanoum in Afghanistan.

334   Expedition of Alexander to Persia and to India.
            ANAXARCHUS OF ABDERA (a student of DEMOCRITUS),
            PYRRHO, and ONESICRITUS all take part in this expedition.

328±ff.   First generation of disciples of DIOGENES THE CYNIC:
            MONIMUS, ONESICRITUS, CRATES, HIPPARCHIA, METROCLES,
            MENIPPUS, and MENEDEMUS.

326–323   The Indian Sage CALANUS meets the Greeks during Alexan-
            der's stay at Taxila, and commits suicide shortly after Alex-
            ander's death.

323   Death of Alexander in Babylon. During the unsettled years
            that follow, various Hellenistic monarchies form.

322±   Death of ARISTOTLE, who is succeeded by THEOPHRASTUS.

321   The comic poet MENANDER, who may have been influenced
            by EPICURUS.

320±   Philosophical activity of PYRRHO OF ELIS. His disciples in-
            clude PHILO OF ATHENS and TIMON OF ATHENS.

312   Death of XENOCRATES. POLEMON succeeds him as head of
            the Academy.

306   EPICURUS founds his school in Athens. His first disciples in-

clude HERODOTUS, PYTHOCLES, HERMARCHUS, METRODORUS, POLYAENUS, LEONTEUS OF LAMPSACUS, THEMISTA, LEONTION, COLOTES, APOLLONIDES, and IDOMENEUS.

301±   ZENO OF CITIUM founds the Stoic school at Athens. His first disciples include PERSEUS, ARISTON OF CHIOS, and CLEANTHES OF ASSOS.

300±   EUCLID (OF ALEXANDRIA) writes his *Elements*.

300±   CRANTOR becomes scholarch of the Academy.

295±   Ptolemy I founds a center of scientific studies in Alexandria called the Museum, with which the Aristotelian DEMETRIUS OF PHALERUM is associated. At the end of the third century, its teachers include the astronomer ARISTARCHUS OF SAMOS and the physician HEROPHILUS.

287–286   STRATO OF LAMPSACUS succeeds THEOPHRASTUS as scholarch of the Peripatetic school.

283–239   Antigonos Gonatas, king of Macedonia, shows favor to philosophers, particularly to Stoics like CLEANTHES.

276–241   ARCESILAUS, scholarch of the Academy, gives the school a "critical" orientation.

268±   LYCON succeeds STRATO OF LAMPSACUS as scholarch of the Peripatetic school.

262±   CLEANTHES becomes head of the Stoic school upon the death of ZENO.

235±   The Stoic SPHAIROS, disciple of ZENO and CLEANTHES, acts as counselor to the Spartan king Cleomenes III, and probably to his predecessor, Agis IV. He recommends social reforms.

230±   CHRYSIPPUS becomes head of the Stoic school upon the death of CLEANTHES.

212   ARCHIMEDES OF SYRACUSE, astronomer, mathematician, and engineer, is killed by Roman soldiers at the siege of Syracuse.

165± CARNEADES is scholarch of the Academy.

155 The Athenians send an embassy to Rome, to request that the city of Athens be exempted from a heavy fine. Its members include three philosophers: the Academic CARNEADES, the Aristotelian CRITOLAUS, and the Stoic DIOGENES OF BABYLON.

150± ANTIPATER (or ANTIPATROS) OF TARSUS is head of the Stoic school.

149–146 Macedonia and Greece submit to Rome.

144± The Stoic PANAETIUS is admitted into the circle of the Scipios. In 129, he succeeds ANTIPATER as head of the Stoic school.

133± In Rome, the Stoic BLOSSIUS, a disciple of ANTIPATER, inspires the social reforms of Tiberius Gracchus, and perhaps also, at Pergamum, the revolt of Aristonicus, who seeks freedom for all slaves and the equality of all citizens.

110± PHILO OF LARISSA and CHARMADAS teach at the Academy.

106–43 CICERO, Roman statesman, whose philosophical treatises are largely inspired by the Academy of his time (CARNEADES, PHILO OF LARISSA, CHARMADAS, ANTIOCHUS OF ASCALON).

99± QUINTUS MUCIUS SCAEVOLA PONTIFEX and RUTILIUS RUFUS, Roman statesmen and Stoics.

97–55 LUCRETIUS, Epicurean philosopher and poet; author of De rerum natura.

95–46 CATO OF UTICA, Roman statesman and Stoic philosopher.

86 Athens is taken by the Romans, and Sulla's troops pillage the city.

79± ANTIOCHUS OF ASCALON opens his own school in Athens and opposes the "critical" attitude (the Academy's stance from the time of ARCESILAUS to that of PHILO OF LARISSA).

60±   Various manifestations of a renewal of Pythagoreanism.

50±?   APOLLOPHANES OF PERGAMUM, Epicurean philosopher.

50±   PHILODEMUS OF GADARA, Epicurean philosopher and friend
           of Calpurnius Piso (father-in-law of Julius Caesar). Many
           of his writings will be found in the Villa of the Papyri at
           Herculaneum.

49±   DIODORUS SICULUS, historian.

44   Julius Caesar is assassinated.

43   Junius Brutus, Roman statesman and assassin of Caesar, at-
           tends classes given in Athens by the Platonist
           THEOMNESTES, who is the last philosopher teaching at Ath-
           ens to be called "Academic"—that is to say, "critical." The
           educational institutions founded by PLATO, ARISTOTLE, and
           ZENO disappear in the last years of the Roman Republic;
           only the institution founded by EPICURUS survives. New
           schools, which take up the doctrinal heritage of PLATO,
           ARISTOTLE, and ZENO, open in Athens and other cities.

35±   EUDORUS OF ALEXANDRIA, Platonic philosopher.

30   Battle of Actium. Death of Cleopatra, last queen of Egypt.
           End of the Hellenistic period.

30?   An Epicurean inscription is engraved by DIOGENES OF
           OINOANDA in his native town. (Some scholars date this in-
           scription to the second century A.D.)

7±   AMYNIAS OF SAMOS, Epicurean philosopher.

                        AFTER CHRIST

                       The Roman Empire

27   Octavian receives *imperium* and the title of Augustus from
           the Senate; end of the Roman Republic and beginning of

the Empire. Flourishing of Latin literature (HORACE, OVID). ARIUS DIDYMUS, counselor to Augustus, writes a doxographic manual on the "dogmas" of the various philosophical schools. SEXTIUS, father and son, Roman philosophers, adopt Stoic and Pythagorean ideas, which also have a great influence on the thought of Seneca.

29–30   JESUS OF NAZARETH is crucified in Jerusalem.

40±   PHILO OF ALEXANDRIA, a Platonist and one of the most important authors of Hellenistic Judaism. He will have a strong influence on Christian "philosophy."

48–65   SENECA, Stoic philosopher, tutor and then counselor to the emperor Nero. After 62, he devotes himself exclusively to philosophical activity. In 65, the emperor forces him to commit suicide.

60   The Platonist AMMONIUS teaches at Athens. PLUTARCH OF CHAERONEA is his auditor.

93–94   The emperor Domitian expels all philosophers from Rome. Chased out of Rome, the Stoic EPICTETUS, student of MUSONIUS RUFUS, founds a school at Nicopolis, on the Greek coast of the Adriatic.

96   The emperor Nerva comes to power.

100±ff. PLUTARCH OF CHAERONEA, Platonist of the "critical" tendency, writes *Parallel Lives* and *Moralia*.

120±   Beginning of literary activity by the Christian Apologists, in particular JUSTIN, ATHENAGORAS, and THEOPHILUS OF ANTIOCH, who present Christianity as a philosophy.

129–200 Life span of GALEN OF PERGAMUM, physician and philosopher.

133±   BASILIDES, the first "historically identifiable" Gnostic, teaches at Alexandria.

140   The Gnostic VALENTINUS teaches at Rome during the reign of Antoninus the Pious.

140±   FAVORINUS OF ARLES, Platonist of the "critical" tendency.

146   The Platonist CALVISIUS TAURUS teaches at Athens. His students include AULUS GELLIUS.

147   CLAUDIUS PTOLEMAEUS (PTOLEMY), astronomer, mathematician, and geographer.

150±   The Platonist APULEIUS OF MADAURA.

150±?   The Platonists NUMENIUS and CRONIUS.

150±?   ALCINOOS, Platonist philosopher and author of *Didaskalikos,* a summary of Platonism.

150±?   The Platonist ALBINUS, author of *Introduction to the Dialogues of Plato,* teaches at Smyrna.

155±   MAXIMUS OF TYRE, rhetor and Platonist philosopher.

160±   The satirist LUCIAN, influenced by Cynicism.

161–180   Reign of the emperor MARCUS AURELIUS, a Stoic highly influenced by EPICTETUS.

176   In Athens, MARCUS AURELIUS founds chairs of philosophy (financed by Imperial funds) for the four principal sects: Platonist, Aristotelian, Stoic, and Epicurean.

176±   ATTICUS occupies the chair in Platonism founded by MARCUS AURELIUS and teaches in Athens.

177±   AULUS GELLIUS composes his *Attic Nights.*

177±   CELSUS, Platonist philosopher and anti-Christian polemicist.

180ff.   Alexandria and Caesarea in Palestine become centers for the teaching of Christian "philosophy." Proponents include PANTAENUS, CLEMENT OF ALEXANDRIA, ORIGEN, GREGORY THE WONDER-WORKER, EUSEBIUS OF CAESAREA.

190±   SEXTUS EMPIRICUS, physician and Skeptic philosopher, spreads the teachings of such earlier Skeptics as

AENESIDEMUS (mid–first century B.C.?) and AGRIPPA (hard to date).

198± ALEXANDER OF APHRODISIAS teaches Aristotelian philosophy, possibly in Athens, and publishes numerous commentaries on ARISTOTLE's works.

200± DIOGENES LAERTIUS writes his *Lives, Doctrines, and Sayings of the Illustrious Philosophers.*

244–270 PLOTINUS, a student of AMMONIUS SACCAS, founds a Platonic (i.e., Neoplatonic) school at Rome. His disciples include PORPHYRY, AMELIUS, CASTRICIUS, and ROGATIANUS. Some of his writings contain discussions with Gnostics.

300± Beginning of Christian monasticism. ANTHONY retires into the desert. ATHANASIUS OF ALEXANDRIA will write a biography of ANTHONY in 356.

The Christian Empire

312–313 The emperor Constantine converts to Christianity. He promulgates the Edict of Milan, which ensures the practices of the Christian cult.

313± IAMBLICHUS founds a Platonic (i.e., Neoplatonic) school in Syria, probably in Apamea. He strongly influences later Neoplatonism through the importance he attributes to the Pythagorean tradition and to theurgic practices. He writes numerous commentaries on PLATO and ARISTOTLE. His disciples include AIDESIOS OF CAPPADOCIA and THEODORUS OF ASINE.

361–363 The reign of the EMPEROR JULIAN, Neoplatonist philosopher and student of MAXIMUS OF EPHESUS, who belongs to the Iamblichean tradition. Beginning of a Neoplatonically inspired reaction against Christianity.

360±ff. Flourishing of "learned monasticism." Adherents include BASIL OF CAESAREA, GREGORY NAZIANZEN, GREGORY OF NYSSA, EVAGRIUS OF PONTUS.

375±ff.   PLUTARCH OF ATHENS. Birth of the Platonic (i.e., Neopla-
            tonic) school of Athens.

386–430   The literary career of AUGUSTINE.

400ff.   Flourishing of Neoplatonic thought in Athens and Alexan-
            dria (private schools); teachers include SYRIANUS, PROCLUS,
            DAMASCIUS, HIEROCLES, HERMIAS, AMMONIUS, SIMPLICIUS,
            OLYMPIODORUS. In the fifth and sixth centuries, there are no
            important doctrinal differences between the Neoplatonists
            teaching in Athens and those who, like HIEROCLES,
            HERMIAS, AMMONIUS, and OLYMPIODORUS, teach in Alexan-
            dria. Numerous commentaries on PLATO and ARISTOTLE are
            written by SYRIANUS, PROCLUS, HERMIAS, AMMONIUS,
            OLYMPIODORUS, PHILOPONUS, SIMPLICIUS, and others. Neo-
            platonism is a center of resistance to Christianity.

529   The emperor Justinian bars pagans from teaching. The
            Neoplatonist philosophers DAMASCIUS, SIMPLICIUS, and
            PRISCIAN leave Athens to take refuge in Persia. After a
            peace treaty is concluded between Chosroes and Justinian,
            they establish themselves in Carrhae (Byzantine territory,
            but under Persian influence), where they continue their
            teaching.

529±   The Neoplatonist JOHN PHILOPONUS converts to Christian-
            ity, probably because of the measures taken by Justinian to
            bar pagans from teaching.

540±   DOROTHEUS OF GAZA, monastic writer.

Index